T0039966

ALSO BY DEREK BICKERTON

Adam's Tongue: How Humans Made Language,
How Language Made Humans

Lingua Ex Machina: Reconciling Darwin and Chomsky
with the Human Brain (with William H. Cavin)

Language and Human Behavior

Language and Species

Roots of Language

BASTARD TONGUES

BASTARD TONGUES

A Trailblazing Linguist Finds Clues to Our Common

Humanity in the World's Lowliest Languages

———

DEREK BICKERTON

Hill and Wang

A division of Farrar, Straus and Giroux

New York

Hill and Wang
A division of Farrar, Straus and Giroux
18 West 18th Street, New York 10011

Printed in the United States of America
Published in 2008 by Hill and Wang
First paperback edition, 2009

The Library of Congress has cataloged the hardcover edition as follows:
Bickerton, Derek.
    Bastard tongues : a trailblazing linguist finds clues to our common
humanity in the world's lowliest languages / Derek Bickerton. — 1st ed.
        p.   cm.
    ISBN-13: 978-0-8090-2817-7 (hardcover : alk. paper)
    ISBN-10: 0-8090-2817-4 (hardcover : alk. paper)
    1. Creole dialects. 2. Bickerton, Derek—Travel.   I. Title.

PM7831.B53 2008
417'.22—dc22
                                                        2007023297

Paperback ISBN-13: 978-0-8090-2816-0
Paperback ISBN-10: 0-8090-2816-6

Designed by Jonathan D. Lippincott

www.fsgbooks.com

P1

For Yvonne, who shared it all with me

"To hold in age's calm
 All the sweets of youth's longings"

CONTENTS

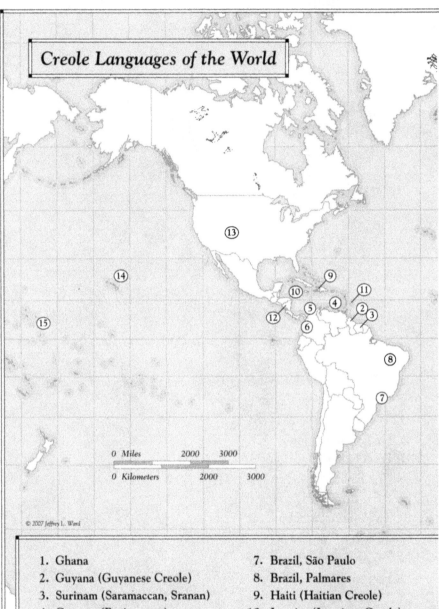

Creole Languages of the World

1. Ghana
2. Guyana (Guyanese Creole)
3. Surinam (Saramaccan, Sranan)
4. Curaçao (Papiamentu)
5. Colombia, Cartagena
   (Palenquero)
6. Colombia, Ure
7. Brazil, São Paulo
8. Brazil, Palmares
9. Haiti (Haitian Creole)
10. Jamaica (Jamaican Creole)
11. Barbados
12. Nicaragua (Nicaraguan
    Sign Language)

© 2007 Jeffrey L. Ward

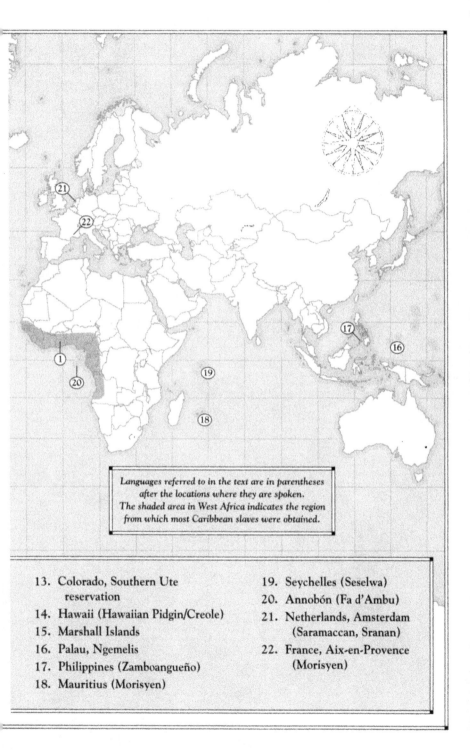

Languages referred to in the text are in parentheses
after the locations where they are spoken.
The shaded area in West Africa indicates the region
from which most Caribbean slaves were obtained.

13. Colorado, Southern Ute
    reservation
14. Hawaii (Hawaiian Pidgin/Creole)
15. Marshall Islands
16. Palau, Ngemelis
17. Philippines (Zamboangueño)
18. Mauritius (Morisyen)

19. Seychelles (Seselwa)
20. Annobón (Fa d'Ambu)
21. Netherlands, Amsterdam
    (Saramaccan, Sranan)
22. France, Aix-en-Provence
    (Morisyen)

BASTARD TONGUES

1

BECOMING A LINGUIST

I waded out of thigh-deep, pellucid water onto a beach of pure yellow sand. Behind, the twin outboards of the motorboat that had brought me churned trails of white foam that dwindled rapidly into the distance. Soon their sound shrank to a murmur, then ceased; the boat vanished in a dazzle of sunlight on the lagoon. I was alone on the island of Ngemelis, in the archipelago of Palau, in the western half of the Pacific Ocean.

I had landed near the northwestern tip of the island. Back of the beach lay a grove of coconut palms, extending southeastward to a low ridge of jagged limestone covered with impenetrable spiny scrub. Hull down on the horizon lay the larger island of Peleliu, scene of ferocious fighting in World War II, home to deadly sea crocodiles, one of which had recently caught a fisherman and stashed his corpse on an underwater ledge, to dine on later. North and east, the central lagoon of Palau spread its vast expanse of tranquil blues and greens, dotted with tiny islands like giant toadstools.

I was marooned on a genuine desert island.

Why on earth would a professor of linguistics have himself marooned on a desert island? Well, that's a long story.

It began eleven years earlier, in West Africa. I was teaching English literature at what was then called the University College of Science Education, located in Cape Coast, Ghana. Science education, what exactly did that mean? Teaching science? Or teaching how science should be taught? Or just teaching everything in a scientific way? Nobody knew, but it sure sounded impressive. Once, in a bar at three in the morning, I stumbled on one of our janitors, paralytic drunk, sitting by himself and repeating, over and over, in tones of rapt adoration: "U-ni-ver-sity Coll-ege of Sci-ence Ed-u-cation! U-ni-ver-sity Coll-ege of Sci-ence Ed-u-cation!"

I wasn't there out of love of Africa or because I particularly wanted to be a literature teacher. There wasn't anything I wanted except to travel and have new experiences. I just did the next thing, whatever that was, and when it got boring I moved on to something else. Yet always at the back of my mind was this feeling that one day I'd meet someone in a bar who'd tell me my true purpose in life.

And believe it or not, this finally happened.

It was just another steamy, sweaty morning on the coast once called the White Man's Graveyard. Thirsty from teaching, I dropped into the Staff Bar for a cold one (faculty are called staff in Britain and its ex-colonies). Somebody called me over to a table and introduced me to an unfamiliar face: John Spencer, Professor of Linguistics, University of Leeds, England, just passing through. I sat down and we talked and drank good Ghanaian beer. To all appearances, a morning like any other.

For some reason I started talking about what it was like teaching English literature to West Africans. The week before we'd been doing George Eliot—I think it was The Mill on the Floss—and we came to the bit where the outraged father drives his daughter and her illegitimate baby out into the snow. Teaching about snow in the tropics is bad enough; likewise explaining how any father who was not an unnatural monster could banish his own child and grandchild just because someone hadn't spoken some words in some church. But then it turned out the whole class thought she was carrying the baby on her back. Naturally, since that's how Ghanaian mothers do it. "No," I said, "in her arms—like this." And I demonstrated. And one of the students said, "What a stupid way to carry a baby."

How could you ever get over cultural barriers like these? And lurking behind my frustration was a still deeper unease. How could you ever make any objective judgments about literature? If I say Joyce is the greatest twentieth-century English novelist, and you say, no, it's Lawrence, how can we ever decide who's right?

"You should study linguistics," John said.

I asked him what that was. I honestly didn't know.

John explained that it was the scientific study of language. And how would that help solve my problems? Well, if you scientifically studied the language writers used, you could get objective measures to compare them with. At least that was what John claimed, and I believed him.

And how could I study it, given that I had my living to earn?

There was a one-year course, John said, at his university. It was primarily designed to train teachers of English as a foreign language, but it mostly consisted of linguistics, and a generous British government would pay me the princely sum of £17 a week (at the 1966 rate of exchange, equivalent to about $45) while I was taking it.

And under normal circumstances that would have been that. Many times in your life you meet someone who suggests something to you and you say, "Hey, yeah, that would be interesting," and promptly forget about it. So why didn't I then? We were happy in Ghana. I was paid well for very little work. We had good friends, we loved the life there: the ratty bars where we all danced the highlife, Biriwa Beach on weekends, servants to do the house and yard, knowing that for as long as we stayed there we'd never feel cold, it would always be summer.

The ironic thing was that until then I'd been a card-carrying grammatophobe. In common with a great many other people, I loathed grammar and anything connected with it. At Cambridge I'd actually switched my major from English to history when I found out that for my finals I'd be expected to take courses in Anglo-Saxon and Italian. All I could remember about grammar from school was diagramming sentences. Why do that, what's it for? Just shut up and diagram, dummy! And here I was, with a wife and three young children to support, gambling my career, such as it was, and my whole way of life on something I'd always hated, on a casual word from a stranger.

I can't really explain it, to this day, but somehow I knew destiny had called me. And I'd always been ready to take a chance, to follow my gut instinct, do whatever it told me and damn the consequences. Luckily Yvonne felt the same way about things as I did.

I handed in my resignation forthwith; in a few months we were in Chapeltown.

Chapeltown is the wrong-side-of-the-tracks section of Leeds where all the immigrants hang out, and on $45 a week it was about the only place a family of five could afford to live. Even if you went without a car. We used to take the bus to the city market on Saturday afternoons, when prices dropped by half, and come home with the platform at the back of the double-decker laden down with our sacks of produce. Home was the rented bottom floor of a big house that had come down in the world, its tall windows still defended by enormous wooden shutters—we did "There's trouble at t' mill, lass" routines every time we closed them.

In retrospect, the course itself wasn't up to much. We had ten lectures on Noam Chomsky's new transformational grammar (as it was then called) given by someone who'd been a student in the course himself the year before. We were taught some British invention called systemic grammar; luckily it never got into my system. We had a ferocious female martinet of a phonetics teacher, a type only Britain can produce—if you've seen *The Weakest Link* you know what I mean—who effectively cured me of any interest in the sounds that make up language.

And yet, for all its flaws, the course was a revelation to me.

I realized that all my life I'd been deaf and blind to an endless string of fascinating mysteries that were there all the time, happening right under my nose, under everyone's nose. For instance, how had I learned language? I couldn't remember. Nobody can. By the time memory starts, language is there already. And once you've learned it, you don't ever have to think about it. You may worry over the content of what you're saying, or your precise choice of words, but how you'll fit the sentences together—never. You never catch yourself thinking things like, "Do I need a relative clause here, or would an infinitival phrase work better?" You may not even know the names for half the things you use, and neither you nor I have the least inkling about how we assemble them. It's as if language was like digestion, or breathing, or circulating the blood—you have no need to know, your brain does it all for you, deep down, below the level of consciousness.

What you speak is English, you think. But listen to a couple of physicists or teenage computer geeks—it's like they were talking in Double Dutch, yet that's English too. Pick up a grammar text, you'd think English was some monolith, but that and all other languages are shifting all the time as you move across professions, situations, classes, races, sexes. Or as you move through time. Grandkids and grandparents understand one another, even if each thinks the other talks weird sometimes, but after a couple of dozen generations the stuff will have become incomprehensible. Or as you move through space. Start walking in the middle of France and finish in the middle of Spain, you'll hear pure French at one end and pure Spanish at the other, yet along the way, any two adjacent villages understand each other perfectly.

Small wonder that many linguists nowadays think first and foremost of Language with a big L, and see the various languages as simply different manifestations of this concept. Chomsky once went so far as to say that there is only one human language, with several thousand varieties. To the layman, stunned by unpronounceable sounds, boggled by barbarous-looking words, this may sound plain ridiculous. But the more you look at languages, the more you realize that (1) it's very hard to draw boundaries between them, and (2) under all those scary but superficial differences, they're much more alike than you'd think.

So what's a language, anyway? According to the mid-century linguist Uriel Weinreich, "A language is a dialect with an army and a navy." That's true because some people try to use language as an instrument of power, to build artificial barriers, keep other people in line, stamp them all into the same mold, but language itself resists power: it's demotic, it's subversive, it slips through the cracks of dictatorships, it makes fools of the powerful. In Spain, Franco tried for over thirty years to destroy the Catalan language. Result: Catalan is now more vigorous than ever before.

For me, the most fascinating things were aspects of my own language that I knew somehow, but knew I had never learned—things that you or I or anyone else wouldn't even know that they knew unless someone pointed them out. Here's just one example. Take simple sentences like:

Mary was too angry to talk to her.
Mary doesn't have anyone to talk to her.

The two sentences look almost identical, but in the first we all know (though I doubt anyone ever told us) that *Mary* and *her* must refer to two different people, while in the second they can (and probably do) refer to the same person. But then look what happens when we just take *her* away:

Mary was too angry to talk to.
Mary doesn't have anyone to talk to.

This time it's the second sentence that involves two different people, and the first that refers back to Mary at the end. And this I'm sure you never learned anywhere, for now there's just empty space at the ends of the sentences, and how could you learn the meanings of nothings? Yet we must somehow know (without knowing we know) the mysterious principles that underlie all this. If we didn't, how could we know instinctively what these sentences mean, and never feel in the least confused by them until, like the centipede wondering how something with a hundred legs could walk, we try to figure out what makes them work that way.

By the end of the course, two things had happened. I now knew with absolute certainty that this was what I wanted to do, if not for the rest of my life, at least for the foreseeable future. And I was no longer interested in using linguistics to evaluate literature. Stylistics, that's called: it's a respectable field of study, I don't want to knock it, I just knew it wasn't for me. Language had too many mansions—far too many mysteries yet to solve.

Now all I had to do was get a job as a linguist.

In these days, when folk with Ph.D.'s from prestigious universities are forced to accept consecutive one-year stints in three different places and then, when they apply for a tenured job, get told, "Uh, you move around too much," you may find what I'm going to tell you hard to believe. But back then, people with anything you could call linguistic qualifications were as rare as hens' teeth. At the same time "Linguistics" was modern and sounded awesomely impressive—like "Sci-ence Ed-u-cation"—so no institute of higher learning felt quite complete without some. Even with my mere diploma, I could have gone to Beirut, to Prague, to Dar es Salaam . . . I very nearly did go to Dar es Salaam. I applied for a job at the University of Tanzania and got it. The family was all geared up for it. There's a big bay there, with lots of islands. We'd buy a boat and sail to the islands on weekends. We'd visit Zanzibar, wake up and smell the cloves. I'd become expert in Swahili . . .

Then the Fickle Finger of Fate took a hand in things.

On the eve of departure I got a phone call from John Spencer. He had a friend, a Professor Bill Murray at the University of Lancaster, who had a deal that might interest me. A job had unexpectedly opened up in Guyana, which had just stopped being British Guiana, a geopolitical anomaly—the sole British colony on the coast of South America—and become an independent state that suddenly realized it didn't have a linguist. Not one! Imagine that! Was I interested?

You bet I was interested. To be the only linguist in a whole country, to have nobody to tell me what to do, that sounded like paradise. On top of which, I'd been there, ten years before, and loved it.

Murray interviewed me. He put himself across as someone not too respectful of authorities and regulations, a trait I've always found appealing. He seemed to assume from the start that it was a done deal, if I wanted it—maybe he had no one else in sight. He spelled out the small print: a five-year contract, four years in Guyana, a year in Lancaster as reward for tropical hardships, plus the high possibility—virtual certainty, he assured me—that I'd then be offered a tenured position there.

There were two small flies in this ointment. One, I wouldn't have quite the hands-free status I'd envisaged. The job came with a remit: to find out why Guyanese children, who everyone agreed were smart, did so poorly at English in the British examinations they had to pass if they wanted tertiary education. People thought this might have something to do with their native language, which was not English but some kind of English-related patois called "Creolese." The theory was that this patois interfered with their learning of English and consequently with their acquisition of any English-based skill or knowledge—after all, they performed above average in nonlinguistic things like art or math, and even in other languages, such as French or Spanish.

The other fly was administrative. I was to head up the English Department, because the current chair, Bill Carr, had done something awful Murray wouldn't talk about, and had been summarily dismissed. I didn't care for the sound of that, but figured I could always delegate. I accepted.

I now had the embarrassing task of dis-accepting the job I'd previously accepted. So embarrassing that exactly how I did it has been permanently erased from my memory bank. But I did it somehow. I knew I had to—destiny had called yet again. Though if anyone was ever less prepared for a job, I'd be surprised.

Well, what cards, if any, did I hold?

Just one. I was a lifelong autodidact.

I'd done some teaching but I'd always disliked being taught. You know the wonderful teacher everyone has at some time in their school career, the one who opens your eyes, inspires you, fills you with enthusiasm . . . Well, I never met that teacher. All the ones I met I either tolerated or flat-out disliked. After the first two days at university I found lectures weren't compulsory and never went to another. I'd figured out how they did it. They just regurgitated their own books. You could read the damn books yourself in one tenth of the time, and leave the rest free for all the fun things undergraduates do.

Most students don't know how to do this, so here's my secret: I read aggressively, and I never hit my head on a brick wall.

Most students read passively. They see themselves as vessels waiting to be filled. They have awe and respect for the printed word. I don't. I want to catch the authors out. I assume, correctly, that part of the stuff, maybe most of it, will be wrong. And I'm going to figure out which part it is. Even if you know nothing about a subject you can spot self-contradictions, and if you read two authors on the same topic you can spot regular contradictions. They can't both be right. (They could both be wrong, though.)

Most students hit their heads on brick walls. They're given a text to read, and somewhere in Chapter 1 or 2 they bog down completely. But they persevere, oh do they persevere! (That's unless they decide to drop out completely.) They feel if they don't absorb Chapter 2 to its very last syllable, they'll be totally lost when they get to Chapter 3. So they keep slugging away until their eyes glaze, trying to force understanding. Finally they sleep on it and start over again the next day.

What I do is skim through the text looking for anything I understand. Sometimes at first it's as little as the introduction and a couple of paragraphs here and there. No matter. I store that in my mind and do something else. Read stuff about the subject that I do understand, stop again the moment it gets to be hard work. Then after a week or two, I come back to the first text, skim it again for anything that makes sense. There will be more this time. I guarantee it. Maybe not much, but a little more will start to make sense. Repeat the process. You'll probably find you're getting patches all over the book. Okay, fine. The patches spread like inkblots; eventually they'll link up. Suddenly, what a few weeks before was a trek into impenetrable jungle becomes a stroll through the park.

You see, evolution has been programming brains for half a billion years. It has been programming them to sort incoming data and make sense out of it. A life-or-death matter: only those who can do it well survive. The brain doesn't care what kind of data. Whistles and roars on the savanna or words on a printed page—it just sorts, interprets, and stores, whether you're conscious of it or not. In fact the brain probably works better when you leave it to its own devices. The French mathematician Henri Poincaré once spent months trying to solve a heavy-duty math problem; finally he put it aside in disgust, and one bright morning a few weeks later,' just as he was boarding a city bus, the solution popped up out of nowhere, ready-made.

I needed these skills now, for I had less than a month to bone up. I knew that "patois" was a rude term for dialects regarded as socially inferior, and that dialects, as Weinreich had said, were just languages that hadn't yet gotten their own armies or navies. So this plus the name "Creolese" led me to suspect that what I'd have to deal with might actually turn out to be something called a Creole language.

I'd vaguely heard of such things. But my total exposure to them consisted of a one-hour lecture by the then-doyen of that then-minuscule field, Robert Hall Jr., a genial old buffer, of which I remembered exactly zero. Grubbing around in libraries (no Internet then!), what I came up with was roughly this:

Creole languages were new languages, things that sprang up seemingly out of nowhere whenever people speaking mutually incomprehensible languages were put in contact with one another over long periods of time. Sometimes this had happened when Europeans set up forts and warehouses on the coasts of Africa or Asia. But it happened most often when slaves were shipped from Africa to the Caribbean, South America, or islands in the Indian Ocean, and where large plantations, mostly sugar plantations, were set up.

Slaves who came to the Americas spoke a variety of West African languages—nobody knows exactly how many. A few of these languages may have been mutually comprehensible, but since slaves were brought from a region stretching from the Gambia to Angola—over three thousand miles—and since many languages were unrelated, a majority of slaves wouldn't have been able to understand one another. And the language barriers were higher still between slaves and their masters, who spoke English, French, Dutch, Portuguese, or Spanish. Yet some way to communicate had to be found if the plantation system was to work.

Why couldn't the slaves, like immigrants elsewhere, simply have learned the ruling language of their new country?

Thick lips and sluggish minds: that was the knee-jerk reaction of the slave owners—slaves could get neither their mouths nor their heads around the intricate subtleties of European languages. In fact, African languages have just as many intricate subtleties as European languages, so you'd think linguists would know better. But barely a lifetime ago, Leonard Bloomfield, founder of the Linguistic Society of America and the leading linguist of his day, produced an only slightly sanitized version of this myth. According to him, slaves first made pathetic, blundering attempts to speak a European language; the masters then imitated their mistakes, whether to facilitate communication or just for ridicule he did not make clear; the slaves then imitated the imitations (badly) and voilà! you had something that could scarcely be regarded as a real language, but that worked, at least for the limited functions of sugar growing and man management.

Whatever processes took place, the immediate result was widely agreed to be a pidgin. A pidgin was a makeshift affair, not a full language and nobody's native tongue. Many believed it was no more than a "reduced" or "simplified" version of some European language; people spoke about languages being "pidginized," about "Pidgin English," "Pidgin French," and the like. Typically, a pidgin had a strictly limited vocabulary and little if anything in the way of grammar, while its speakers, whether African or European, were mostly adults. But then the slaves had children, and when the children learned the pidgin they somehow managed to transform it— they "creolized" it—resulting in a Creole language. A Creole might not (due to its pidgin past) have the wide range of words and structures found in older languages, but it was still a full human language, able to discharge all the functions that human languages are expected to discharge. In a phrase common at the time, the Creole "expanded" the pidgin.

Exactly how languages "reduced" or "expanded" one another was still, I discovered, something on which there was little or no agreement. For instance, there were three competing theories about how Creoles came to be.

One was "superstrate" theory. This approach regarded Creoles as no more than deviant dialects of whichever European language had been dominant at the place and time in question. Some even saw Creoles as carrying to extremes tendencies already implicit in that European language: *français avancé*, advanced French, was one description sometimes used for French-based Creoles.

Another was "substrate" theory. While the vocabulary of a Creole language came mostly from its dominant European language, substrate theorists pointed out that many grammatical structures did not look like anything European, though they did resemble similar structures in African languages. Hence they argued that, as one linguist put it, a language like Haitian Creole was "a West African language with French words."

A third theory was known as "monogenesis." It took off from a very odd fact about Creoles, first noticed by a nineteenth-century Portuguese linguist, but generally ignored by both substratists and superstratists. The grammars of Creoles, wherever these had sprung up—even thousands of miles apart—were surprisingly similar to one another, far more similar than anyone would have predicted, given the different mixtures of very different languages that had presumably gone into their making. When such similarities are found in more traditional languages, the usual explanation is that they are historically related in some way. Therefore the monogeneticists hypothesized that Creole languages must be the descendants of some kind of Mother of All Creoles, a language—probably some Afro-Portuguese mix—that had developed in West Africa five centuries ago and then spread via the slave trade, changing its vocabulary as it traveled but keeping its basic structure intact.

As for the status of these languages, they were regarded by most people—even some linguists—as "imbecile jargons," "infantile languages," "debased languages," "a cognitive handicap," or even as "the blind groping of minds too primitive for expression in modes of speech beyond their capabilities." Wherever they were spoken, educators made war on them. Children were routinely beaten for speaking them, and not just for speaking them in school. In Hawaii, many schools used to require students to report any other student they heard speaking Creole (still called "Pidgin" there) in the street, in the home, or anywhere else. Popular humor reinforced the stereotype of Creole as a sign of retardation, like the one about the guy who before a botched brain operation "talked like this" and after it "wen tok la'dis."

Of dubious and disputed parentage, despised and abused, Creole languages surely were, in every sense of the word, bastard tongues.

A few days before I was due to leave, Murray called me. There had been a slight glitch. Bill Carr wasn't going to be fired after all.

As I found out later, what had happened was this. After two weeks of binge-drinking, he had thrown his English wife and four children out of the house and ordered them back to England so he could live with the Afro-Guyanese daughter of the Guyanese prime minister's personal physician (you can read the details in his son Matthew Carr's memoir, My Father's House). But Bill had now gotten himself a lawyer, who informed the university that no matter how steamy a mix of sex, race, and substance abuse one might brew in one's private life, it does not afford grounds for breaking a legally binding contract. Fortunately my contract was signed and sealed and they couldn't get rid of me either. But I would be a colleague of the man I'd been supposed to replace—an embarrassing situation indeed.

I flew alone to what might now be unfriendly territory, leaving the family to follow if and when I established a beachhead there.

2

GRAPPLING WITH GUYANA

As the plane bounced to a stop at Atkinson Field, I felt a tremor of nervousness that had nothing to do with the quality of the landing. Nor was it the country or the job; it was the fact that within moments I would be confronting the man I'd been supposed to replace, who would now remain as the head of my department.

And there he was, a bluff, blunt, stocky Yorkshireman, and at his side a smaller, elfin-faced man of mixed blood whose eyes sparkled with intelligence and mischief. Bill introduced him: Professor Harry Drayton, chair of the biology department. Together they took me into what passed for the VIP lounge and began to grill me with a barrage of questions about my background, my politics, and my motives.

I realized why, immediately. They saw me as an establishment tool in the plot against Bill Carr. They would first expose me, then humiliate me and make it clear that whatever dastardly designs I might harbor would be thwarted. But as I answered their questions I sensed their hostility changing to puzzlement. Clearly I was far from what they'd expected. The glacial chill with which our meeting had started gradually began to thaw.

After an hour or so we headed for the capital, Georgetown. Halfway there we stopped and went into a rough black-working-class bar. Since Harry was not, at least as Guyanese go, a drinking man, I'm sure this was a test. He and Bill were doubtless hoping

that the liberal sentiments I'd expressed in the airport were a cha-
rade, that I'd somehow reveal the acute discomfort many middle-
class white people might feel in that kind of environment, thereby
outing myself as a closet racist. How were they to know that
Yvonne and I had frequented such places every weekend while we
were in Ghana, because in Ghana (though not in Guyana) that
was where the dancing happened?

After a couple of drinks we went out, stood shoulder to shoulder by the wayside, and relieved ourselves in the long grass.
Whether this was a final test, an act of male bonding, or simply because the bar's toilet was too disgusting, I'll never know. But while
we were doing it, a truckload of black laborers drove by, and one of
them shouted:

"Look a red man a piss a road corner!"

They all roared with laughter, and the truck vanished into the
night.

Although it was a while before I fully understood it, you can learn
a lot about Guyana from just that one sentence—about both
Guyanese society and Guyanese language.

Take the expression "red man." In America, a "red man" would
be a Native American. For centuries, you were either black or
white, and you can still be considered black even if your skin is
paler than mine. In Guyana, and the Caribbean generally, there are
three categories, black, white, and red, and you are red if you are
anything between stove-top black and pillow white. Why red and
not brown? For the same reason a Guyanese, hurt in the leg, will
yell, "Ow, me foot!" To us it seems obvious how the world is divided up, and hence how a well-behaved language should divide it.
West Africans would disagree. In many of their languages, everything in the spectrum from coffee to crimson is marked by a word
for which we have no equivalent—our nearest term is "red"—while
the organ we have to translate as "foot" reaches up to their knees.
One way is as good as the other; the world is full of stuff that
doesn't really have boundaries, however "natural" the ones our language selects may seem to us.

Red men hold an ambiguous position in Caribbean society.

They are both envied and despised. Because they had some European blood, the colonial regime used them as a buffer between black and white, giving them preferential treatment that black people naturally resented.

Two white men were also pissing by the roadside. Why didn't the black workmen pick on us?

I learned why later, when I asked a black colleague to accompany me to a bar like the one we were in that night. He refused. I asked why. "You go in there, when you come out, you're still white. I go in there, when I come out, I'm an ignorant black *rassole*." In other words, if you're not white in the Caribbean, certain kinds of behavior, like drinking in low bars, will destroy whatever hard-earned status you may have won. But if you're white, nothing can take away from your whiteness. And it's your whiteness, not your morals, that folk will judge you by.

So there was nothing particularly remarkable to our black workmen about two white men urinating in public. White men had been doing as they pleased in black men's countries for hundreds of years. They were a law unto themselves. But it was a surprise and a delight and a piece of real one-upmanship to see a red man disgracing himself. Not that this worried Harry. A natural rebel, he just grinned and waved to them.

But what about the language itself?

The meaning of the sentence may seem obvious enough to you (although in at least a couple of respects it isn't). But the grammar of the sentence differs radically from the grammar of English. Since it was quite a while before I really understood these differences, let me first tell you how I started to learn what people in Guyana still referred to as "Creolese."

Obviously, if I was going to find out how Creolese interfered with Guyanese students' English, the first thing I had to do was learn how Creolese worked. And I had been told in my one-year course at Leeds that if you wanted to study a previously unstudied language or dialect, the first thing you had to do was find a native speaker who would help you out.

My first helper was a very forthright Afro-Guyanese lady called

Joyce Trotman. Joyce was the principal of the Teachers' Training
College, and as such could present herself as a fearsome dragoness
of the Queen's English and bourgeois respectability whenever circumstances required. At the same time, when she let her hair down
among friends, she could be as earthy as they come, shooting out
sentences like

She mosi de bad mek she tek he.

which means, believe it or not, "She could only have married him
because she was completely broke."

Joyce agreed on one condition: that she could bring a chaperone. That surprised me. Not because of the condition itself. All
social codes are a mix of license and strictness; Caribbean and
American codes just mix the ingredients in different ways. It surprised me because of her choice of chaperone: her best friend, Beebie Beekie.

You could hardly imagine two people more different. Where
Joyce was abrasive and all business, Beebie was feminine and
pillow-soft. But the difference in personality wasn't the oddest
thing about their friendship. The oddest thing was that one was
Afro-Guyanese and the other was Indo-Guyanese.

Workers from India were brought to Guyana to cut sugar cane
after the abolition of slavery in the 1830s, when the Afro-
Guyanese, almost to a man, walked off the plantations and set up
as subsistence homesteaders. All through the subsequent years of
colonial rule, the British played the two races off against one another. But in the rising tide of anticolonialism that followed World
War II, they joined together to demand independence, and for a
few years it looked like Guyana might become a haven of interethnic harmony. But the Brits rallied, worked the divide-and-rule
routine they'd mastered over centuries, exploited personal jeal-
ousies between Cheddi Jagan, the Indo leader, and Forbes Burn-
ham, the Afro leader, and in no time brought the country to the
brink of an undeclared civil war in which, with British boots back
on Guyanese streets, they could pose as the peacemakers.

But not until the Guyanese had pioneered ethnic cleansing. Before that term was even a twinkle in Slobodan Milosevic's eye, they had forcibly homogenized a majority of Guyana's formerly mixed-race villages by beating, raping, and killing members of whichever race was in a minority in any given village, by burning their homes and stealing their possessions. You couldn't blame one side more than the other: Africans and Indians were equally ruthless in hounding out the other race wherever they could. The country became polarized. Few interethnic friendships survived: Joyce and Beebie weren't unique, but they came close.

I started work. What's the Creolese for such-and-such? Joyce answered, so-and-so. Beebie immediately protested. The real answer was something quite different. Joyce got indignant, and in seconds the two were going at each other hammer and tongs. "Ladies, please," I said, and as soon as I'd managed to calm them, meantime scribbling down both their answers, I tried another phrase or sentence. Joyce responded, Beebie protested, and they were at it again. Not just once or twice, but over and over.

I was totally buffaloed. Nothing in my training had led me to anticipate this. According to that training, the native speaker of any language was the ultimate authority on it. If that speaker said something was right, it was right. If, very occasionally, what one native speaker said contradicted what another native speaker said, then both were right—for their own particular dialects. But no one, apparently, had anticipated two native speakers who disagreed on virtually everything. What was the matter with them? Didn't they know their own language?

I decided the only thing I could do was find a third party to serve as tiebreaker, and the person I chose was George Cave.

People who knew him sometimes said that George—a high school teacher when I first met him, but soon to become a colleague at the university—had been deliberately invented by the Almighty to disprove all the stereotypes that whites have of blacks. He couldn't sing to save his life. He danced as badly as the most inept *bakra* (what white folks are called in the Caribbean). But he was a one-man army of tireless energy and furious efficiency. I'll never forget the day I accompanied him to a school sports meeting where for some reason several hundred students' lunches failed to show up. George went into overdrive, phoning, cursing, and when finally a truck arrived with the chow, unpacking and distributing cardboard boxes virtually single-handed (I tried to help, but couldn't keep up with him) at a bewildering speed. Here, surely, was a man whose yea was yea and his nay, nay, whose final judgment I could thoroughly trust.

I told him what Joyce had said and what Beebie had said. "Which is right?" I asked. "Neither of them," George said in his take-no-prisoners voice, handing me a third alternative. And again the process repeated itself, over and over.

By now I was getting really worried. Was it me? Was I a hopeless incompetent at the job? Or could it be true after all what denigrators of these languages had always said, that they had no grammar, you could just string things together anyhow you liked? It was blasphemy for a linguist to even think such thoughts, but suppose after all they were the truth?

At the last minute, I was saved by my own students.

I was teaching introductory linguistics to a class of twenty. I set them an assignment: translate this English passage into Creolese. The first three words were, "I was sitting . . ."; I forget what followed, and it hardly mattered, since for just those three words, from twenty students, I got thirteen different versions: *Me bina sit, Me did sittin', Ah de sittin'*, and on and on.

I had a sudden flash of inspiration. I wrote one of the versions on the blackboard, and asked, "What kind of person would be the most likely to say this?" Answer: an illiterate female rice-grower in Berbice. I wrote another. "And this one?" A middle-aged black stevedore on the Georgetown docks. By the end of the class, we had a "most probable speaker" for each of the thirteen variants.

Now at least I had some inkling of what I had to deal with, although I didn't as yet have the faintest idea how it could have come about. I was dealing with what were coming to be known as "sociolects"—dialects based not on geographic location but on social criteria: education, age, class, sex, occupation. Sociolects are found in all languages. I know of no language where Ivy Leaguers and street people speak the same way, even when they inhabit the same city. But nowhere else were the sociolects so different from one another. And yet this was in a country with less than a million people, almost all of them sandwiched into a strip of coastline a couple of hundred miles long and seldom more than ten miles wide. How could there be so much variation in so little space?

I began to collect variants and play around with them. Could you mix them up any old way? I did just that, and tried the mixes out on my informants, my students, and anyone I met. Could you say, for instance, *Ah bina sittin'*? No way! The reactions I got were like those of an old-time English teacher to things like "Nobody don't know nothing." In other words, certain expressions were ungrammatical for everyone. I knew then that there had to be a system in this apparent chaos, if I could only find it.

I began to shuffle and reshuffle the variants. Some looked more like English than others. I took the extremes—the ones most like English and the ones least like it—and tried to find out if it was possible to get from one to the other in a series of steps, changing just one word or one sound at a time. It was. The extremes were linked by a series of linguistic stepping stones.

A hypothesis popped into my mind. It was logical, it was plausible, and for many years I and many others believed that it was right.

The hypothesis was this. Suppose that, in slavery days, a Creole language had formed that was radically different from English. Nothing surprising in that, even if *how* it had formed remained a black box. Masters and slaves inhabited separate universes. Masters didn't want slaves to speak English, the tongue of the prestigious and powerful. Slaves needed to speak to one another far more than they needed to speak with masters. So between English and Creole there'd be a gulf, seemingly unbridgeable.

But then slavery ended and the descendants of slaves became, to a greater or lesser extent, socially mobile. Schools were set up. All were supposed to, and many did, become at least marginally literate in English. What would happen? Surely the higher you rose in the social pyramid, the more you'd see your native Creole as a hindrance to your social advancement, hence the more you'd want your speech to approximate English. So, after a century or so, the Guyanese would be strung out like runners in a race, with Standard English as the goal and finish line. But because of different degrees of exposure to English and different levels of motivation for getting there, the pace of the runners would vary far more than in other races. Some would have barely left the starting gate while others were almost breasting the tape, and the rest would be strung out all across the space between them.

What followed from this was a really exciting notion. Normally when you look at any language, even if you look at all the variation in it, what you are seeing is no more than a cross section of that language as it is right now. If you want to know about its past, you have to consult written records. But most of the world's languages and a large number of Creoles don't have any written records, and those Creoles that do have little if any for the crucial early stages. There is a process known as reconstruction that is standard for use with unwritten languages, but to use it you have to be able to compare sister languages. Since the ancestry of Creoles was still up for grabs, you couldn't tell which were sister languages, or even if there were any sister languages. So all avenues to the Creole past seemed blocked.

However, if I was correct, you *could* get at the past. In fact the past sat there right in front of your eyes. The variation I was charting constituted a literal cross section of history; the sociolects furthest from English were the oldest, the ones with a little more English influence were a little younger, and so on up to the most English-like varieties, which must have developed only in recent decades.

It was such a great idea that it took me a long time to find out what was wrong with it.

Meantime I was settling into my new routine. I had no more problems with Bill Carr, who, once he realized I had not the slightest interest in usurping his position, soon became a friend. Or with Harry Drayton, to whom, over time, I became indebted in ways that form part of another story. Because most of the students came from a working-class background (the middle and upper classes sent their children to more prestigious universities overseas) and therefore had to support themselves with day jobs, most classes took place in the evening, leaving my days free for study and research. And my purported task of solving Guyana's educational problems got shoved further and further into the background, never to emerge again.

Then, a few months into my new job, notice came of an international conference on Creole languages to be held on the Mona campus of the University of the West Indies in Jamaica. I eagerly applied for, and was promptly granted, travel funds to attend it. I sat there in genuine awe of the scholars who attended. A mere neophyte, I shut my big trap and opened my ears wide.

At that time, you could have numbered the world's Creole scholars on three or four pairs of hands, and few even of these had Creoles as their primary specialty. Almost all of them came to Mona; many were meeting one another for the first time. Some told how, as students, they had been warned off the study of Creoles. Weren't there more than enough *real* languages to go round? Becoming a creolist was regarded, in most universities, as professional suicide. I had the sense of being in on the ground floor of something. Quite what, nobody yet knew—there were almost as many theories as attendees. But for anyone in my shoes it was all thrilling and all new.

Two things about that conference stuck in my mind.

First was the paper presented by David DeCamp from the University of Texas. He had been working in Jamaica on the exact same kind of language variation that I had been struggling with. His analysis was far more sophisticated than my hopeful scribblings, but it was along the lines I had been pursuing. Yes, things had begun with English on the one hand, a radically different Creole on the other, and a huge and empty gap between. Over the years, just as I had thought, changing social circumstances had caused the gap to fill up. The variation found today simply reflected this process: it was living history, as if three centuries of language change and development had been frozen in time. I was delighted, and shyly congratulated him when we bumped into each other in the men's room. That was the start of a friendship sadly cut short by his untimely death.

David called the Jamaican situation a "post-Creole continuum." I agreed with all of it bar the name; to my mind, it wasn't "post"; the original Creole was still alive and well at the far end of the continuum. In that continuum you could not only rank varieties in order, from nearest-to-English to furthest-from-English, you could actually predict a good deal of what any given Jamaican would say. For instance, if someone used the expression *nyam*, meaning "eat," you would know immediately that he would say *no ben* rather than "didn't," *pikni* rather than "child," and that he'd pronounce /d/ and /t/ like /th/. With the statistical method David used, which is called implicational scaling, I knew I could begin to make sense of Guyanese variation.

The other thing that stuck was Douglas Taylor. Douglas had an unusual history. Unlike the rest of us, he had private means and could have led a life of leisure if he'd wanted to. But in college he became fascinated by the Garifuna, or Black Caribs—a strange community formed on the island of St. Vincent from the union of local Carib Indians with slaves who had escaped from shipwrecks. They fought the colonial powers for over a century until the British conquered them and shipped them off to Central America. There, Douglas studied their language, culture, and history. Since their language was a form of Carib rather than a Creole, he went on to the island of Dominica, the last refuge in the Caribbean of the people who'd given the sea its name. His first visit coincided with a brief uprising—the so-called Carib War of 1930—which the British authorities publicly accused him of fomenting. It was nonsense, of course; Douglas always took the side of the underdog, but violence was wholly foreign to his nature. Anyway, he was never prosecuted, and in 1938 he returned to Dominica, where he married a Carib woman and settled down.

So Carib rather than Creole was Douglas's main focus, which made it all the more remarkable that he not only knew Creole languages but could actually speak them fluently—something hardly any of the others could. His talk included several examples that bowled me over. Here's one of them, the same sentence in São

Tomense (a Portuguese Creole spoken on an island off the coast of West Africa) and Lesser Antillean (a French Creole spoken on Guadeloupe, Martinique, and other Caribbean islands, but somewhat different from Haitian)—two languages several thousand miles apart, whose speakers, so far as we know, had never been in contact with one another:

São Tomense:	Ke	nge	ka	bali	kee-se	da	bo?
Lesser Antillean:	Ki	mun	ka	balie	kay-la	ba	u?
Literal for both:	What person ASP sweep house-you give you?						
English for both:	"Who sweeps the house for you?"						
(ASP = aspect marker)							

And there were more.

How could these two languages be so alike? Could Douglas's own theory—monogenesis—possibly be right? Could there have been a single original Creole language that had spread all over the world, wherever sugar and slavery existed, changing words as it moved but keeping its basic grammar the same? His examples stuck in my mind like burrs, but it would be some years before the seeds they carried bore fruit.

Meanwhile I had a more pressing issue, to try and determine the full range of variation in Guyana and sort it all into some kind of meaningful order. In other words, I had to gather data, and that meant going out into the field.

If I'd been one of those systematic, methodical people, I would have studied the demographics of Guyana and selected a random sample that would proportionately represent all the classes, sexes, races, and age groups in the country, then interviewed them, one after another. I don't want to knock this approach, but it's not mine. I'm far too undisciplined, a fault I excuse by claiming to believe in serendipity. I'd cast myself on the waters and see what I dredged up.

I made use of contacts obtained through my students and other

people I knew, but my favorite modus operandi was simply to drive
around until I saw a bar I liked the look of. I'm still not sure what
my criteria were, for they all looked pretty much alike: bare rooms
with a counter at the back and a few rickety chairs and tables, the
front as often as not open to the street. The only real difference
was that some, amazingly, had "Club" in their names. I would walk
in, buy a beer, and get talking to someone—anyone. I carried the
cheapest Philips portable tape recorder slung over one shoulder,
and I would make no effort to hide it or the fact that it was running. The idea of surreptitious recording repelled me, convenient
though it might be.

It was, and is, convenient because of a phenomenon known as
code-switching.

Code-switching is one of those things, like talking prose, that
you've been doing all your life without realizing it. Would you talk
to your boss the same way you talk to your high school buddies?
Giving testimony in court, wouldn't you become still more formal?
In a language like English, the range through which you shift in
these switches is not great: it affects mostly the degree of care with
which you pronounce things and the kind of vocabulary you
choose, but has little effect on the basic grammar that most varieties of English share. In Guyana, differences were much greater
and affected every aspect of speech. And although, as my class had
taught me, a certain variety of speech might be typical of a Georgetown dock worker, that didn't mean the dock worker would always
talk that way. It just meant that it was his home ground, the kind of
speech in which he felt most comfortable and natural. He might
not be able to talk down as far as a Berbice rice-grower or up as far
as a high school teacher, but he could shift around quite a bit in the
middle. Others might have a much wider range. Suppose you were
a shop steward in a rural trade union. You'd have to speak something pretty close to English when you were negotiating with the
bosses, but you'd have to speak the deepest Creole if rank-and-file
union members were going to believe you and trust you. And quite
likely you'd control the intermediate varieties as well.

So, when suddenly confronted by a large white stranger driving
a Land Rover with a university logo, people were not about to

speak in the way most natural to them. I couldn't talk to them in Creole: they would have regarded that as patronizing, or presumptuous, or just weird. I could, and did, roughen my speech and manner, to that extent taking off some of the curse of color and education, but I couldn't totally efface myself, and the fact that they were being recorded added a further element of unnaturalness to the scene. To record surreptitiously would have at least removed one factor from the equation, but it would also have violated my most deeply held beliefs about the rights of others. I sometimes wondered what I'd do if someone confessed to a murder on tape; unless it was especially heinous, I decided, I'd keep my mouth shut.

As it happened, after a couple of drinks people usually ceased to be aware of the tape recorder and began to talk more naturally. Better still, they'd get into conversations with one another in which I became a mere bystander. And then, maybe someone would suggest moving on to someone's house and sampling a bottle of "bushy."

"Bushy" is home-brewed rum, double the strength of the legal, excised kind. There is a rule of hospitality in Guyana that says if there's a bottle on the table, nobody gets up until it's finished. Trouble is, just at that point someone may come in with another bottle. If you don't have a good head for liquor, don't even try to do fieldwork this way.

My experiences provided objective evidence for something I'd subjectively known for years. Most of the Spanish I speak was learned from drunks in bars. In fact, drunks are the world's most underrated language teaching resource. The stereotypic drunk speaker slurs his speech to the point of unintelligibility, but in real life this happens only in the final, immediate-pre-collapse phase of drunkenness. Prior to that, drunks speak slowly and with exaggerated care, because they know they are drunk but don't want other people to know. Moreover, since they're already too drunk to remember what they just said, they repeat themselves over and over, and don't mind if you do the same. If you're gregarious and a drinker, it's by far the easiest way to learn a new language.

But because drunks are conscientiously monitoring their speech, it's not the best way to elicit the deepest Creole. Accordingly I curtailed my nighttime investigations, though days do have a habit of turning into nights when you're in the field. The one thing I got right from the start was to focus my research on working-class speakers, and in particular on that section of the working class most resistant to bourgeois values. Most academics can't or won't do this, as Beryl Bailey demonstrated statistically.

Beryl was a wholly engaging and feisty black Jamaican woman who wasn't afraid to go up against her own teachers. She wrote the first generative grammar of a Creole language. She also reanalyzed the samples of Jamaican speech that had been presented by Bob LePage, her mentor, as the deepest form of Jamaican Creole, and by an ingenious system of giving numerical values to the various expressions proved beyond any doubt that his samples came not from the deep end but from about halfway across the continuum—precisely because LePage had failed to find the right informants. It was a brilliant piece of work, but Beryl's life, like Dave DeCamp's, was cut tragically short. I was shocked the other day when I Googled her and got fewer than two dozen hits, all tangential. Someone should memorialize her.

In any Creole-speaking community, the people who speak the deepest Creole are what you might call the unrighteous working class. I chose to work with working-class rather than middle-class people, and with the unrighteous versus the righteous working class, by sheer gut feeling. I didn't even realize what I was doing or even that there were righteous and unrighteous classes until one Sunday morning when I was working out in Berbice, the remotest coastal district. I was driving along in the university's Land Rover when I spotted a bar where a bunch of men in torn and dirty shorts and T-shirts were leaning on the front rail of its verandah *gyaffin*, which is Guyanese for shooting the breeze. I braked immediately and joined them. After a few drinks someone suggested we move to their place for some bushy, so we all piled into the Land Rover and set out.

At that moment, the service finished in the local church, and suddenly the twisting dirt road filled with men in collars and ties and neat, if shiny or threadbare, suits, and women in flowered dresses with hats from another epoch, all of them still clutching prayer books in their fists. They walked in front of us at a solemn, decorous pace. Damned if they were going to get out of the way of a 4WD full of boozing heathens.

The road was too narrow for me to pass. I had no recourse but to crawl after them at walking pace while my passengers turned the air blue with their comments. The righteous studiously ignored these. But then as we crept along, first one, then another, peeled off to enter their homes. And those homes were all little wooden boxes on stilts—exactly like all the other homes in the village, including the one we would shortly enter for our Sabbath-defying booze-up. The fundamental difference between my passengers and the worshippers was not one of class, or income, or education—it was one of attitude. My passengers rejected the authority structure, the worshippers accepted it. If I'd recorded the worshippers instead of the passengers, I'd have gotten something about three times closer to English.

I collected some wonderful stories: about adventures in the bush (Guyana's vast untrodden hinterland where none but the intrepid go—call it "jungle" and you brand yourself a tenderfoot); about atrocities committed in the Disturbances, that epoch of ethnic cleansing I mentioned earlier; and about strange supernatural beings, of which Guyana hosts more than its fair share. Like the Water-Mamma, a female creature some Guyanese will refer to only by her euphemism, Fair-Maid; she appears to young men as a seductive woman who lures them to a river bank, then seizes them and drags them under. One of my informants told me, in all seriousness, that an uncle of his had been pulled under by a Water-Mamma only to surface three weeks later in Trinidad, so his folks had to wire him the money to fly home. But for me the scariest was the Moon-Gazer, a spectral creature fifty feet high that appeared on nights of full moon, and it scared me because I'd seen it, when I was about five, in a dream I remember to this day; I crept through a hole in a hedge into a fallow, moon-drenched field, and there it was, towering over me, stooping . . . At that point, fortunately, I woke.

And there were adventures that were neither hearsay nor dream. What was perhaps the strangest happened when I was chatting with the uncle of one of my students in his home in a village twenty miles west of Georgetown. Suddenly a guy waving a cutlass (as the machete is still called in the Caribbean) burst in, screaming obscenities. I knew at once who he was because the uncle had just been telling me about him. He had already hacked one neighbor to death and had escaped justice only because his lawyer was a man known as "the Guyanese Perry Mason," who'd gotten dozens of other murderers acquitted. And of course, at that very moment, a soft click informed me that the tape in my trusty Philips had just run out.

Dare I put in a new cassette? The stream of profanity that was pouring from the murderer's mouth represented perhaps the most comprehensive anthology of Guyanese cusswords ever uttered. I would have given anything to record it. Well, almost anything. Obviously not my life. But if he saw me putting in a cassette, what was that life worth? Not much, given that a well-aimed cutlass stroke can take off a limb or a head.

Self-preservation trumped science. Meanwhile, the uncle was magnificent. Neither showing fear nor giving provocation, he spoke calmly and logically to his uninvited guest until the latter lowered his weapon. Seizing the initiative, the uncle suggested a drink. The murderer assented. We adjourned to a bar across the street. The murderer got very drunk very fast. He began to rave about white folk. White folk, he assured us, were God. And I was white folk. So, logically, I too was God.

Wholly without warning he fell on his knees and embraced my legs, crying out at the top of his voice, "You are God!" I've never been more embarrassed in my life. Fortunately the other patrons of the bar, ordinary working folk, had the decency not to laugh. And after a while the murderer picked himself up, staggered out of the bar, and collapsed on a footbridge over a canal. A light rain began to fall. While the uncle and I sat there drinking, analyzing and reanalyzing the incident, we could see him lying unconscious in rain that turned slowly to a steady downpour. When we left, he was still there.

3

A DIFFERENT KIND OF SYSTEM

———

By now I was getting used to the intricacies of Guyanese grammar. There weren't supposed to be any, of course. Creoles were supposed to be "simple" languages; many regarded them as just "simplified" European languages. At the Mona conference we'd wasted a whole morning discussing "simplicity" and what it might mean in a Creole context. Unsurprisingly, nobody could agree on this. Creoles may look simple. They're not.

Take the sentence we met at the beginning of the previous chapter:

Look a red man a piss a road corner.

As this sentence suggests, most of the words in Guyanese Creole are immediately recognizable as English words, just as in a French Creole, most of the words are recognizable as French words (and the same goes for Spanish, Dutch, and Portuguese Creoles, though there's a handful of exceptions I'll discuss in a later chapter). But the fact that the words look the same doesn't mean that they mean the same.

For instance, you probably thought, just as I did, that *road corner* meant "the corner of the road." But there were no corners in sight: the road was straight. In fact it means "by the side of the road."

Why should some of the most common words change their

meanings in Creole? Until recently, almost anyone would have said, "Because it's just broken English." And left it at that. The obvious questions any serious inquirer would ask—who broke it, how did they break it, why is it broken the way it is and not some other way?—they would have dismissed as unworthy of consideration, thereby demonstrating their contempt for both the language and the people who spoke it.

Words in Creoles change their meaning for a variety of reasons. Perhaps the most common is the fact that a lot of words were simply lost in the extraordinary circumstances that gave birth to Creoles. Take a typical Guyanese query: *What time we go reach?* Reach what? Well, wherever you're headed for. *Reach* simply means "arrive," and means it because "arrive" got lost in the shuffle: if you're Guyanese and you ask another Guyanese, "When will we arrive?" they'll probably respond with a *chups*, or *suck-teeth* (a Caribbean-wide expression of contempt, made by literally sucking one's teeth), and call you an "English duck." In other words, when words are lost from the vocabulary, other words move over to fill the gaps.

The change in meaning of *road corner*, however, is due to another common cause—the original meaning of one word can be preempted by a change in another word's meaning. You can't say "the side of the road" because "side" has already been co-opted for a different function.

You might think that in any contact between folk speaking mutually unintelligible languages, some of the few things that would surely get through would be question words: who? what? when? which? where? how? why? After all, people who have trouble understanding one another must be constantly asking questions. Well, you'd be wrong. Typically, a Creole will acquire just one question word from its dominant European language. It might be "who," or "what," or "which"—it makes no difference, that word henceforth will signify just "Q for question." Then to this you have to add another word: "Q person" for "who?" "Q time" for "when?" "Q place" for "where?" and so on. Often it's even more opaque. Haitian Creole for "who?" is *ki moun. Moun* is the Haitian version of French *monde*, "world," so you might initially translate this as "who world?" Then you'd remember that *le monde* is used by the

French to mean "people in general," so *ki moun* really does mean "Q person," or "who?"

Not all Creoles have the full deck of two-piece question words—for a variety of reasons, some got lost or never took shape—but almost every Creole has at least one or two. In the oldest form of Guyanese, *wissaid*, derived from "which side," was the chosen form for "Q place." That meant that *side* could thereafter mean "place" and only "place" and therefore could no longer mean "side." But something meaning "side" still had to be said, so they co-opted "corner"; *a road corner* now means "by the side of the road."

And these are only a few of the kinds of thing that can happen to words. For example, nouns can and often do turn into verbs. You don't dust a room, you *cobweb* it; you don't steal something, you *thief* (pronounced *teef*) it. This creates new gaps, which in turn have to be filled; since *thief* is now a verb, a thief has to become a *teefman*.

Things lost from the ends of words cause a different kind of change. Take a word like "stupidity." Like most abstract words, that one was unlikely to be used much down on the plantation ("stupid" was another matter, of course). So "stupid" survived but "stupidity" didn't. But there was still need for a word that would mean the condition of being stupid. One of the few suffixes that survived was "-ness," so that word is *stupidness* (correct pronunciation, *chupitness*).

Then there are the things you can't say, like "mashed potatoes." You can't say "mashed potatoes" because *mash* means "to press or crush with the feet." When I went for my car's first safety check, the cop in charge said, "Mash you brakes." I hesitated, bewildered. "Mash you brakes, mon!" Only then did I realize he meant for me to press the brake pedal. It was for this reason that the housekeeper of a government rest house in the interior (a couple miles from where, seven years later, the Jonestown massacre took place) offered me "beef with crushed potatoes"—who'd want potatoes that had been tràmpled underfoot?

Or take my favorite Guyanese headline, MAN GETS FOUR YEARS FOR BORING A WOMAN. The most radical feminist might think this excessive, but of course it doesn't mean what it seems to mean. The Guyanese word in the reporter's mind was *jook*, but he couldn't use that, and the editor would have cut it if he had. *Jook* is a word of African, possibly Bambara, origin which means "pierce, stab, penetrate," and from this it has acquired the further meaning of "to have sexual intercourse." (It's likely "jukebox" comes from the same source, but that's another story.) Thus there were three good reasons why the newspaper couldn't use *jook*. One, it was an African word, and African words were looked down on. Two, it was also a "dirty word." Three, the story concerned a stabbing, not a rape case. And the replacement word for *jook* in that sense is "bore"—as in to bore a hole in something, or someone. Thus "bore" replaces "pierce," "stab," "penetrate," and all the similar words that got lost when the Creole was formed.

But sometimes it's the other way round: Guyana has preserved the old meanings of words that English has lost. I was baffled at first when a woman told me she had to *naint baby*. In modern English, the word "anoint" hardly occurs except in a handful of old-fashioned expressions like "the Lord's anointed." But in the seventeenth century, it simply meant "to put oil on someone"—only later did it shrink to its present quasi-liturgical meaning. In Guyana, the initial vowel was lost (a common fate—"America" is still *Meriki* for some older speakers) but the old meaning remained.

Then there are the words for which there's no equivalent in English. Such as the word for the smallest possible quantity—a *kn*. Or what looks like a related word but isn't—*kina*. "Da mi kina," someone will say, explaining why they can't eat a particular dish they've been offered. They mean it's been made from their totemic animal—part of a belief system inherited from Africa—and therefore they're prohibited from eating it. But I've heard people of Indian descent using the expression, since many, though not all, practices and beliefs are shared by everyone in the Creole culture, regardless of origins.

I could fill the rest of this chapter, maybe even the book, with ways in which the Guyanese vocabulary differs from English. Some readers may wish I would. One of the differences between linguists and people is that people like words better than grammar and linguists like grammar better than words—they're looking for systems, and words just aren't systematic. But unless we grapple with grammar, we'll never really understand Guyanese, or Creoles in general.

Let's start with something relatively straightforward—the three *a*'s in "Look a red man a piss a road corner." All of these *a*'s are different, and not one of them is the English indefinite article "a." (Of course you'll find English indefinite articles in the varieties closest to English, but in what follows I'll be talking about the "deepest" kind of Creole, the kind that differs most radically from English.)

The first *a* is a definite, not an indefinite, article. It's a reduced form of *da*, which was the archaic, original form, and which most likely derives from "that" (you could hardly get more definite than that!); it has nothing, beyond a shared meaning, in common with the English definite article "the." The second *a* marks aspect, the category that tells us not the time of an action (that's tense) but its nature, whether it's ongoing, completed, habitual, or whatever. Here it means the verb is the equivalent of our present progressive "is pissing." It may or may not have something to do with archaic English expressions like "he's a-going." The third *a* is a reduced form of *na*, the archaic, all-purpose locative marker, which can stand for "in" or "on" or "at" or any other locative preposition. It may come from Portuguese *na*, "in the/on the," or it may be that it happened when an epenthetic vowel (a vowel added for ease of pronunciation by speakers of a language whose words must end in vowels) was added to "in," giving *ina*, and then *ina* was generalized to other locative expressions (just as "who" or "which" was generalized to all question words), losing its initial vowel in the process, just like *naint* did. Multiple possible derivations are the bane of Creole etymologists.

This gives you at least a taste of what makes Creoles look simple: they use, compared to older languages, a far smaller inventory of items. But since they perform all the functions that other languages perform, they have to work harder, so to speak, and put more weight on syntactic structures than on individual words. You can easily distinguish the meanings of the three *a*'s once you realize that one only comes with nouns or noun phrases, one only comes with verbs (and must always be directly before a verb), and one always comes with adverbial expressions of place.

The reductio ad absurdum of putting syntax before words appears in the sentence Guyanese love to tease newbie *bakras* with:

De de de.

"Tell us what that means," they say to the bewildered American or Englishman. Well, it means "They are there." The first *de* is just "they" with its interdental fricative replaced by a stop consonant. Same with the third *de*: just a rephonologized "there." But the second *de* is much more interesting, because it takes us into an area where Guyanese grammar is not simpler but actually more complex than English.

English has a single verb "to be," which occurs in a variety of contexts. The Guyanese have three verbs for the same set of functions. Or rather two verbs plus what we linguists call a "zero form," a verb that is "not phonologically realized" and looks to the layman like nothing at all:

I am hungry = me hongry.
The boy is lazy = di bai lazy.

This is typically what happens when the predicate is an adjective. If it's a noun, you get yet another *a*:

I am captain = me a kyapn.

However, if the predicate is an expression indicating location, *de* must be used:

I am in Georgetown = me de a Jarjtong.

If there is no predicate (as in Descartes' "I think, therefore I am") then the meaning must be the same as "exist," and again *de* is used:

God is/exists = Gad de.

Actually, for ease of exposition, I've oversimplified this description. Take the contrast between *he sick* (a permanent condition) and *he de sick* (a temporary illness), or between *he bad* (morally evil) and *he de bad* (short of money): this helps explain Joyce Trotman's "She mosi de bad mek she tek he," quoted in the previous chapter. And if you say simply *de de*, that means they're shacking up together. Just a simple language for simple folk, right?

Another area where Guyanese Creole is more complex than English—and for that matter more logical than English—lies in its article system. In English, you can't use a count noun without either an article or a plural. You can say "bread" by itself (you can't count it) but you can't say "loaf" by itself (you can count them). You can say, "I bought *a* loaf" or "I bought *the* loaf" or "I bought loaves," but you can't say, "I bought loaf." In Guyana you can. Indeed you have to, if you don't know or if it just doesn't matter whether you're talking about one or several, or perhaps even none.

Say for example you want some books. You can say in English, "I'm going to buy books," but in point of fact you don't yet know whether you'll actually buy some, or just one, or perhaps not find any of the ones you're looking for. But you can't say, "I'm going to buy book." The best you can do is, "I'm going book-buying," but this is the kind of stilted expression no one ever uses. However, in Guyana, *me go buy book* is just fine. This very natural and logical state of affairs extends even into Guyanese official English: in the Georgetown Zoo, the cage of a particular bird species included a note that said, "Frequents tall tree." Not "tall trees"; that would suggest that, if there were just one tall tree among smaller trees, the bird would scorn it. Not "a tall tree"; that would suggest there was just one particular tall tree the bird would condescend to live in. "Tall tree" fits the facts better than either of the English alternatives.

And talking about logic, people frequently claim that while Creole languages may be just fine for schmoozing in, they can't handle heavy-duty stuff like science or philosophy. Well, take the

Descartes dictum I quoted just now: "I think, therefore I am." Can you translate that into Creole?

Sure. While the verb "think" is widely used, there is a much older and more typically Creole equivalent, *mi mind gi' me*. But this, unlike "think," demands an object, introduced by the particle *se*. What object could you have, in this context? Only the fact that you exist. So the translation is:

Mi mind gi' me se me de mek me de.
[My mind gives me that I exist] causes [(the fact that) I exist].

Tautologous? Well, yes. But when you think about it, so's Descartes' original. Indeed, the ruthless honesty of Creole (in Haitian, *pale kreol* means "to speak the truth," *pale franse*—"speak French"—means "to lie") exposes the essential circularity and vacuity of the celebrated philosopher's historic phrase.

This should already be enough to convince you that the old belief "Creoles have no grammar" is about as far from the truth as you could get. They have grammar, an enormous amount of grammar, but it's not English or French or Portuguese grammar, it's something completely different. Whatever the first Guyanese Creole speakers did, they didn't "simplify" English—they didn't know enough English to be able to simplify it—and they didn't "creolize" it, whatever that means (the title of the Mona conference was "The Pidginization and Creolization of Languages"—as if creolization was a generally accepted and well-understood process, a kind of mincing machine where if you put a European language in one end, a Creole would come out the other). Instead, Creoles were going their own way. They were working to some kind of pattern of their own. But what was that pattern, and where had it come from?

The place where the pattern was most striking was in the tense-modality-aspect (TMA) system.

This is what the layman usually thinks of as just tense. Teaching grammars of languages are no better; they talk about "perfect tense" and "conditional tense," though these things aren't really tenses at all. Tense simply tells you when the action took place, aspect (as we saw just now) tells you the type of action that's being talked about, and modality tells you whether it's a real, a hypothetical, or a possible-in-the-future kind of action. So English perfect tense—"I have done"—mixes tense with aspect, showing that you're talking about a completed rather than an uncompleted action, while conditional tense—"I would do"—is really modality, showing that you're talking about a hypothetical rather than a real action.

The first thing you notice about tense in Guyana is that it doesn't work the same way as in English. Look at the default form— the verb stem that doesn't have any "-ing" or "-ed" tacked onto it. In English, this indicates what grammar books call the "simple present" or "present indicative." The term is a bit misleading, because if you say "I play tennis" it's unlikely that you're playing tennis at this present moment. What it means is that the reference point for the English TMA system—what it takes as its fixed point for measuring time from—is the present moment. It means that you play tennis around that point, so to speak: you have played it before and you expect to go on playing it in the future. Whereas if you say "I played tennis," this means that you played tennis at some time in the past, and may or may not imply, depending on context, that you don't play anymore.

The Guyanese TMA system is completely different. Me *play tennis* means that you played tennis on some particular occasion in the past. In other words, the reference point for Guyanese (and other Creoles) is *not* the present moment, but whatever point in the past you're talking about. And if you were to say Me *bin play tennis*, that would mean you had played tennis at some time *before* the time you are talking about.

If this sounds weird to you, think about it. You could argue that the Guyanese system is the more logical. After all, what exactly is the present moment? It's a constantly moving target; before you can grasp it, it's gone already. As a fixed reference point, it leaves much to be desired. But a definite action in the past occurred at a fixed time and will always stay that way.

, So how would you say "I play tennis" in Guyana? Answer: Me a play tennis, using the second a in "Look a red man a piss a road corner." Once again, the Creole is more logical. English (like most European languages) mixes tense, aspect, and modality in really messy ways. For instance, English "present tense" marks habitual aspect as well as tense—things you do regularly and repeatedly. Guyanese a marks both habitual and ongoing actions—I call it a "nonpunctual" marker because it can indicate any action that's not a single event at a particular point in time. It follows that Me a play tennis can mean either "I play tennis" or "I am playing tennis." Is this a weakness? Not really. Context usually disambiguates it. If you're talking about something you're doing right now, I can see that you're doing it. If I can't, I assume you do it habitually.

The Guyanese TMA system has a logical elegance that you very seldom find in the systems of older languages. It has one tense marker, bin, one modality marker, go, and one aspect marker, a. Given that there is only one possible order—first tense, then modality, then aspect—these can combine in all possible ways, as follows (I use "V" to indicate the default form, the bare stem of the verb, and to simplify matters, I'm talking only about verbs that express an action, like "do" or "play," rather than a state, like "know" or "love"—they behave slightly differently):

V	punctual action, past
bin V	punctual action, past-before-past
go V	irrealis (hypothetical or future action)
a V	nonpunctual, present or past
bin a V	nonpunctual, past-before-past
bin go V	irrealis, past-before-past
go a V	irrealis, nonpunctual
bin go a V	irrealis, nonpunctual, past-before-past

None of these corresponds exactly with any of the English "tenses," which is why I'm not giving you English translations for them; me do might sometimes translate as "I did," sometimes as "I have done," and me go do as sometimes "I will do," sometimes "I would do." Instead, each TMA marker is like an independent atom of meaning, and each keeps its meaning constant so that you can deductively derive the meanings of the combined forms. What's more, in contrast with the things the English TMA system uses, these atoms don't have any other functions besides expressing tense, modality, and aspect. Take a sentence like "If it hadn't started to rain, I would have been playing tennis by now"—a sentence in the Guyanese equivalent of which you would use all three markers, *bin go a play*. For that, English has to use "have," which is also its regular verb for possession, and "be," also its verb for equivalence/existence, in addition to the "-en" and "-ing" suffixes that have functions similar to (but not quite the same as) *bin* and *a*. Compared to Guyanese Creole, English TMA is a mess.

But what's more to the point is that, as the Maine farmer said, you can't get there from here. There is no way in which you could derive the Guyanese system from the English system by modifying it, simplifying it, chopping it up and rearranging it, or any other conceivable procedure. It had to come from somewhere else. But where?

I began to think about this more and more. But as far as my everyday work was concerned, I was still busy with my continuum of varieties.

I was lucky in that variation was currently a hot topic in the U.S. Several factors contributed to this. One was a negative reaction to Chomsky's take on what linguists ought to be studying. In 1965, Chomsky had written, "Linguistic theory is concerned primarily with an ideal speaker-listener, in a completely homogeneous speech-community, who knows its language perfectly and is unaffected by such grammatically irrelevant conditions as memory limitations, distractions, shifts of attention and interest, and errors (random or characteristic) in applying his knowledge of the language in actual performance." This uncompromising sentence served as a red rag to the bull for folk who believed language was a highly variable social construct. In fact, it's a perfectly legitimate scientific generalization, like what Newton did when he investigated the tides. He did not rent a boy and a rowboat and tour the harbors of the world with a plumb bob, measuring high and low tide wherever he went. He hypothesized an earth covered by an ocean of uniform depth, worked out mathematically what effect the moon's pull would have on that, and thus produced a model from which you could calculate what the tides would be anywhere in the world. Fact may be the flesh of science; idealization is its lifeblood.

But the reaction of the social constructionists was fueled by, well, social forces.

In the 1960s, America experienced a wave of race riots that focused attention on the deep rifts still dividing American society. Americans were made forcibly aware that the melting pot hadn't melted. Blacks and whites were still miles apart in their culture, their lifestyles, their values . . . and their language. How could whites understand what blacks wanted if whites couldn't even understand what blacks meant?

So the study of what they said and what they meant by it became a growth industry in academia. But to study what was variously known as Afro-American Vernacular English or Black English, you couldn't do what the Chomskyan linguist did, sit in your office and study your own intuitions. When it came to Black English, white intuitions weren't worth a dime. But, thanks to just the kind of thing blacks were protesting, the vast majority of linguists were still white. So the only thing they could do was exactly what I did in Guyana—go out in the street and record the actual speech Afro-Americans used. Once you'd got that, you could start dealing with the "memory limitations, distractions, shifts of attention and interest, and errors (random or characteristic)" that had Chomsky so worried. Until you got real data, you could do nothing.

Linguists soon found out that there wasn't a single, monolithic Black English, but rather a continuum, nothing like as broad but similar in kind to the one in Guyana. So people who'd already started studying language variation took a front seat, and the frontest seat of all was occupied by Bill Labov.

Labov, originally trained as an industrial chemist, had switched to linguistics, and his doctoral dissertation, on speech variation in Martha's Vineyard, quickly followed by a massive and meticulously documented study of speech variation in New York City, had established him as America's number-one sociolinguist. Now he had turned to the complexities of Black English. But he dealt with variation in a way very different from that of DeCamp and me. He had invented what he called "variable rules." These were not the rigid rules of orthodox grammars; what they did was estimate the frequency with which people of particular ethnic groups, social classes, or educational backgrounds would use particular pronunciations or particular grammatical expressions. To write a variable rule, you first had to sort speakers into classes based on these and other social conditions.

To me, this was putting the cart before the horse. And a horse with a cart in front of it is going nowhere. Once you had cataloged who spoke what when and where, where were you going to go with it all? It seemed to me to lead only to more and more purely descriptive studies, studies that would explain none of the things about language I wanted to know. So DeCamp and I had adopted the reverse procedure, sorting people according to the variety of language they used. Once you'd done that, you could match types of language with clusters of social variables, if you wanted to, or you could look at what interested me far more: the way in which all the parts of a linguistic continuum fitted together, out of which you might (or so I dreamed) extract basic principles that would explain how and why languages are constantly changing.

Moreover, looking at my growing data collection and testing out Labovian variable rules on it, I found cases where Bill's approach seemed to produce misleading or even incorrect results. If you grouped people according to social variables, you'd find anomalies; a deep Creole speaker in a middle-class urban group, a speaker close to English in a group of rural peasants. Obviously there were variables of motivation and self-identification that crosscut social strata and influenced people just as much as the familiar factors of age, education, income, and so on. But my main complaint was that "variable rules" didn't reflect the realities of language. For a group of people it might be true, if unilluminating, to say they did something with a 30 or 75 percent probability. But individuals don't work that way, at least not when it comes to grammar. With the sounds of speech, maybe: half the time I don't know whether I'm pronouncing "French" as *frentch* or *frensh*, and I bet you don't, either. But when people say sometimes *me bin do* and sometimes *ah did do*, that conveys subtle differences in the way they look at the situation they're in, or the way they feel about the people they're speaking to.

So I wrote a paper entitled "Inherent Variability and Variable Rules," and sent it off to a journal called *Foundations of Language*. Bingo! It was accepted. Pure merit, I told myself. That it was a hot topic, that the editor might have been happy to see Labov put down, that someone may even have thought that, writing from Guyana about Guyana, I could be black and therefore deserved a little equal opportunity—it never occurred to me, innocent as I then was, that considerations of this kind might have played a part. Anyway, before it hit the streets I sent a manuscript copy to Labov.

I suspect many scholars of Bill's eminence would have simply ignored this unsolicited approach from a brash upstart. Some would have been livid, and would have told me so. Bill's response was to send me, almost by return mail, a single-spaced twelve-page letter analyzing our points of difference, defending some of his views, accepting a few of mine, all in the most cordial and collegial of tones. I would learn, as we became friends, that this was typical of him. He "has no side," as we used to say in the old country, meaning no pretensions, no exaggerated care for his own dignity. On top of which he has a degree of emotional detachment from his own work that is very rare in academia.

I think what appealed to him most was that, like him but unlike most linguists, I was prepared to go down mean streets and get my hands dirty with raw data. There was at the time a kind of macho camaraderie among those who called themselves "street linguists," as opposed to "closet linguists" who worked mainly in their own heads. We were a minority, but the future was ours, or at least so some of us thought. I was somewhat skeptical from the start. Although I enjoyed field work, I was a street linguist from necessity more than from conviction. But it was fun to go along with, while it lasted.

And that first exchange of letters led to one of those episodes I can only call "intellectual infatuations," of which I've probably had a dozen or so in the course of my life. They are indeed like love affairs without sex: they begin abruptly and without warning, they involve intense, rapid, and passionate exchanges of correspondence, they don't last very long, and they give way to complete indifference or occasionally, as was the case with Bill, a calmer but more lasting relationship. A relationship that, a couple of years later, would open perhaps the most crucial door in my career.

Although I still had a ways to go before I knew and thoroughly understood the full range of Guyanese variation, I could already see that this wasn't going to be my life's work. I was thinking more and more about how Creoles could have begun, and in particular about where the Guyanese TMA system could have come from. Long before Morris Goodman hammered the last nail into the coffin of monogenesis, I found that hypothesis hard to accept. How could a single language spread all over the world, keeping its original grammar virtually intact? Who could have spread it, given that slaves relatively seldom moved from country to country, and even when they did, seldom if ever moved outside the domain of one or another colonial power?

Such a language could have existed only if, very soon after if not before the start of slavery, Africans living on a stretch of coastline from the Gambia to Angola, well over three thousand miles long, had all spoken the same contact language, whether a pidgin or a Creole. Moreover, that language could not have been some makeshift affair; it must have already developed a complex and highly stable grammar. How could this have come about? Before the arrival of Europeans, Africans had few contacts outside their local communities; they had no sailing ships, no long-distance roads, and the area was split into a host of tiny states, frequently at war with one another, which would have made travel a risky business even if it had been possible. Improbability piled on improbability until the whole edifice collapsed.

But what was the alternative? Only the substrate languages, the

unnumbered tongues spoken by Africans at the time of their en-
slavement. The secret must surely lie there somewhere. There was
little I could do in Guyana, given its meager library resources. But
as soon as my four-year stint was over, I'd go back to England and
delve into all the grammars of African languages I could find,
searching for the one—there must surely be one—that had the exact same TMA system Guyana had.

Meantime, a creolist with only one Creole (and there are still
too many of these, even today) was like a bird with only one wing.
Consequently, long before the point I've now reached—back as far
as the Mona conference of 1968—I'd already set myself to remedy
this by looking in the one place where, the conventional wisdom
said, there weren't any Creoles and indeed couldn't be any Creoles
at all.

4

COLOMBIA BEFORE COCAINE

———

B ack then it was the conventional wisdom that there couldn't
be any Creole languages in Latin America. Race relations,
the story went, were much healthier in Latin than in Anglo
or other Euro cultures. Blacks had been absorbed into the general
population. No race distinction meant no linguistic distinction.
Descendants of African slaves would speak the same kind of Spanish as descendants of free white immigrants from Extremadura or
Andalusia.

I suspected, and later found, that the sociological side of this is
nonsense. Of course there were distinctions of color, not the same
as U.S. distinctions, but distinctions nonetheless. And I reasoned
that if there were distinctions of color, distinctions of language
would surely follow, as night follows day, in at least some places.

But where to look?

I got hold of a demographic atlas of the Americas and checked
out the population balance in every country in or near the tropics.
Leaving Brazil aside (I wasn't interested in Portuguese-based languages at this stage), the highest concentration of black people was
in Colombia, particularly in the north, on the Caribbean coast,
where they amounted to 30 percent of the population. I guessed,
again correctly, that the distribution would be skewed, giving the
possibility of black majorities locally. Bingo, I thought. If Creole
Spanish exists anywhere, it'll be here.

At the Mona conference, I asked everyone if they'd ever heard of anything that might possibly be a Creole or semi-creolized form of Spanish in Colombia. Nobody had. Bill Stewart, who looked more like a tugboat skipper than a prof, claimed to have heard some funny-sounding Spanish when he was hanging out in Santa Marta, near the east end of Colombia's north coast, but that was all the information I got.

I phoned the airline office, and found that for no additional cost they could reroute my return trip to Guyana via Colombia. Around midnight my plane landed in Barranquilla. The place looked dead. Three dispirited-looking taxis waited outside the airport. I took the first, and asked the driver, "Is there anywhere around here where they speak a funny kind of Spanish?"

"Sure," he said. "Village the other side of Cartagena—El Palenque de San Basilio."

I couldn't believe my ears. But still I dared to ask, "You wouldn't happen to know if there's anyone around here who knows about it, would you?"

"Well," he said, "I've heard there's a guy at the Universidad del Atlántico, but I'm sorry I don't know his name."

If you want to find out anything, don't ask the experts, ask the locals.

After a grueling night in a Barranquilla fleabag, with no air conditioning but plenty of mosquitoes that a highly audible electric fan did nothing to dispel, I set out. When I asked a traffic cop how to get to the center of town, he looked at me reproachfully and said, "This is the center of town." Eventually I found my way to the Universidad del Atlántico, a huddle of narrow, cement-block, louvered-window buildings, at an angle to the prevailing wind, standard issue for new third-world universities; the concrete had as usual started crumbling already. There, after a half hour of asking around, I found my man, Aquilas Escalante.

Later, a bearded Colombian professor of anthropology (who on one memorable evening rode his mountain bike through the best nightclub in Popayán) told me that Escalante was known in his profession as "El Moreno," the Dark Guy. In other words, he was the only anthropologist in Colombia who wasn't lily-white—so much for that famous Latin color blindness. In Guyana he would have been a red man, a stocky individual who bore psychic scars from getting to where he'd gotten to. He had indeed been studying the Palenqueros for many years, though his main interest was their culture rather than their language. And he told me all he knew about them.

In the early 1600s, or so the story goes, Domingo Bioho, a.k.a. El Rey Benkos, was a slave working on the fortifications of Cartagena (you can still see these structures today, and massive they are). He was from Angola, and claimed to have been a king there. With some thirty followers he escaped, and settled in the still-virgin forests fifty kilometers south of the city. There he, his followers, and their descendants fought off Spanish attacks for a century and finally signed the standard treaty between slave states and maroons: stop raiding our plantations and freeing our slaves, and we'll leave you alone.

Since maroons will play an important role in my story, this is as good a time as any to introduce them.

The word "maroon" comes from the Spanish *cimarrón*, which means "wild," as in "wild animal." The Spanish used it to describe escaped slaves, and the word, losing its first syllable, passed into both French and English. In Spanish-speaking areas, a settlement of maroons was referred to as a *palenque*, a word meaning "fence" or "stockade"; if you see Palenque in any place-name in Latin America, odds are it was once a maroon colony. In these colonies, African belief systems and cultural practices survived, as well as isolated African words, but not, so far as we know, African languages. Maroons today are Creole speakers, but if there is also a Creole in the surrounding countryside (the case in Jamaica and Suriname), the maroon Creole will be further from the dominant, European language, hence harder for white folk to understand, than the Creole of those whose forebears remained in slavery.

But further from the European language meant nearer to . . . what exactly? That was the big question.

Escalante didn't have a car (they don't pay Colombian profs that much), so we caught the bus to Cartagena and then an open truck with wooden bench seats to El Palenque de San Basilio. I was in luck, because until a year earlier, the only way you could get there was on horseback. Now they'd built a dirt road that wound through a range of low, densely wooded hills into an area of mixed woodland and pasture, and there it was, a village of wattle-and-daub huts with mud floors and palm-thatch roofs, but no electricity, no pavement, no running water, and no sewer system. It was one of the most impoverished villages I've ever seen. We wandered from house to house; Escalante knew everyone, and he loosened up a lot, even made a joke or two. I kept my trusty Philips running, and I soon knew that, beyond any doubt, the language was a Creole.

I didn't find this out until later, but I wasn't the first linguist to visit El Palenque. Someone from the Caro y Cuervo Institute in Bogotá, Colombia's premier school of linguistics and anthropology, had visited the village, and according to him its speech consisted of all the worst features of every dialect of Latin American Spanish. In other words, Palenquero was a kind of septic tank into which all linguistic drains had emptied.

Now you don't need any data to know that this is total nonsense, and prejudiced nonsense at that. Dialects don't work that way. Every dialect feature has geographic boundaries, and every dialect is a structured, integrated whole; it's just not possible for isolated features to detach themselves from their homes and congregate in a single place. The guy must have seen that the people were very black and very poor and decided he could dump on them with impunity—if what he said didn't make sense, who'd care? It saved him from having to take them seriously.

But on top of this, he was ignoring the obvious fact that the local speech contained features found in no other Latin American dialect, however substandard it might be regarded. Take this, for example:

Mailo mi kele nu.
Husband my want not.

Or: "My husband doesn't want [it, understood]." Now the standard Spanish for this sentence (and the dialects don't differ except in pronunciation) is:

Mi marido no lo quiere.
My husband not it wants.

The main differences here are that Palenquero puts the possessive adjective after its noun (instead of before, like both English and Spanish) and the negative marker at the end of the sentence (instead of in the middle, again like English and Spanish). The first trait is noteworthy because it contradicts the myth that Creoles "have no grammar" so you can just put anything anywhere. Creoles have grammars that are often stricter and more regular than those of European languages. It's more regular, for instance, to put all your adjectives, whether possessives or just ordinary ones, either before or after nouns. Palenquero does (they all follow the noun) but Spanish puts possessive adjectives before and the rest after. The second trait is weirder, never occurring in any European language and hardly ever in Creoles, though it is found in some languages in the Congo basin, which is where many of the original speakers of Palenquero came from. In fact it's variable; you could say *mailo mi nu kele* or even *mailo mi nu kele nu*. But the fact that final negation is there at all makes one of the few really clear examples of "substrate influence"—cases where a grammatical feature is transferred from a non-European language to a Creole.

In addition, as the example shows, you can drop object pronouns (the "it"), but, as I soon learned, you can't drop subject pronouns, which is the exact reverse of Spanish, and for a very good reason. Spanish can drop subject pronouns (and in fact almost always does, except when emphasis is needed) because subject agreement is marked on the verb, so that the verb ending tells you whether the subject is I, you, he/she, we, or they (*quiero*, "I want," *quieres*, "you want," *quiere*, "he/she wants," and so on). Palenquero doesn't have different person or tense marking; verbs never vary in form (*kele*, "want"). Tense or aspect are indicated by a particle that goes in front of the verb, just as in Guyanese Creole.

This state of affairs follows naturally from the processes through which Creole languages are born. When speakers of many different languages are brought into contact with one another, communication is reduced to a minimum, and anything not essential for communication is stripped off. That includes the inflections that express things like tense, aspect, number (singular versus plural), and person; it's much easier, at first contact, to use invariant pronouns and verbs than to try to remember all those bits at the ends of words. That's fine if the language is just an auxiliary, one you use when you have to, when your own won't be understood. It's not fine if it's the only one you've got. People have a built-in need to indicate when actions happened or might happen and whether you're talking about something that repeated itself or was a background condition or just happened one time. So Creoles all have some kind of system of preverbal particles to take the place of end-of-verb inflections.

Some words, too, were markedly un-Spanish, and not found in any other Latin American dialect—things like *nguba* ("peanut"—compare Southern States English "goober," from the same source in an African language, Kimbundu), *ngombe* ("cattle"), *bumbula* ("swollen testicle"), *kobeho* ("vagina"), *mambengo* ("pubic hair"). Words like these are sometimes called "loan words," but they're not really borrowed; they're part of the native languages of the parents of the first Palenquero speakers—a better term would be "survivals." Typically, as the last three suggest, they're drawn from the part of the vocabulary that you might describe as "intimate." Note the prenasalized consonants at the beginning of words like *nguba*. These are not just un-Spanish—you don't find them in any European language, and non-Africans almost always make a mess of them. Those old enough to remember the days when Kwame Nkrumah ruled in Ghana will remember how radio and TV announcers constantly referred to him as "En-krumah" or "Nuh-krumah." Yet prenasalized consonants are really easy to pronounce; you're pronouncing them all the time, but only at the ends of words—just say "sing" or "sink"—not at the beginnings.

As Creoles go, Palenquero wasn't a really *deep* Creole; that's to say it wasn't among those Creoles that differ most radically from

their related European language. The furthest from Spanish it gets
is in things like

Ane ba kamino ane.
They go way they.

Or: "They went on their way." The Spanish is

Se fueron por su camino.

But there aren't any of the un-European features like serial verbs or
verb-fronting that we'll meet in later chapters. That's hardly surprising. Palenquero and Spanish have been in contact for the better part of four hundred years, and, for all their poverty and poor
transportation links, its speakers have lived within thirty miles of a
major city all that time, so the surprising thing is that it is still, so
very obviously, a Creole language.

My rerouting via Colombia was less successful travelwise. The
flight to Curaçao was delayed ten hours. By this time I'd spent literally every penny and was saved by a kindly American fellow pas-
senger who lent me $20; otherwise, in the roasting oven of the
Barranquilla terminal, I couldn't even have bought a bottle of
water. And the airline, KLM, wasn't handing out any freebies.

By the time we arrived, after midnight, I'd missed my connection to Trinidad, and, since the Caribbean hadn't yet become a major travel destination, there wasn't another for two days. According
to KLM, my stay, although their fault, would be at my expense.
We'll see about that tomorrow, I thought.

This was before the days of universal credit cards. Somehow I
bluffed my way into a luxury beachside hotel. It was too late and
I was too disorganized to sleep, so I turned on the radio, and heard,
just as I'd hoped, another Creole: Papiamentu.

The name Papiamentu comes from an old Portuguese verb, pa-
pear, "to chat," which is found in the name of another Creole on
the opposite side of the world, on the coast of Malaysia: Papia Kris-

tang, literally, "Christian chat." Papiamentu is spoken in the ABC islands, the three members of the Netherlands Antilles (Aruba, Bonaire, and Curaçao, occupied by the Dutch since 1634, and before that by the Spanish), and it has the dubious parentage that's typical of almost all bastard tongues.

Was it (as some claim) part of an original, widespread Afro-Spanish Creole, spoken widely in South America, of which it and Palenquero are isolated survivors? If so, why does so much of it look like Portuguese? Well, in 1493 the pope divvied up the non-Christian world between Spain and Portugal, who he reckoned were its most reliable Catholic flag-bearers, the boundary line being down the middle of the North Atlantic—everything to the left (Central and most of South America) was Spanish, everything to the right (Brazil and Africa) Portuguese. So if Spain wanted African slaves, she had to buy them from Portugal. In other words, any slave coming from Portuguese territory could have already picked up the Afro-Portuguese contact language claimed—on negligible evidence—to have been spoken throughout Portuguese territory. But the main ingredient of Papiamentu was Spanish, not Portuguese, and it dates from the original Spanish occupation of the island, way back in the early 1500s.

That's the Hispanophile story.

No, said others. The Spanish occupation of the ABC islands was minimal, a few hundred people, few of them slaves, and all of these were forcibly shipped out when the Dutch took over. The true origins of Papiamentu lie with the slaves of Portuguese-Jewish plantation owners who, in a little-known episode of the Jewish diaspora (but one we'll meet again in later chapters) arrived in Curaçao from Brazil, or Suriname, or both, during the seventeenth century; they already spoke a Portuguese-based Creole that had nothing to do with Spanish but became the lingua franca of the Netherlands Antilles, a cosmopolitan community with no common language of its own. So why does Papiamentu now sound much more like Spanish than Portuguese? That's obvious. The islands are only a few miles off the coast of Venezuela, smugglers go back and forth all the time, Spanish is a world language and Portuguese isn't, so what would you expect?

That's what I guess you could call the Lusitanophile (pro-Portuguese) story.

And you can spin either story so it reinforces the theory of monogenesis described in Chapter 1: that all Creoles stem from a single, original contact language based largely on Portuguese, spoken first in Africa, spread worldwide by slaves. But no monogeneticist that I know of spotted the flaw. This Ur-Creole was supposed to have relexified wherever it went, switching its Portuguese words for English, French, or whatever. In most places it must have done this pretty thoroughly; well over 90 percent of Guyanese Creole words are English, well over 90 percent of Haitian Creole words are French, and so on, while only a handful of the words in English Creoles (like *sabe*, "know," or *pikni/piccaninny*, a corruption of Portuguese *pequenino*, "very small") come from Portuguese. But the Antilles had been occupied by the Dutch for much longer than Guyana had been occupied by the English or Haiti by the French. So why did only about a quarter of the Papiamentu vocabulary consist of Dutch words, while 60 percent was still Portuguese?

Regardless of where it came from, it seemed pretty obvious where Papiamentu was headed now. As I listened to my hotel radio in the small hours, I was forcibly struck by the extent to which Spanish had penetrated the language. Not just words, but whole phrases were almost identical with Spanish; sometimes it was only when I heard the suffix *-nan* used in Papiamentu to form plurals that I realized it wasn't Spanish I was hearing.

Of course I was up against the register factor. A register is a type of speech used for a particular function, like radio announcing or newscasting. Registers can have amazing effects in some languages. For instance, if you go to Romania and know Spanish or Portuguese or Italian, you can pick up a newspaper and follow the stories on the world news pages with only a little guesswork. But turn to the literary pages and you're totally lost. That's because Romanian has a mixed vocabulary, part Romance, part Slav; the kind of words used in news items mostly have Latin roots, the kind used to discuss literature have a high Slavic content.

Creoles are typically intimate, home languages—you don't do science or foreign policy in them. So long words, complex words, highfalutin words in general, have to be borrowed from whatever language happens to be top dog in the vicinity—in this case, Spanish. When, after a very late breakfast, I went out on the street and talked to real people, the Spanish invasion did not loom anywhere near so large as it had on the radio.

First, though, I had to settle with KLM. The guy I talked to hung tough at first, so I told him I was secretary of the University of Guyana faculty union (this wasn't a total lie; I'd subbed for the real secretary while he was on a trip) and that if he didn't pay my room and board for the whole time I was in Curaçao I'd make sure that no member of our faculty ever flew KLM again. The guy looked disconcerted, vanished for a while, then came back with a bundle of vouchers and a pretty bad grace.

I enjoyed my stay but didn't try to do any serious work on Papiamentu. It was already well-known and moderately well studied. Palenquero, though, was another matter, if only because I felt certain there were more Creole enclaves in Spanish America, if you only looked for them.

I visited Colombia several times over the next few years. It's bigger than Texas and California put together. It has, and always has had, a reputation for violence. When I was there, there were four separate *focos*, guerrilla insurgencies, going at the same time. Bands of "anti-socials," as they were called, roamed the outskirts of cities, robbing and killing. Outside the locked gates of a university, I saw tanks with their turret guns trained inward. A sit-in was in progress, following a more than usually severe riot. A Colombian explained to me how those riots worked. Students would start throwing rocks at cars with *placas negras*, black license plates, because those plates meant the cars belonged to foreigners, probably Americans. The police did nothing, because they didn't like Americans either, and because the fathers of many of the students were lawyers, politicians, industrialists, members of the moneyed elite. Gradually word got around, and the supply of *placas negras* started to dry up. But by now the students were into it, so they started throwing rocks at police cruisers. And that was too much. Rich kids or no rich kids, it was git-down time. Once the cops had shot a couple of them the rest would usually go back to class.

Yet despite all of this violence I never felt the way I've felt walking through Bed-Stuy in Brooklyn or Chicago's South Side. The country seemed relaxed, even welcoming. The bad things were always happening somewhere else. I've noticed this all over the world; the press reports make it sound like the country you're in is in turmoil, folks write and ask if you are okay, and you wonder, What is it with these people? Things couldn't be calmer. There was none of the tense atmosphere, the greed and suspicion that grew in later years as Colombia sank deeper and deeper into the cocaine trade.

I went to a conference in Popayán, one of the world's loveliest cities until an earthquake devastated it. Popayán lies at the head of the Cauca valley, a long and deep basin between spurs of the Andes. In earlier years there had been rich sugar plantations along the Cauca, worked by slaves. If I'd been a slave, I thought, where would I have run to? Obviously, the mountains surrounding the valley.

So I explored a couple of side valleys, but there was nothing, no trace in local memory that there'd ever been any *palenques* there. I formed a theory that people of African descent, accustomed to tropical lowlands, wouldn't go above 5,000 feet. That theory foundered almost immediately because, riding a bus across Ecuador at around 8,500 feet, I came on a village with circular huts roofed with dunce's caps of straw. I jumped off the bus and sure enough, everyone in the village was black. But when I started talking to them, they answered me in what, despite its odd intonation patterns and slurred, elided consonants, was clearly still Spanish. I still couldn't help feeling that there was more Creole Spanish to be found somewhere.

Then I heard of a village called Ure (pronounced like "hooray" without the "h") where, again, something not really Spanish was alleged to be spoken.

Ure was way out in the hills of the northwest. To get there, you first took a bus ride of several hours from Medellín (not yet the capital of the drug trade) to a place called Planeta Rica, rich planet. When the bus lurched to a stop in its dusty main street I thought I'd entered a time warp. There were the false-front buildings and the roaring saloons with the low-swing double doors, there were the cowpokes in their chaps and spurred boots with six-shooters on their hips, and the lone riders with dust-whitened gear and Winchesters across their saddles—all the paraphernalia you see in Western movies.

A cattle boom was going on. But the range wasn't your classic Western range, sparse of grass, spotted with brushwood and cactus. It was thick, knee-high, virulently green tropical grassland. And instead of roaming the range in freedom, the cattle were penned into enclosures of a few acres each, behind six-foot fences of multi-stranded barbed wire. This went on mile after mile as the open truck bound for Ure headed westward. Jeeploads of troops in leopard-spotted camouflage suits roared past us, bound for one of the *focos*. As dark fell, we arrived.

If anything the village was poorer even than El Palenque. The nearest thing to a bed they could offer me was a half-collapsed pool table in what looked like a wrecked rec center. For washing there was a black, greasy-looking river; for all other bodily functions, ditto.

"You're out of luck," they told me.

"How come?"

"Well, there used to be a funny dialect here, but the last person who spoke it died a year ago. He was nearly a hundred," they added, in a consolatory way, as if the poor guy had been desperately hanging on to meet me, but couldn't quite make it.

I kept looking.

In Cartagena, the Palenqueros had gotten themselves a corner of the produce market where they sold their fruit and vegetables. There I got talking to a bootblack who told me some interesting things. He'd traveled as an illegal immigrant into Venezuela, and worked for a time at a sugar town near the head of Lake Maracaibo, a place called Bobures. And in Bobures, he told me, they spoke a language that was quite like Palenquero. But there was a catch. It was a secret language, a bond of intimacy among pure-black sugar workers.

"Be a waste of time for Escalante to go there," he said.

"Why?"

"Too light-skinned. They wouldn't give him the time of day."

Not much point in me going, then. But the guy told me there were other places he'd been—places way off the map, in the region at the extreme northwestern end of Colombia, adjacent to Panama, called the Chocó.

The Chocó is the reason why there's no real Pan-American highway, why you can't get in your car in Alaska and drive all the way to Tierra del Fuego. It's a region of dense and swampy lowland forest with no roads and very few people, a land of suffocating heat and torrential rains. The only way into it is along the Río Atrato, a river that corkscrews for hundreds of miles through the swamps to empty into the Caribbean just south of the Panama border.

Years afterward, in a nightclub in Cartagena, I met an American called Parrett who claimed that he owned the only boat that went up the Atrato.

"How long does it take?" I asked.

"Oh, about two weeks."

"What do you do for food?"

"We serve food on the boat."

"What's it like?"

He rolled his eyes. "Horrible!"

For all that, I was tempted. But I was on my way to Costa Rica and I had other plans. Someday I'll go, I told myself. But I never did.

Those places, Bobures, the Chocó, are still there, and to this day I don't know of anyone who's investigated them. Someone should. Preferably some smart Afro-American grad student who speaks Spanish and doesn't mind a spot of hardship when it comes to marking up a career notch. I wish him or her the very best of luck, and please write me if you find anything. If you don't look, you'll never find; if you look where no one else has looked, or where others have looked but only superficially, you'll always find something new.

My visits to Colombia didn't really further my career. But to identify a language nobody had known about, so early in that career, gave me a lot of confidence, and convinced me that when I took that leap in the dark, back in Ghana, I'd made the right choice. I knew with growing certainty that what I had to do was find out where Creoles came from, how they were born, why they were the way they were and not some other way. Palenquero, interesting as it was, wouldn't help me much in that. It wasn't deep enough, near enough to the source. I had to find either a Creole that had been out of contact with its dominant language almost since birth, or one formed so recently that traces of its birth pangs were still accessible.

Or, preferably, both.

5

THE ROAD TO THE ISLES

M y time in Guyana was winding down. I was having a farewell drink with a Guyanese friend when a mangy, yellowish cur slunk onto the porch looking for what he could steal. "Get out, you congalong!" Ivan yelled at him.

"You what?" I asked.

"Congalong."

"What's a congalong?"

"Well . . . kind of dog looks like that."

In four years in-country I'd never heard that word. Any language, even a bastard tongue, is a truly inexhaustible thing.

But its etymology was clear enough. In slavery days, *Congo* was a term of abuse used by older hands, who scorned newcomers from Africa for what they regarded as their barbarism and ignorance. For instance, there's an old Guyanese song that contains the line "On'y las' year me come, an' dem call me 'Congo fool.'"

For that matter I was pretty convinced by now that wherever Guyanese differed from English, the cause lay in the substrate—the African languages that the early arrivals spoke. Among other things, Guyanese was full of what linguists call calques, literal translations from another language. "Dizziness" is *eye-turn*; "obstinacy" is *hard-ears*; both these and many more are word-for-word translations of common African expressions. For some of these compounds, there isn't even an English equivalent: *suck-teeth*, which we met in Chapter 3, for example, or *cut-eye*, a Caribbean-wide expression for a sidelong glance of contempt, the eyes quickly moving past their target (not to be confused with Hawaiian *stink-eye*, a baleful, persistent stare). In addition there were African survivals like *juk* or *nyam* or *potopoto*, a lovely word that means a muddy puddle and crops up in several languages in and around southern Nigeria. It seemed only reasonable to suppose that the non-English features in Guyanese grammar had arisen in a similar way.

Supporting this view was the indisputable fact that Guyanese, and indeed a large number of Creoles, have grammatical structures typical of West African languages. Among the commonest of these are what are known as "serial verbs."

A serial verb construction is one containing at least two verbs but no conjunction or any other linking device, in which no subject or object can be repeated. Like this, for example:

Me carry book come give you.

This simply means "I brought you a book." What seems bizarre from an English perspective is not just the fact that three verbs are used where one looks like it should do, but that the subjects and objects of some of these verbs are missing. This is all the stranger because as a general rule such things can't be left out even where English leaves them out. We can say:

I went home and then ate dinner.

But in Guyana you have to say the equivalent of

I went home and then *I* ate dinner.

Unless you turn the whole thing into a serial, without any kind of conjunction in it:

Me walk go a house go nyam.

There are lots more things to say about serial verbs, but for now it's sufficient to note that they appear with great frequency in many

West African languages. People have written whole papers that simply list serial verbs in African languages, then list serial verbs in Creole languages, then put them together and say, "Look! It's obvious that the second lot comes from the first."

Things aren't always what they seem, though.

Meanwhile I had another intellectual infatuation going. This time its object was a Kentucky colonel, of all things.

I started getting letters from someone calling himself C.-J. (for Charles-James, as it turned out) Bailey, located at the University of Hawaii. In Hawaii, apparently, they had a linguistic continuum situation pretty similar to that of Guyana, which nobody had been able to do much with. Just as in Guyana, there was a Creole at one end that differed radically from English, a dialect at the other that differed little, except in accent and some peculiar words, from Standard American English, and a whole range of intermediate dialects. But since there was still a large segment of the population that hadn't been born in Hawaii, but had immigrated (mostly from Japan and the Philippines, but also from places as far away as Puerto Rico, Norway, and Russia), there was also what might actually represent the pidgin that had been spoken before Creole ever developed. (To make it even more confusing, Creole in Hawaii is known universally as "Pidgin"!)

Apparently Bill Labov had just paid a visit to Hawaii and happened to mention my work in Guyana. It had therefore occurred to the folks in the linguistics department of the University of Hawaii that I might be able to help them describe the situation. C.-J. confided it was not beyond the bounds of possibility that I might even be invited to work there.

Well, as far as I was concerned, that was beyond the bounds of possibility. I'd always thought of America as some kind of mythical land, somewhere between Utopia and Tir nan Og, where you maybe went when you died but not before. And this in spite of the fact that my best buddy from high school, Donald Higginbotham, had not only gone to America but returned with an American bride, who asked me if I would care to leaf through some magazines while they got ready to go out. Leaf through? That wasn't part of any language I spoke. And to make matters stranger still, I'd actually been there myself and it still didn't seem real to me. Waking in a Manhattan hotel to see our two sons playing horsey on a seventh-floor balcony balustrade, going down to the lobby to blaring tabloid headlines: TOT FALLS SEVEN STORIES—AND LIVES! Ordering root beer at a wayside stop under the impression that it was beer. Being greeted on the street by an upstate sheriff and invited to go for a ride in his cruiser. These were obviously things that didn't happen in the real world. America was a place they'd invented so they could make movies about it. It had never occurred to me that it was somewhere you could actually go and stay and make a life.

When we finally flew from Guyana back to England our plane made an intermediate stop in Bermuda.

As we hung around the almost-deserted airport in the middle of the night, my eldest son, Jim, then thirteen, came to me with a strange linguistic confession.

In Guyana, both my sons quickly picked up the local vernacular, as they did wherever we went. With us, they continued to speak British English; with their friends, they spoke the working-class Creole dialect of Georgetown, which was what kids spoke regardless of class. One of Jim's school friends was on our flight, and they'd been talking together. "But you know, Dad," he said with a worried air, "it somehow doesn't feel right. I don't feel comfortable talking Creolese anymore."

Language has roots in where you are as well as who you are. Six hours out, he was already a citizen of a different linguistic world.

England came as a shock. Well, it had always come as a shock, every time I'd returned there over the last twenty years, but this time the shock was worse. I was going to the University of Lancaster, for the final year of my five-year contract, which was the prize for four years of tropical hardship (second prize, two years in Lancaster). But Yvonne wasn't.

During the previous four years she had earned a degree in sociology at the University of Guyana, where she won the President's Prize for the best graduating student of her year. Despite this, and despite the fact that I was going to work there, Lancaster had turned down her application for their doctoral program. I don't to this day know why; I suspected—this was before the days of equal opportunity and political correctness—that because she had graduated from a black university in a black country, they thought she was black. Whatever the reason, it didn't stop her from being accepted by the University of Sussex, a more prestigious university in much nicer surroundings. So she would live there with the kids in the driest and sunniest part of the country while I lived in Lancaster in a corner of the northwest where it had always just rained or was just about to rain. You may rightly conclude that the mood in which I started my new job was, as they say in the old country, distinctly Bolshie.

Over the summer we'd bought a camper van to tour France and Spain. In Lancaster, thinking there was no reason I should pay two rents because of other people's stupidity, I lived out of the van. I'd park it in a remote corner of campus, shower in the gym, move the van every few days so as not to alert campus security, and eat in disgusting university cafeterias. Every other weekend I'd fire up the van and head south out of the clouds for the three-hundred-mile run to sunny south-coast Brighton.

They say every cloud has a silver lining. And that grueling six-hundred-mile round trip opened up a professional window that I might otherwise never have seen.

Smack in the middle of the Lancaster-Brighton route sat London, and smack in the middle of London sits SOAS—London University's School of African and Oriental Studies. And in the basement of SOAS there were grammars of every African language for which grammars had been written. But not, it seemed, read. My most vivid memory of that basement is the puffs of dust that exploded from books as you opened them—books that looked like they hadn't been opened in forty years.

I would time my trips so that on either the inward or outward journey I could spend a few hours going through these grammars in search of the African tense-aspect system that had given rise to the Guyanese TMA system. I'd pull out an armful of volumes, turn to the sections on tense and aspect, and jot down the results. Those results were frustrating. There were tantalizing resemblances: in grammar after grammar, for instance, I found the same use of the bare stem of the verb to express past events, rather than present reference, as in English and (if it comes to that) most European languages. Yet none of the systems quite fit. All of them had features that weren't there in Guyanese and all of them lacked features that Guyanese had.

I don't remember how many African languages I'd looked at— dozens, certainly, maybe going on a hundred—when an awkward thought hit me.

Suppose I was successful. Suppose the next grammar I opened had the exact same TMA system that Guyanese had. That was just one language—maybe the only one that had it. How many African languages had gone into the linguistic melting pot that produced Guyanese? Nobody knew, there were no records, but it was safe to assume not less than a dozen or two. West Africa has several hundred languages, the area in which each is spoken is quite small, but the slave dealers bought slaves wherever they could get them. Many slaves were in fact prisoners of war captured in battles between African mini-states deep in the interior and then marched to the coast and sold for whatever they would fetch.

So why would all the slaves have given up the systems of their own native languages and learned someone else's system? It didn't make sense. Unless of course the speakers of the language with the winning system had either outnumbered everyone else or enjoyed some kind of dominance due to their greater strength or intelligence or simply because the slave owners liked them better and gave them positions of control. These possibilities didn't look likely, but I couldn't rule them out. So I kept looking, though with diminished enthusiasm.

In London I met Ian Hancock. We'd exchanged a couple of letters while I was in Guyana; Ian was working on a comparison of English-based Creoles and had developed a kind of scaled-down version of monogenesis. According to him, the close resemblances between all of these—and the closer he looked, the more resemblances he found—were due to the fact that they'd all originated from a single Anglo-Creole spoken originally in West Africa. And this Creole had arisen among children with English-speaking fathers and African mothers who grew up speaking some kind of Anglo-African mix. The fact that in mixed-language marriages children normally learn both the mommy-language and the daddy-language, and seldom if ever mix them, did not deter him from what he called the domestic hypothesis.

Ian was not the kind of person you usually meet in academia. In the first place, he was a Gypsy, a member of a large family of fruit-pickers and fairground workers none of whom had ever been to college—maybe not even school in some cases. Ian too had never gone to college. But he had made friends with someone from Sierra Leone, and became so fascinated by Krio, the English-related Creole spoken there, that he went there himself and, without having had any linguistic training, wrote a complete grammar of the language.

His modus operandi was both brilliant and typically Ian. He had found out the catch-22 for white folk learning a Creole. If you try to speak it yourself, you are regarded as patronizing if not downright insulting and people clam up on you. If on the other hand you address them in English, then they speak something as close to English as they can. To get around this, he posed as a French sailor who knew not a word of English but had managed to pick up a little Krio. So the only way they could talk to him was in Krio and they had no reason to modify whatever they normally spoke.

When he'd finished his grammar he sent it to one of the linguists at SOAS. The guy was astounded; solemn conclaves were held to decide what to do about it. Finally SOAS waived its normal entrance requirements and admitted Ian to its doctoral program without even a single semester of college.

Ian and I seldom agreed about anything in Creoles. That didn't matter. We were kindred spirits. We shared a taste for low life and scatological humor, and a total lack of respect for the respectable.

In Lancaster, things were rapidly going from bad to worse.

I thought I might as well check my future prospects, so I reminded Professor Murray that, when he first hired me, he had promised me a tenured position at the end of my five-year contract. He began to hem and haw. Well, he hadn't actually promised. It was all contingent on . . . well, contingencies. There simply wasn't a vacant position for the next year. Unless they got enough Arabic-speaking students. If they got enough Arabic-speaking students (translate: enough petrodollars), then there just might be a position teaching English as a second language to Arabic speakers. Not tenured, though—oh no. Year to year, for as long as the petrodollars kept flowing.

I was livid. Quite perversely so—I hated the place so much I would almost have paid them not to have to work there—but I felt both that I'd been cheated and that I was being seriously undervalued. Both were unacceptable. Either one meant war.

The department was already in turmoil. It was an English department; that is to say literary and language studies cohabited uneasily under the same roof, with language definitely the junior partner—you felt like you were a plumber on call to fix flaws in student essays. But what became known as the Craig affair was between literature guys, although the split ran right through the department.

David Craig was a senior lecturer (more or less equivalent to an associate professor) and Murray, as department head, had removed him from teaching a course on nineteenth-century literature because of alleged communist content. Craig contested the decision, through both legitimate and illegitimate channels. The department was split more or less fifty-fifty. It was already getting ugly; junior lecturers on one-year contracts had been warned that if they supported Craig, they wouldn't get renewed. I had stayed out of it—it was no concern of mine, and I was actually pissed at the lefties who supported Craig, for the following reason.

That fall, a thirteen-year-old English boy had been thrown into a Turkish jail for dealing drugs. The reason he dealt drugs was that he, his hippie mother, and his younger siblings had been deserted and stranded in Turkey by their hippie dad, and it was the only way he could support them. Just imagine what is likely to happen to a thirteen-year-old boy in a Turkish jail (later he said it hadn't, which I hope was true and not just quid pro quo for getting out in one piece). Anyway, I tried to get my lefty colleagues to write letters to the Turkish Embassy to get him out. They refused. They were quite indignant about it. How dare I ask them to engage in some sentimental, petit bourgeois crusade and distract them from their Mighty Struggle to Free All Members of the Working Class?

But, as they say, my enemy's enemy is my friend, so I openly and very publicly allied myself with the Craig faction.

And then, like a deus ex machina, like a life jacket hurled to one drowning in stormy seas, there came the letter from Hawaii, with a round-trip ticket to Honolulu and the offer I couldn't refuse: spend a week here and if we like you and you like us, maybe there's a job in it for you.

November in Hawaii is usually the wettest month, and this was no exception. My first, confused impression was of mountains steeper than they had any business to be, clouds huger and blacker than I'd ever seen, and bursts of torrential rain punctuated by ominous stillnesses. There were parties in houses on the slopes of mountains overlooking a vast acreage of city lights, where faculty and students exchanged cigarettes that contained no tobacco, where everything, at least compared with poker-assed British universities, seemed deliciously loosey-goosey.

Would I like to sample local dialects? That could be arranged. With a sociology prof as my guide, I spent an evening in a Leeward Coast bar, talking to the locals. After a couple of hours the barman confided, "You're lucky you picked this bar—if you'd gone to such-and-such a bar down the road . . ." and he rolled his eyes and drew his finger across his throat. I said, "Oh, er, thanks," not having the heart to tell him that I'd heard this same story in other parts of the world, and would bet that if we'd gone to the bar down the road we'd have been told the same thing about the bar we were in.

Unfortunately there was no sign of my latest postal infatuee. C.-J. had been denied tenure. Nobody seemed to want to talk about it, and I was reminded of Bill Carr. But it was nothing like that. I later learned that he had been too free with his opinions of some other faculty members—even while talking to students. Under all the loosey-goosey, lines were drawn that you crossed at your peril.

The week passed in a blur. Whether, after that, they still wanted me, I had no idea. I just knew what I wanted.

Back in Lancaster, l'affaire Craig pursued its course. Due to the English Channel, there was a four-year time lag behind Europe, so now it was 1968 all over again. Students marched, demonstrated, blockaded the administration building, seized the computer building—it was always the computer building they seized. Craig and his minions rabble-roused the students. Murray and the establishment denounced Craig and his minions for rabble-rousing the students. Faculty marched, demonstrated, held endless meetings— after all, talking is what they're best at, they even get paid for it— but did not seize buildings; they're not so good at that.

In the middle of this came another letter from Hawaii. It had good news and bad news. The good news was they were willing to offer me a job. The bad news was that they had a hiring freeze, so they didn't know when or even if I would ever get it.

While things were still in limbo, Bill Labov invited me to a conference. He drove me from the Philadelphia airport to his home. Throughout the drive he neither stopped talking nor looked where he was going; his car, like an old mule, seemed to know the way. Horns blared at us as we lurched through stop signs, paused un-accountably in crowded intersections, made abrupt, unsignaled changes of course. How could he have survived so long, I wondered? He finally stopped talking around 3:00 a.m. At 6:00 he was back up, waking me by continuing from the exact place in the argument at which he had stopped.

The conference was in Washington, and basically it was a debate between those who, like Labov, believed in variable rules tied to social variables, and people like me and Dave DeCamp, who believed in analyzing the variation and letting the social chips fall where they may. It was as totally inconclusive as these things usually are. But I was happy to finally meet C.-J., and even more so to find we were on the same side.

C.-J. was as charismatic in the flesh as on paper, a patrician from the Old South unaccountably obsessed with linguistic variation. To him, the fact that all languages varied all the time, from district to district, from person to person, even from situation to situation with the same person, was the most important fact about language, and he believed that the study of variation, when it happened, where it happened, how it happened, why it happened, was on the brink of becoming the central topic of language studies everywhere. He was wrong, of course, and a bad career move didn't help his cause—he wound up in Berlin, and for American scholars, Europe is where you go on vacation, not where ideas come from.

As for the Kentucky colonel bit, I'd always thought that was some obscure American joke until I saw the framed certificate on his apartment wall. One evening we were drinking in a D.C. restaurant and a waiter asked us to leave, since they wanted to serve dinner in that section. C.-J. refused. The waiter went away and came back with someone in a suit. The suit asked us to leave.

"Get me the manager," C.-J. said.

"I am the manager," said the suit.

"Then get me the owner."

You may think Brits can be frosty, but a Kentucky colonel can give them points any day. I don't know if the suit was scared that C.-J. would buy the restaurant and fire him, but anyway he vanished and we finished our drinks in peace.

Back to Lancaster again. The contrast between America, where I was wined and dined, and England, where they treated me like shit, was made all the more vivid by the speed of these jet-fueled transitions. I'd had enough. I went to Murray and threatened him and the university with a lawsuit for breach of contract.

I didn't have much of a case. It was my word against Murray's. I didn't care, I didn't even want tenure there, but they had disrupted my family, and I was going to give them all the grief I could. My timing, though, was perfect. Embroiled as they were in the Craig affair, the last thing they wanted was more trouble.

In due course I was summoned by the vice-chancellor, Charles Carter. Carter began by trying to explain to me that whatever Murray had promised me was irrelevant, since he had no authority to speak in the university's name. I countered that any rational person, such as a member of a jury considering an action for damages, would assume that anything coming from a highly placed faculty member with the right to hire would be backed by the university, and they would decide accordingly. Since I've always found that coming on strong in a confrontation beats subtle diplomacy every time, I then showed him the brochure from the Washington conference, where my affiliation was listed as "University of Lancaster, England."

"Look," I said, "people over there have never even heard of you. They have to be told where your university is."

He didn't like that, but it got his attention. I pointed out that the university for which he was responsible was already in a mess and that the last thing he needed was more bad publicity. However, there was a simple solution. If he would give me leave on full pay for the six-month balance of my contract, I would withdraw my support from the Craig faction and drop all claims against the university.

He bought the deal.

The next day the department faculty had scheduled a one-day strike.

I was in a quandary. It would be a couple of days before I got anything in writing, but I had promised to stop supporting Craig, and the university would surely jump at any reason to renege on the deal. On the other hand I was a lifelong union man. At seventeen, I tried to organize a strike of fruit-pickers, but they just ran wild and trashed the orchard. In Guyana I did eventually become the union secretary I'd posed as for KLM; it was a really solid union, a vertical union containing everyone from full professor to janitor, which both pleased my egalitarian heart and exposed for the nonsense it is the myth, sedulously fostered by administrators, that faculty play any real role in university governance. How could I become a scab?

I could and I did. There was no price I wouldn't have paid to be reunited with my family. I spent two hours in empty classrooms—the students were on strike too—feeling like an idiot, but who knew who was watching? I couldn't even tell anyone why I was doing it; secrecy was a condition of the deal. I told people I'd been out of town when the decision to strike had been made. That was true, but ridiculous as an excuse; union members are supposed to abide by majority decisions no matter what, but I couldn't think of anything else to say.

Two days later my letter of confirmation arrived and within the hour I was heading south for the last time. A hundred miles down the road, the sun broke through the cloud layer. It was suddenly spring, and the world was my oyster.

In Brighton we'd rented a half-timbered seventeenth-century cottage that had somehow survived progress on a corner of the beach promenade. It was an ideal situation; the kids were in school, Yvonne was at the university, I had the whole day to myself to get on with my book, and the sea was fifty yards away if I wanted a break from it.

The book was the second reason for the deal I'd made. Publishing papers was okay, but to make your scholarly bones you needed a book under your belt. I had masses of data from Guyana, but with all the politicking on top of my teaching load I'd hardly had time even to start organizing it. I wanted to write more than just a descriptive grammar; I wanted to show how, as I then thought, an original strongly African-influenced Creole had gradually morphed into something close to Standard English, leaving its history spread out for view in a chain of dialects running from the speech of illiterate rice-growers in Berbice to that of educated professionals in Georgetown.

Then, in the same mail, I got two letters. One announced that the hiring freeze in Hawaii had ended and there was a job for me in the fall. The other was from the University of Texas offering me a job in Austin—DeCamp's doing, I'm sure.

Which should I take? A family conclave took place; the issue was examined from every angle. Texas was the more prestigious university, though how much more so I had no idea at the time. It was within easy reach of the Caribbean, my old stamping ground and home to more than a dozen Creole languages. On the other hand, Hawaii offered a higher rank—associate, as against assistant, professor—and a salary 20 percent higher. (We had no notion then that 80 percent in Texas would buy you more than 100 percent in Hawaii.) Hawaii offered the kind of multiracial, multicultural background we were used to, while Texas had the reputation (undeserved, as I later found) of being wall-to-wall bigoted white braggarts. Hawaii was in the tropics, and we had spent nine out of the past fourteen years in the tropics. And Hawaii was . . . well, Hawaii. There would never be any winter. We could swim all year round. The boys could learn to surf (they did, and still do). In Texas, who could tell? They might grow up to be cowboys.

I accepted the Hawaii job, and regretfully turned down the Texas one. It all turned out for the best, because Texas immediately offered it to Ian Hancock, who accepted.

My next mail was a large parcel from Lancaster. It contained examination papers, with instructions for grading them.

I promptly mailed them back, with a note regretting that I could not grade them, as I was on leave. By return I got a very snotty letter explaining to me that I had certain responsibilities for the courses I had taught, and it was my obvious duty to grade the papers.

I wrote back politely and pointed out that being on leave meant being on leave, which meant no academic duties, no exceptions, period. I could have added, but felt it unnecessary to do so, that when an institution, for no conceivable reason, refuses admission to your spouse, thereby dividing your family, and in addition breaks its solemn promises and tries to humiliate you by demoting you to some language-mill dogsbody, you owe them nothing, nada, zip.

They wrote back again threatening dire consequence. I ignored them. I was a little worried in case they stopped paying me, but relied on the fact that in universities the right hand knoweth not what the left hand doeth—or at worst, there's a six-month time lag involved.

I was right. The checks kept coming until the end.

Then we all went riding on a United rainbow, to a new land very far away.

6

UNDER THE RAINBOW

———

Talking of rainbows, Hawaii has more of them than I've seen anywhere else; their brilliance is unsurpassed, and the best are doubles, one perfect arc inside another. And one of the best places to see them from is the University of Hawaii, especially on days, and they are frequent, when trade winds blow a fine mist of rain across the Ko'olau Mountains and the slant beams of a late afternoon sun cut through it. This lovely campus with its ugly buildings would be base camp throughout my career as an American academic.

I only gradually came to realize how ill-equipped I was for such a role.

Anyone who'd gone to graduate school in America would have mentors—older scholars who had taught them, who had a vested interest in their careers, who would use their influence to advance those careers in a dozen ways.

I had no mentors.

Anyone who'd gone to graduate school in America would have cohorts—fellow students who would rise with them through the system, with whom they could network, who would keep them constantly informed of job opportunities, trends, scuttlebutt, you name it.

I had no cohorts.

Anyone who'd gone to graduate school in America would probably have a Ph.D. to prove it.

I had not gone to graduate school anywhere and did not have a Ph.D. I had been appointed at associate level, almost unheard-of for anyone without a doctorate. This would not have presented a problem in the U.K., where at that time many full professors (and a full professor in the U.K. is a far rarer and more exalted figure than a full professor in the U.S.) held nothing higher than a master's or even a bachelor's degree. In fact, there was definitely a feeling, in British academic circles back then, that it was really a bit common to have a Ph.D., that if you were one of us it was both unnecessary and vulgarly ostentatious to have a Ph.D.—anyone who had one verged on being a bounder and was certainly no one that one would want to know socially.

As an associate, in four years I would come up for promotion and tenure. And it was tactfully made known to me that by that time I had better have a Ph.D., because it was up or out, and they surely would never appoint me to full without the magic parchment. (And that's all it is—it's no guarantee of excellence. I've known people with doctorates who were thicker than two planks. Anyone who can stay the course and faithfully regurgitate their teachers' opinions should be able to get one.)

How, with a full-time job, was I supposed to get a Ph.D.? Well, that was my problem.

Nowadays, Hawaii is marketed as tourist heaven, all luaus and aloha, full of charming nonwhite people in subordinate positions who perform for your pleasure in a vacuum without a past. It has been marketed thus for a long time. As early as 1888 a magazine called *Paradise of the Pacific* was commissioned by King Kalakaua to boost Hawaii as a tourist destination. But under paradise there was already a plantation hellhole where workers from all around the globe were treated little better than slaves in Caribbean sugar colonies.

Once there was only ocean. Then, millions of years ago, a tectonic plate inched its way northwestward over a hot spot in the earth's mantle. Volcanoes flared. Molten lava cooled into islands. The plate kept moving, forming a long chain of islands.

For untold millennia the Hawaiian islands remained uninhabited save for the few plants, birds, and insects carried there on driftwood or by storms. Polynesians came in canoes some twelve hundred years ago. Caucasians came in sailing ships just over two centuries ago. They found a highly organized authoritarian state, its population close to the million-plus it has today, saved from the famine that afflicted other Polynesian colonies by wise ecological practices. Conquest was out of the question. Infiltration, unfortunately, wasn't.

A minority of haoles—the Hawaiian word used to mean just "stranger," but naturally it came to mean "Caucasian"—settled to trade and service the sandalwood collectors and the whaling fleets. A few grew sugar. There seemed no future in it. A U.S. tariff barrier blocked exports to Hawaii's natural market, the western states of America.

All that changed when America began to sniff the heady perfume of empire. To extend its hegemony into the Pacific required a safe naval base way off the West Coast—2,500 miles off, too far for anyone to pretend it was just for the defense of the realm. Pearl Harbor looked perfect, so in 1876 the United States did a deal with the still-independent Hawaiian state: use of Pearl Harbor as à naval base in exchange for removing the tariff on Hawaiian sugar.

The sugar industry exploded. Recruiters scoured the world for labor. First China, then Portugal's Madeira and Azores islands, then Japan, then Korea, Puerto Rico, Norway, Germany, Russia, and finally the Philippines. Hawaiians, reduced by 90 percent from their pre-"discovery" levels by foreign diseases, became a minority in their own land. Immigrants came as indentured labor, and could be tried and jailed for leaving their employment before they had worked out their term—could be, and often were, savagely beaten, sometimes to the point of death, by ruthless overseers. Sometimes they responded with violence. As late as 1922, a revolt of Filipino sugar workers cost twenty lives, sixteen of them workers, and was suppressed only by troops with heavy machine guns.

In 1893, a cabal of American businessmen, supported by troops from an American warship, overthrew the Hawaiian monarchy and declared a haole-dominated republic. Five years later, the United

States annexed the islands. This was not a case of enterprising Westerners taking over some backward and incompetent indigenous regime. Hawaii under the monarchy was, by any valid criteria, among the most advanced and civilized nations on earth. Honolulu was lit by electric street lamps within a few years of their first appearance and before most U.S. cities got them. In the 1880s, Hawaii's literacy rate was higher than that of the United States. The unprovoked rape of Hawaii was comparable with Saddam Hussein's unprovoked seizure of Kuwait.

The United States liberated Kuwait in a matter of weeks.

The United States apologized to Hawaii after a hundred years.

What was known about the linguistic consequences of these events was mostly due to the work of John Reinecke, a farm boy from Kansas who had come to Hawaii as a schoolteacher in the 1920s and in the thirties wrote an M.A. thesis that eventually became his 1969 book *Language and Dialect in Hawaii*. He then won a scholarship to Yale and wrote, for his 1937 doctorate, a dissertation on what he called "marginal languages"—no one had yet made a clear distinction between pidgins and Creoles—that was far ahead of its time. But his promising academic career was cut short when the University of Hawaii failed to renew his teaching contract, almost certainly due to the fact that he was an avowed Marxist. When red paranoia hit Hawaii in the late forties, he was permanently prohibited from teaching, arrested, tried, jailed, and finally had his conviction overturned by the Supreme Court.

The persecution of John Reinecke was one of the nastiest of the little worms that wriggle around the underside of paradise. Nearly a quarter century after his death (and over a quarter century after the State of Hawaii paid him a quarter million dollars in compensation) people still write ridiculous nonsense about him. "Morally he was unfit to teach or even be around impressionable young people," according to one self-appointed arbiter of morality. John was, in fact, kindly and peace-loving, generous to a fault, and one of the tiny handful of genuinely good people I've met in my life (two of the others were Catholics; virtue knows no dogma). Knowing what was then known about Creoles, what's surprising is not that he got some things wrong, but that he got so much right.

According to John, language contact prior to 1876 had been limited to English and Hawaiian. There had existed, then, something he called hapa-haole ("half Caucasian"), an extremely unstable medium based on Hawaiians' attempts to learn English, with a heavy admixture of Hawaiian words. Though he admitted that some haoles learned a little Hawaiian, he regarded this hapa-haole as "the most common means of communication between Haole residents and Hawaiians." However, with the influx of labor after 1876, hapa-haole developed into what he called "the creole dialect." He failed to make a clear distinction between the speech of immigrants and that of the locally born, although he did note that while the speech of immigrants varied sharply according to their national origins, that of the locally born was much more uniform.

I would have to do what I did in Guyana—immerse myself in the community, absorb the linguistic situation by a kind of osmosis. With the wisdom of hindsight, I now see what I should have done. I should, right away, have explored the historical record. There were three reasons why I didn't.

First, according to John and his collaborator, Stanley Tsuzaki, there wasn't a historical record. They had published, in 1966, an annotated bibliography of English in Hawaii that had exactly three pre-1900 entries. I believed them. I still hadn't fully absorbed the lesson of Palenquero: never say it's not there till you've looked for yourself.

Second, I still believed that a Creole's history was alive and well and fully visible in contemporary speech. All I had to do was chart the full spectrum of that speech and it would reveal its past and its origins. The fact that here, unlike Guyana, the pidgin that had preceded the Creole was still in evidence merely added an extra dimension to my task.

Third, I simply didn't have the Sitzfleisch to park myself in libraries and hunt patiently and laboriously through old books and documents. The true history of language in Hawaii would have to await someone who did.

It did not look like the best of times for a haole to be immersing himself in the community. The statehood awarded Hawaii a dozen years earlier had not led to the hoped-for prosperity and equality between locals and haoles; rather it had relatively impoverished and marginalized large sections of the local population. Caucasians unwise enough to camp in certain beach parks ran the risk of assault, rape, robbery, and occasionally murder. Tour buses returning from the Polynesian Cultural Center—a kind of human zoo where people from the various Pacific islands performed their arts and crafts for the entertainment of tourists—were routinely stoned. But the worst I ever experienced was a little stink-eye, which I simply ignored.

Hawaii was just like Guyana in that the further you got from the cities and the lower on the social scale, the more un-English speech became. In Hawaii, the deepest Creole was spoken by members of the working class in rural areas of the islands of Kauai and Hawaii (the Big Island with the active volcano, not to be confused with Oahu, where Honolulu is located). It wasn't as deep, as different from English, as Creole in Guyana; more English had leaked into even the deepest levels, and English forms would alternate with genuine Creole forms even in the most natural speech. Yet the overall similarities with Guyana were amazing to me.

Take the TMA system. In Guyana, the bare stem of the verb represented past, not present time; same in Hawaii. If you were talking about something further back in time—past-before-past, I called it in Chapter 3—you used *bin* with the verb; same in Hawaii. If you were talking about something in the future, or hypothetical, you used *go* with the verb; same in Hawaii. If you were talking about something ongoing or recurrent—what I called nonpunctual in Chapter 3—you had a special form for that, too. Hawaii didn't have the same marker as Guyana, but it went one better: it chose as its nonpunctual marker the verb *stay*, which is also the locative copula, so you get this:

Da book stay onna table.
"The book is on the table."

He stay kakaroch [cockroach] da money.
"He is stealing/habitually steals the money."

This—the use of the locative verb as the nonpunctual marker—is found in a Creole more radical than those of Hawaii and Guyana, Sranan (much more on this language in Chapter 11), where the locative verb *de* provides the nonpunctual marker *de* (usually reduced in speech to *e*).

In fact, the only real difference between Guyanese and Hawaiian TMA systems lay in the fact that in Hawaii the combination of past-before-past and irrealis markers—*bin go*—either never had been or was no longer used to express counterfactuals like "I would have done such-and-such."

When it came to definite and indefinite articles, the story was the same. Guyanese had three ways of distinguishing nouns, all three of which were found, with an identical range of meanings, in Hawaii:

- *da* (equivalent to Guyanese *di*) for definite things known to the speaker—corresponding in meaning, very roughly indeed, to English "the"
- *wan* for indefinite things presumed unknown to the speaker—derived from English "one," and corresponding even more roughly to English "a/an"
- zero, nothing, for truly indefinite things—when you were unsure of a number, when you were talking about things in general, or when it simply didn't matter whether what you were referring to was singular or plural

For instance, in English if you want to say "X is a mammal," with X equal to "dog," you can say "a dog" or "the dog" or "dogs." But not in Guyana or Hawaii; there you can say only "dog." And just the same as in Guyana, this usage had even leaked into public announcements.

Remember the "frequents tall tree" notice in the Georgetown zoo? I spotted the exact same thing on a long-defunct little greasy spoon in Honolulu: "We take order." Not "an order," because if you wanted more than one, you might think you wouldn't get it there.

Not "orders," because if you wanted just one *malasada, loco moco,* or *spam musubi* you might think you had to order at least two.

When it came to dealing with that "simple" (!) English verb "to be," it was the same story: three different forms, one before nouns, one before locative expressions (*da book stay onna table*), and another—another zero in fact—before adjectives. The only difference: in Hawaii they co-opted English "is" for before nouns:

Who go down first is loser.

(This was an old guy telling me about fights when he was a kid.) But an even more striking similarity was the use of *stay* with adjectives to indicate temporary states. Remember the Guyanese contrast between *he sick* (permanent condition) and *he de sick* (temporary condition)? Here's the exact same thing from a locally born plantation worker and pig hunter of Filipino ancestry on the island of Kauai (I should mention that the hunting of wild pigs in the mountains is the sport par excellence for macho working-class males, and thus a great topic for getting people to produce their most natural speech):

"You know the best kind mountain pig, eh, one sow, when you catch um an' just *hanau* [given birth] eh? Bugger STAY crisp—oh no, not *hanau*, I mean when the bugger STAY *hapai* [pregnant]."

These are just a few of the more striking resemblances between the Creole of Guyana and the Creole of Hawaii. How to explain them?

When linguists find resemblances between languages their immediate reaction is that there must be some kind of genetic relationship. Thus when we find Spanish *dos*, French *deux*, Portuguese *duas/dois*, Italian *due*, Romanian *doi*, we assume that these languages have a common parent, and indeed they do—it's Latin, where "two" is *duo*, and of course this is just one of the many resemblances showing that all of the so-called Romance languages are related by their common ancestry. Such resemblances are indeed convincing where the countries concerned all formed part of the Roman Empire, or where (as in the Spanish ex-colonies of Latin America or the Portuguese ex-colony of Brazil) the languages are known to have been exported. Indeed, so reliable is the "comparative method" that migrations have been deduced from such data, even when there were no historical records.

Thus when we find that "woman" is *fefine* in Tongan, *fafine* in Samoan, *vahine* in Tahitian, and *wahine* in Maori and Hawaiian, and when such resemblances aren't limited to odd words but run right through the vocabulary, we don't assume there's just a lot of coincidence around—we assume that Tonga, Samoa, Tahiti, New Zealand, and Hawaii were all settled by the same people. Nowadays these assumptions can be checked by DNA, but long before we knew about DNA, people figured out migrations on the basis of language alone.

I wasn't the first by any means to spot the similarities between the Creole of Hawaii and what are known as the "Atlantic Creoles"—Creoles related to English that are spoken in the Caribbean or on the coasts of Central or (like Guyanese) South America (although, coming almost directly from Guyana, more of these similarities were more obvious to me than to most other linguists). Indeed, Bill Stewart, the guy who'd told me about "funny Spanish" spoken in the Santa Marta area, along with other scholars such as John Holm, was convinced that the Creole of Hawaii was simply another member of the family, an Atlantic Creole somehow transplanted to the middle of the Pacific.

Wait a minute, I thought. There were two things seriously wrong with this proposal.

The first related to the kind of similarity. The kind of similarity on which the comparative method was based had to do with words, not grammar. If the words in two languages looked similar enough to be related to one another, and the phonetic differences between them could be explained either by general principles of sound change or well-documented trends in the language family concerned, common ancestry was assumed. Nothing at all was assumed from grammatical resemblances. No two languages had ever been assigned to the same family on the basis of grammatical resemblances unless they also shared a sizable stock of cognates (words clearly related to one another by both sound and meaning).

But the only cognates common to the Atlantic Creoles and

Hawaii were words derived or directly borrowed from English. None of the non-English words in Atlantic Creoles ever found its way to Hawaii. You can find words like *nyam*, "eat," or *unu*, "you (pl.)," or *obeah*, "witchcraft," in most if not all of the Atlantic Creoles, but never in Hawaii; similarly, you never find words like *hapai*, "pregnant," or *wahine*, "woman," or *akamai*, "clever, skilled," common in Hawaii, in any of the Atlantic Creoles. In other words, diffusion between the two areas wasn't even a one-way street—it was a blind alley, a dead end. Even English-derived words with changed meanings didn't migrate—you can't *cobweb* your house in Hawaii, any more than you can *lawnmower* your lawn in the Caribbean.

In other words, people who asked you to believe that the structural similarities between Hawaii and Guyana sprang from some kind of genetic relationship were doing this on the basis of evidence no one would even have dreamed of using anywhere else in the world.

The second thing wrong with the genetic-relatedness hypothesis was the absence of any plausible means of transmission. Everyone knows how Portuguese got to Brazil or English to India, but how had any Atlantic Creole ever reached Hawaii? The two are separated by about five thousand miles of mostly ocean. Slaves from the Caribbean were never transported to Hawaii. To the best of my knowledge, the first time people from the Caribbean even met people from Hawaii was at the conference on Creoles we held in Honolulu in 1975, and a real eye-opener that was for both parties, culturally and linguistically (the evening they learned one another's songs was a truly memorable one). So who could have brought the language?

There was only one possible answer: sailors.

Sailors have been blamed for lots of things, but this is their bummest rap. One of the oldest myths in Creole studies is that there was some kind of "nautical jargon" spoken worldwide. There's not one single citation of this fabulous tongue, not one iota of empirical evidence that there was ever anything onboard ships but a constantly shifting mélange of scraps of different languages that depended on the constantly changing ethnic composition of ships' crews (and given mortality rates and desertion rates up to and including the nineteenth century, those were no mean changes).

But absence of evidence has never stopped scholars from making stuff up whenever it suited them. Look at "land bridges." In 1915 the German meteorologist Alfred Wegener published his claim that existing continents had once been joined, citing among his evidence the undisputed fact that fossils of the same prehistoric species were often found in sites separated by thousands of miles of water. The geophysical establishment poured scorn on him. Everyone knew that continents were where they'd been ever since they jelled out of the primordial magma.

So how had the animals gotten from one continent to another? Simple. Land bridges had conveniently risen out of the ocean, the animals marched across them, and then the land bridges conveniently sank back beneath the waves—just like the Red Sea parted for Moses. There was, of course, not an iota of evidence that these land bridges had ever existed, but of course they must have existed; otherwise people would have had to change their precious beliefs about the permanent stability of continents.

In just the same way, if there wasn't a nautical jargon, people would have to change their precious belief that genetic relationship was the only possible cause of similarities between languages. So let's be kind to them and pretend that there was a universal nautical jargon. What would it have been like? Well, only a very few Caribbean Creole speakers joined the merchant marine, so the vast majority of seamen would have been non-Creole speakers. What are the chances that this majority would have acquired, from a tiny Creole-speaking minority, not just words, but entire Creole grammars, down to points as subtle as the use of locative copulas to indicate temporary states? What are the chances they would do this when they didn't even acquire Creole words (as shown above, there are no words of distinctively Caribbean provenance in Hawaii)? And, suspending disbelief yet again, just supposing they had acquired such a grammar, when, where, and how would they have transmitted it to Hawaiians? On weeklong benders in the bars of Honolulu and Lahaina?

Sure, sailors not infrequently jumped ship and entered the community—one even rose to become governor of the Big Island under King Kamehameha. But the community they entered was an independent Hawaiian-speaking nation, and what's the probability that the Hawaiians would have learned anything that such immigrants spoke? Exactly the same as the probability that English-speaking natives of Wisconsin would have learned Norwegian, instead of expecting Norwegian immigrants to learn English. The by now definitely ex-seamen would surely have learned Hawaiian, well or badly—close to natively, one would assume, in the case of the governor at least.

Bottom line: the only reason for believing that Creole in the Pacific came from Creoles in the Atlantic was that nobody could think of an alternative explanation.

On realizing which, any rational observer would conclude that there just had to be an alternative explanation.

The only question was—what was it?

I'd been given to understand that I was expected not only to obtain a doctorate from somewhere somehow in the next four years but to earn my keep by obtaining a substantial amount of grant money for the university. Yet another new skill now had to be learned: how to write grant proposals with six-figure budgets. The obvious thing to do was to carry out an overall survey of all the varieties of English and English-related speech to be found in Hawaii, a survey of the type pioneered by Bill Labov. Labov's recommendation, I now learned, had been instrumental in getting me my job; it looked like he'd also given them instructions on what to do with me once I'd got it.

I was lucky in that this kind of survey was still in vogue. I put into the proposal all the right words about how I'd obtain a representative random sample of the population, knowing that once I had the money I could do the job the way I wanted to. The core of the survey would be a standardized one-hour interview administered to over two hundred Hawaii residents, supplemented by participant-observation and other techniques. Interviewees would be compensated at a rate of $5 per hour, not a princely sum but enough for a six-pack of Bud back then. All materials would be tape-recorded, transcribed, and statistically analyzed.

Off went the proposal to the National Science Foundation. Back it came with the news that, well, it could be accepted, but only if I made one small alteration—dropping the $5 fee for interviews. Apparently the scholars who reviewed the proposal felt that if I got away with this, nobody would ever again talk to them for free.

I was livid. What kind of linguistic droit du seigneur did these profs think they had, to waste an hour of working people's time and not provide even a token recompense? Summoning all my eloquence I wrote back an impassioned letter where I laid out all the arguments why paying for interviews was the only just and equitable procedure. It worked: the NSF agreed to pay.*

By rights I suppose I should have sent someone to every nth house, or something along those lines, in order to randomize my sample. But that approach, what's called a cold canvass in the soliciting trade, is not the best way to elicit the kind of relaxed speech I was looking for. Networking was a far better approach. I had assembled an excellent team of student assistants, all local bar one haole (there is a category, "local haole," for white folk born in the islands, but in general "local" is a code-word for non-Caucasian), and they had connections in the community, and their connections had connections, so we could know in advance that everyone we interviewed was someone willing and ready to cooperate. You could argue the sample was biased—"people willing to talk to strangers"—but what would have been the point in finding people who weren't willing to talk to strangers?

Anyway, I kept a running tally so that our sample stayed more or less representative, with the right proportions of Japanese to Hawaiians to Filipinos, women to men, young to middle-aged, immigrants to locally born, working- to middle-class, rural to urban, and so on and so forth. I'd say things like, "We can't use so-and-so; we've got enough Koreans" or "Do all the Chinese live in Honolulu? Doesn't anybody know any from outside?"

I trained the students in how to interview. Novice interviewers talk too much. They tend to be nervous with strangers, so if there's more than a second or two of silence they feel impelled to fill it with speech. I pointed out that if they were talking, the interviewee wasn't. Interviewers have to learn to efface themselves, act like a sponge, drawing out by osmosis the true nature, and the true language, of their subjects.

I also tried to train them in sensitivity. There were, of course, certain basic questions the subjects had to answer: age, education, profession, and so on. After that there was a list of suggested topics, which I told them not to take too seriously. They were suggestions only. An interviewer is like a fisherman. When the fish takes the hook, you let it run, wherever it wants to, as long as it can, and your advantage over the fisherman is that your line is endless.

There was one interview, from a book on sociolinguistics, that I used as a cautionary tale. The subject tells the interviewer how his eldest son just died of liver failure. After a couple of perfunctory inquiries—no condolences, no sympathy, nothing—the interviewer plows straight into the next topic: "What do people round here grow in their gardens?" "Oh, potatoes, tomatoes," the guy says, "*or did you want me to say 'maters' and 'taters'?*" You could hear his suppressed fury even in the cold print. And, believe it or not, this was from an interview given as an example of how to do it.

A lot of the interviewing I did myself; I needed to run a hands-on operation. The oldest speaker I interviewed was ninety-eight. He had no teeth, so what came out was too mushy for anyone to transcribe it. The oldest intelligible speaker I interviewed was ninety-two; he was still pretty spry, but thinking of building a temple before he passed on, because *money no can hapai*—"You can't take it with you."

As in Guyana, the supernatural was a fertile topic. My favorite story came from a Hawaiian on Kauai who had inadvertently built an outdoor toilet smack in the route of the Night Marchers.

The Night Marchers are the ghosts of the Alii, the aristocratic warriors of old Hawaii, who on nights in the dark of the moon patrol their old territories. If their gaze falls on you, you die. So this guy was in his toilet one night, taking a dump, when suddenly in the distance he heard a sound of muffled drums and tramping feet. He didn't wait. Pants around his ankles, he took off like a rocket; by first light, his outhouse was history.

I learned the Filipino way to find your way if you get lost. Take all your clothes off, put them back on inside out, and away you go.

I learned odd facts about language. There were Japanese immigrants whose pidgin was more Japanese than English; as one of these said:

Hapa-hapa shite—all time the nani ni watashi mo
   hanashite mo wakaranai.

which, literally translated, means "Half-half do—all time the what in I either speak either don't know." And if that doesn't make it much clearer, what she meant was: "I speak half-and-half—I never know whether I'm speaking one or the other."

Because Japanese is a language of prestige, even second- and third-generation children of immigrants often speak it. Because Filipino languages—Ilocano, Tagalog, and the like—are not languages of prestige, no locally born persons of Filipino ancestry (with the rarest of rare exceptions) speak them. I talked to one of the exceptions, a youngish guy with a black belt in karate. He was at a cockfight—cockfights, or chicken fights as they are more frequently called, are illegal in Hawaii, but they go on all the time, and there are few working-class districts where you won't hear the crowing of "fighting chicken"—when he overheard some old Filipino immigrants discussing him most offensively in Ilocano. So certain were they that he couldn't understand them, they didn't even bother to lower their voices. "I broke a guy's arm," my informant confessed, with a rueful mix of pride and shame.

But the best work I did was outside of formal interviews. I worked with a group of pig hunters on Kauai, one of whom supplied the pregnant-sow recommendation I quoted earlier. We'd drink beer together; I'd take one of them off for a formal interview and leave another tape recorder running on the table. One day I got graphic proof of how well this method worked. When I played the tape I was amazed to find an animated discussion of my own personality, behavior, and possible motivation. They must have totally forgotten that the machine was there.

It was fascinating to hear how the Creole got deeper as soon as I left the room and shallower when I returned; you could actually measure the amount it changed by the percentages of distinctively non-English forms in their speech. Even types of structure were affected. In one hour, five guys talking together produced not a single relative clause. In the first five minutes after I returned, three came out. But the mechanism there was pretty obvious. You use relative clauses to describe things you don't think the hearer will readily identify. These five guys worked together, hunted together, and had been buddies since high school; they didn't need signposts when they talked with one another. I, the outsider, did.

On the Big Island I had Joe Abril. I found Joe through one of my students, Nancy Nakamatsu; she'd made a surreptitious recording of her uncle talking to him, and I was impressed both by his skill as a raconteur and the depth of his Creole. Joe was a construction worker, an extrovert, a drinking man with a wide circle of friends who controlled the whole range of the Hawaiian continuum from Japanese-related pidgin through all the layers of Creole to Standard American English. To accompany him on his travels around the island was like a seminar in code-switching, and if any of his friends were linguistically affected by my presence, he'd call them on it: "Eh, brah, how come you stay talk like dakine *haole*, ah?" Some of my best data came from those trips.

I was one of a panel on a call-in radio show talking about local language, Pidgin, as everyone called it, and I played a tape of Joe and asked if anyone could identify his ethnic background. The other panel members all tried, and then several callers, and not one of them got it right. Joe's ancestry is pure Filipino, but a plurality guessed Hawaiian, and all of a sudden I realized why—they were basing their choices not on language but on content. The tape described incidents in a wild night out, and while Filipinos drink and party relatively little, Hawaiians do it a lot (at least, those are part of the local stereotypes). And indeed, except for a Chinese guy who'd apparently spent his whole life as a cook in a Chinese restaurant, and a small group known as the *kibei* that we'll meet in the next chapter, I never met any locally born individual whose origins you could identify on the basis of his speech.

Conversely, I never met any pidgin-speaking immigrants whose origins you couldn't identify as soon as they opened their mouths. Mostly they were either Japanese or Filipino, with an occasional Korean. Chinese and Portuguese, the earliest arrivals, were all native-born by the time I arrived in Hawaii. So the difference between Creole and pidgin was absolute, and in the next chapter we'll look at the differences and see all the things that can be learned from them.

Meantime I'd found out how to get a Ph.D. without going through grad school or even mail-order college.

My first degree was from Cambridge University. If you got a bachelor's from Cambridge, you were entitled, at a later date, to obtain a master's by the simple act of paying them £5 (at the rate of exchange back then, about $12.50). Think of the chutzpah of it—they're saying, in effect, our B.A. is as good as anyone else's M.A.

So, in order to obtain a Ph.D. . . .

No, you're wrong. They weren't offering a special on doctorates for $29.95. What they would do, however, and I think they're virtually the only university that does this, was award you a Ph.D. on the basis of published work.

Well, there was my book on Guyanese Creole, by now all ready to go. So I submitted it to Cambridge University Press, on the principle that, as the old adage has it, dog doesn't eat dog.

It took a while. The mills of God grind slow, but the mills of university presses grind even slower. I answered all kinds of nitpicky questions, but the most grief they gave me was over the title: *Dynamics of a Creole System*. This was a little too dynamic for some reviewers—they demanded something duller. My greatest ally was Dave DeCamp, who said no, that was exactly what the book was about; it was a description of how a Creole continuum worked, how all the parts of it related to one another, so any other title would be a misdescription. He won me the point.

There was one condition. Whoever submitted published work

had to pass an oral exam on it, to make the process at least look a little more like your traditional dissertation defense. (For those of you unfamiliar with this arcane process, a doctoral candidate, once A.B.D.—all but dissertation, i.e., having satisfactorily completed all relevant courses—normally goes through several rounds of revising the dissertation, supposedly "a substantive contribution to knowledge," with a supervisor and a committee of four other scholars, one from a discipline different from the candidate's, and then the process, one that may take years, ends up with a two- or three-hour grilling by the committee where you "defend" your work against every conceivable criticism.)

So, with only months to spare before my promotion-and-tenure decision, I was summoned to Cambridge, where on a chill gray day in the middle of winter I was grilled for a couple of hours by Bob LePage, whom you may recall was the scholar whose account of Jamaican Creole Beryl Bailey had dissed, and a Cambridge phonetician called John Trim (there was nothing about phonetics in the book). At the end of this, they just got up and started to leave.

This wasn't how they did things in America. By that time I'd been on several Ph.D. committees and chaired a couple, so I knew that you sent the candidate out of the room and discussed for a few minutes, then called the candidate back in, announced your verdict—seldom negative; you'd worked together over the thing for so long you'd be condemning yourselves if you nixed it—after which everyone, chair, committee, candidate, and anyone else who happened to be around repaired to the nearest bar to celebrate the new inductee into the halls of academe.

"Did I pass?" I asked them outright.

They looked shocked. "Oh, we can't tell you that. We have to send a report to the committee."

The cheapskates didn't even buy me a drink.

I wasn't worried about a negative verdict. I figured correctly · that they wouldn't dare fail me on a book their own press had published. All I worried about was, would they come through in time?

They did, with only days to spare.

Now I was a full professor with tenure. At this point, many profs relax and just coast through the rest of their career. In Germany, I've heard, some even take off for years at a time, and a full professor over there—Herr Doktor Doktor Professor—is so exalted a being that no one dares complain about it. As far as I was concerned, I'd gotten the bullshit out of the way so I could now get on with the serious business of life.

Which is, of course, finding out stuff.

7

FROM PIDGIN TO CREOLE

Rai . . .

"Rai . . .

"Ano book anything borrow dekiru tokoro."

The penny dropped. "Oh," I said, "you mean a library?"

"Yeah. There work husband."

The sixty-six-year-old Japanese woman was trying to tell me her daughter's husband worked in a library ("That book-anything-borrow-can place"). People sometimes act as if pidgin speakers were stupid, but they're far from stupid. They're really ingenious; when they don't remember a word they'll work around it until you get the message. They'll use words from your language if they know them; if not, they'll use words from their own, and hope you know them, and failing that, words from any other language that might happen to be around. That's pidgin.

By rights, this woman shouldn't have been a pidgin speaker. She was what is known as a *kibei*: that is, someone born in Hawaii but sent back to Japan for her education. This one left at age five and returned at eighteen. According to gospel, she should have been a Creole speaker, since "pidgin speaker" is usually defined as "non-native" and "Creole speaker" as "native, locally born." In general, this is true. But length and time of exposure are the critical factors—not brute location.

Take my own children. Up until they were four and six respectively, Ash and Jim lived a good part of their lives in Spain, spoke kiddie Spanish indistinguishable from that of Spanish kids, and learned to read in Spanish. In a matter of months after they stopped speaking it, they lost it entirely. Or almost entirely. A few years later we gave them a Spanish newspaper. They read from it fluently, with perfect accents—but they couldn't understand a word of it.

To speak a language fluently, natively, you have to learn it before a critical age—thirteen or so, at the latest. But this doesn't mean you get to keep it. You also have to use it, maybe right up to that critical age if not beyond. Our Japanese lady may well have learned Creole up to the age of five, but when she came back to Hawaii thirteen years later, she was in exactly the same position as some naïve immigrant fresh off the boat.

But what position was that, exactly? Remember the conventional wisdom I described in Chapter 1: when immigrants speaking several different languages arrive in such numbers that the dominant ethnic group becomes a minority, the language of that dominant group somehow gets "pidginized," reduced, stripped of all its complexities—turned into a means of communication that can be quickly learned by newcomers and thus keep society functioning. You'll still see this, or something like it, in books on pidgins and Creoles or introductions to general linguistics, mindlessly repeated. It's hard to throw off conventional notions when there's no clear alternative.

So, even several years after I arrived in Hawaii, I was still claiming that pidginization was "second-language learning with inadequate input." One reason I clung to the conventional wisdom was that this made a neat contrast with my definition of creolization: "first-language learning with inadequate input." It's always nice when you can solve problems just by balancing a pair of clauses. But my data were telling me a very different story.

In fact, one of my informants had told me in plain words. She was an old Hawaiian lady who had spent a large part of her life alone with her husband in the mountains of Kauai, looking after a small, isolated hydroelectric plant; they would stay up there for months on end, coming down only to buy the next few months' supplies, bringing them back on donkeys, since there was no road. But before that she had grown up in the sugar-growing lowlands at a time when a large majority of the island's inhabitants were pidgin-speaking immigrants.

"So we use the Hawaiian and the Chinese together in one sentence, see?" she told me. "And they ask me if that's a Hawaiian word, I said no, maybe that's a Japanese word we put it in, to make a sentence with a Hawaiian word. And the Chinese the same way too, in order to make a sentence for them to understand you."

I could have just believed her. But to have done so would have violated a basic law of academic inquiry, which is, don't pay any attention to people who've actually done something—listen to people with the right credentials who've dreamed up their own explanation.

But the data reinforced her picture, not the conventional one. Nobody was trying to learn English and failing at it. A few thought they'd already learned it; John Reinecke had a lovely story about a cane-cutter who had complained to the big boss after a new overseer fresh from the Carolinas had addressed him in Southern States' English: "Wassamatta dis *haole*? He no can speak *haole*!" But most were simply trying to communicate with whatever scraps of whatever language they'd managed to pick up. Since English was the dominant language, it followed that, sooner or later, there would be many more words from English than from anything else, so that when you looked at the result, you could easily convince yourself that they'd been trying to learn English all along, but just couldn't get a handle on it until they'd "reduced" it somehow.

There were other facts that didn't fit the conventional story. The older the immigrants, the more Hawaiian words they used. Occasionally you'd even run into sentences with more Hawaiian than English in them, like this from an old guy describing an incident in the cane fields:

Luna, who hapai? Hapai all, hemo all.
Foreman, who carry? Carry all, cut all.
"Who'll carry it, boss?" "Everyone'll cut it and everyone'll
    carry it."

Moreover, from early in the century, the Hawaii Sugar Producers Association had been putting out little phrase books containing all the technical terms needed for sugar production. The earliest of these ran to several hundred items, the vast majority of which consisted of Hawaiian words. Well, almost Hawaiian words—while they looked like Hawaiian, many differed from standard Hawaiian forms. For instance, while Hawaiian for "irrigate" is *ho'okahe wai*, the phrase book entry was *hanawai*, which literally means "work water." In other words, the entries seemed to represent some simplified form of Hawaiian. This was funny, because the influx of foreign labor in the late nineteenth century supposedly came about because there were too few Hawaiians to work the booming sugar plantations, and most of that few didn't want to anyway. But if Hawaiians made up only a fraction of the workforce, and if the plantations were owned and controlled by haoles, how did the Hawaiian language get to provide almost the entire technical vocabulary for the industry?

All the bits and pieces were there to explain this, but I still wasn't able to put them together.

There were other ways in which pidgin in Hawaii was not acting like a well-behaved pidgin should. Once a language had been pidginized, it was supposed to "stabilize," to develop some kind of simple but regular structure. But by the time I got to Hawaii, English in some shape or form had been around for nearly two centuries. Even allowing for the fact that my immigrants, all elderly now, had probably acquired their pidgin up to half a century previously, that still gave pidgin a life of nearly a century and a half. Surely if it was ever going to stabilize it should have done so in that amount of time?

Yet, as I noted in the last chapter, I never met any immigrants whose origins weren't obvious from the brand of pidgin they spoke. And I don't mean just from the stereotyped sound-changes they made, the Japanese /r/ for /l/ ("Honoruru"), the Filipino /p/ for /f/ ("chicken pight"). I didn't need to hear them. I could pick blindly from a pile of transcripts and after reading a few lines I would know immediately not only whether the speaker was native or foreign-born, but (if the latter) what his or her native language was, even when no non-English words were used:

"Us kerosene plantation one month, four gallon give."
Japanese!
"Only two hundred forty the salary."
Filipino!

You can do it too. In the Japanese sentence, the subject ("plantation") is in the middle and the verb ("give") at the end. In the Filipino sentence, the normal English order (subject first, predicate last) is reversed. If people had done this all the time, things would have been easy: I could have said there was a Japanese-influenced pidgin and a Filipino-influenced pidgin. But they didn't do it all the time. Often they'd use an English-type order, subject first, verb next to it. Then in the next sentence they'd put words in an order that wasn't English or Japanese or Filipino. And, once in a while, a Japanese speaker would put a subject at the end of a sentence, like Filipinos sometimes did—you can catch one doing it in the fifth line of this chapter—or a Filipino would put a verb there, like Japanese did. Pidgin in Hawaii just didn't have any regular structure.

If a Creole language somehow grew out of a pidgin, this made it even harder to see how. For most people, the big problem had been the fact that pidgins were too simple to make a proper human language—they had to be "expanded," whatever that meant. But clearly now there was an additional problem, equally large. For children to acquire language, they were supposed to receive what's known in the trade as "robust data"—that's to say abundant samples of a single language that had clear and regular structure. Even children growing up bilingual get this: they are presented with two sets of robust data instead of one, and they very seldom mix them up.

Nobody knew how children would manage things if instead of this kind of input they received data that were not only too basic to constitute a real language, but where verbs and subjects could pop out all over the place, quite unpredictably. If indeed they appeared at all—they could just as often be "unexpressed," left for the hearer to figure out from context. I've often read transcripts of scenes I actually took part in, and have been quite unable to make out what pidgin speakers meant, even though I must have understood them perfectly at the time—so much depends, where pidgin is concerned, on where you are, who's there, what you've been talking about, what things are visible in your surroundings, and I don't know what else, though I'd like to exclude weather and time of day.

And there was another even weirder thing about the pidgin-Creole interface. I learned about it the first time I heard Creole-speaking adults talking to their immigrant parents. To make those parents understand them, they had to repidginize their Creole!

I was flabbergasted. This was the exact opposite of what's supposed to happen in the acquisition of language. Under normal circumstances, children are supposed to learn language from their parents. There's even a special kind of talk, called "motherese," which mothers (and, let's not be sexist, fathers and other caregivers) use when talking to their children—a radically simplified, heavily accented, slowly enunciated, often repetitive version of English or whatever the mother tongue is. Some researchers (not I) even claim that without motherese children couldn't learn language. But here were children talking motherese to their parents!

And, in some cases, the parents seemed to be learning.

Here we need to look at a little history. Around 1930, the steady wave of immigration that had continued unchecked for more than half a century was brought to a screeching halt by the Great Depression. There was no money to ship in new immigrants and no work for them even if they came. After the Depression came World War II, so it wasn't until the late 1940s that immigration resumed, and even then on a far smaller scale than before. By that time, the vast majority of Hawaii residents were locally born Creole speakers, so new immigrants acquired the local language, well or badly, just as they would have done anywhere else.

But until 1920 or so, Creole speakers—the native-born—had been a minority consisting mostly of adolescents and children. It was only after this date that the numbers of Creole-speaking adults really took off. And here an interesting correlation emerged. All of the immigrants in my sample who had arrived before 1920 spoke the kind of pidgin shown in the examples I've given: highly variable, mother-tongue influenced, and extremely basic. They couldn't speak anything else (apart, of course, from their own native languages). But among those who came after 1920—at a time, that is, when they could get ready access to Creole speakers of their own age—were some whose pidgin was getting closer and closer to the Creole. In other words, when they were fully exposed to the Creole, they began to learn it.

The most Creole-like speaker was a Filipino guy, now retired, who'd arrived in 1930 and risen from cane-cutter to supervisor on the Honolulu docks, where he was constantly interacting with tough young Hawaiian Creole–speaking longshoremen. He had almost got the Creole down, but not quite.

One Creole rule is, if the subject is indefinite, it has to be followed by a pronoun:

Some guys they no like play.
"Some guys don't want to play."

But note that the pronoun follows the sentence subject, not the noun, so that if you add a relative clause to "some guys," the pronoun follows the clause:

Some guys no like play they gone awready.
"Some guys who don't want to play have already left."

Now there are three other logically possible things you could do with the pronoun. You could keep it next to the noun that heads the subject (an asterisk before a sentence indicates that the sentence is ungrammatical in the language or dialect in question):

*Some guys they no like play gone awready.

Or you could play safe by putting it in both places at once.

*Some guys they no like play they gone awready.

Or you could leave it out altogether:

*Some guys no like play gone awready.

In the course of my conversation with the dock supervisor, he produced all four constructions, the correct one and the three incorrect ones. In other words, he knew, at some obscure, unconscious level of knowledge, that in sentences like these there was something funny going on with pronouns. He just wasn't quite sure what.

But then he did something glaringly un-Creole. We were talking about how badly young people behaved nowadays (always a hot topic for older people) and he said, "I blame the farens."

The foreigns? The fair ones?

No, he was hypercorrecting. Filipinos with little exposure to English commonly turn all the /f/s into /p/s. This guy knew that, and was so afraid of branding himself as a *bukbuk* (the pejorative term in Hawaii for Filipinos) that he not only avoided the mistake but went too far by turning some genuine /p/s into /f/s. Who he blamed were, of course, "the parents."

But apart from a few similar post-1920 arrivals, the gulf between pidgin speakers and Creole speakers was not only absolute, but vast.

Take just the speed at which they spoke. Creole speakers typically spoke fast. There were a few, like Nancy Nakamatsu's uncle, who carefully doled out their words, but most spoke at a machine-gun pace, sometimes so fast that even when you were familiar with their pronunciation, grammar, and vocabulary, there were sections of tape you had to play several times before you could transcribe them. But pidgin speakers, even if you discounted the long pauses while they fished for the right word, spoke about three times more slowly.

Pidgin had no rules or consistent structure. Creole was as structured as any human language.

Pidgin varied according to the ethnicity of its speakers. There were no Creole speakers whose ethnicity you could guess from their speech.

Of course Creole wasn't invariant. It varied just like it did in Guyana, as a function of distance from urban centers and of social and occupational variables, skewed heavily by the righteous/unrighteous distinction I'd seen in Guyana. But even when I first arrived, decreolization had gone much further and faster than in Guyana. That was only to be expected, now that Hawaii was one of the fifty states, with over a quarter of its population native speakers of English.

I was most interested in the deepest surviving Creole, the variety most different from English, for this should represent the earliest variety, the one that emerged first from the pidgin. To hear that, you already had to go to the outer islands, more particularly the Big Island and Kauai—you had to go into the rural areas of those islands and among people who worked with their hands. Elsewhere, particularly in and around Honolulu, what you heard were only watered-down versions of the original.

For instance, you would hardly ever, if ever, hear anyone say *bin* in Honolulu. There it had been replaced by *wen*, which in the rapid speech of adolescents reduced to *we*, or even just /w/ or /n/. According to folk etymology—the way naïve speakers explain the origins of words—*wen* came from English "went." Of course this gave the "Creole equals stupid" school a big laugh, because the past of "go" became *wen go*—saying the same thing twice, ha ha ha.

In actual fact, *wen* derives from *bin* by a simple set of sound changes; if you want to get technical, the bilabial stop /b/ weakens to the bilabial semi-vowel /w/ in contexts where low stress and rapid enunciation co-occur, as they typically do in preverbal tense markers, and in the same contexts contrast between adjacent front vowels /i/ and /e/ tends also to weaken through centralization, a tendency reinforced, in this case, by general front-vowel instability among Filipino speakers. Indeed, a few speakers used *bin* and *wen* indiscriminately, and one old Filipino guy, in a single conversation, produced not only these but the two intermediate forms, *win* and *ben*, not to mention forms with a sound intermediate between /b/

and /w/, the bilabial fricative that linguists indicate with a Greek beta (β).

As for *stay*, that got gradually replaced too (the parenthesized comments are rough guides to whereabouts you are on the continuum, not separate and distinct dialects):

> He stay work. (deepest variety)
> He stay workin. (low intermediate)
> He workin. (high intermediate)
> "He is working."

And *go* as an irrealis marker was similarly replaced by *gon*, slightly downmarket from *gonna*.

> I go tok to om.
> I gon tok to om.
> I gonna talk to 'im.
> "I'm going to talk to him."

But anyone whose main interest is in how Creoles began isn't going to spend too much time on the intermediate varieties. The big question was, and remained, how could anything like a Creole emerge from the kind of pidgin I've described?

It looked as if it should have been impossible. From the fact that locally born adults spoke Creole, while their immigrant parents spoke pidgin, it didn't take Sherlock Holmes to figure out that the Creole could only have been created by those adults when they were children. But how could a child have learned anything from the formless, shifting, rudimentary input that their parents had given them? Well, they hadn't. Under normal circumstances, children end up reproducing (with subtle differences—otherwise languages would never change) whatever their parents spoke. But children in Hawaii must have gone far beyond their parents' language, taking from their input only a stock of words and ways of pronouncing them, creating a grammar almost from ground zero.

On top of which, the grammar they created wasn't just any old grammar. It was a grammar that, if not quite identical to the one I'd found in Guyana, contained far more similarities than anyone could have expected. And those similarities were not, by any stretch of the imagination, a result of the fact that English was the major supplier of words for both languages. The most striking similarities between the Creoles of Guyana and Hawaii were in things that they didn't share with English.

We've looked at TMA marking and articles and ways of handling what are delightfully called "copulative" structures—things expressed by the verb "to be" in English—but there are lots more with which I won't bore you by going into them in depth: ways of making questions and negative sentences, existential constructions ("There is a . . ."), passive equivalents, relative clauses without relative pronouns, finite clauses of purpose, and on and on. And those are just the full-blown similarities; I'm not including things that were full-blown in Guyana but only partially developed in Hawaii (probably due to the far stronger impact of English on the latter)—things like serial verbs and plural markers that occurred sporadically or in limited contexts but never really got off the ground.

The obvious explanation, the explanation any linguist in his right mind would go for, was that Creole had been introduced from somewhere else. But how, and by whom? There had been no contact between Hawaii and any Creole-speaking area, no immigration, nothing. Except . . .

Except for the tiny portion of the Hawaiian population known as Bravas. Some seven hundred immigrants from the Cape Verde Islands, mostly from the island of Brava, had come to work on the plantations. And the language of the Cape Verdes is a Portuguese Creole.

Believe it or not, it's been seriously suggested that these seven hundred are responsible for Hawaiian Creole. It's what I call the bacterial theory of language transmission. Everyone in Hawaii—tens of thousands of them—hung around wondering what they were going to do for a language until suddenly, in the nick of time, the Bravas showed up, their tongue swept the islands like a flu epidemic (translating itself as it went, of course) and voilà, if you'll pardon my French. Ian Hancock went so far as to make a bogus tape in which some individual (actually him; he's a great mimic) is interviewed on the beach in Waikiki and claims that, yes, he's descended from these people and they did indeed bring the Creole with them. Some creolists were actually fooled by it.

But leaving aside the absence of evidence for contact, there's a purely logical reason why no diffusion theory can fly. Suppose for a minute it was true—suppose Creole had been brought in by the Bravas or by some other group, any group. That group would have had to speak only to locally born children. If they'd spoken to anyone else, then at least a handful of our immigrant subjects should have picked up some of their language. After all, as I've shown, as soon as a locally born Creole got going, pidgin speakers started picking it up. If Creole had been there earlier, why wouldn't they have picked up at least as much of that?

But if you ruled out importation from elsewhere, you were back with the original, seemingly insoluble problem—how could children have learned rules of grammar for which there was no evidence in any input they had received? And how could they wind up with the same kind of grammar in very different parts of the world?

For the more I read about other Creoles, the more apparent it became that the similarities I was finding between Creole in Hawaii and in Guyana were far from unique. They were no more than a special case of what was happening throughout the world. Over and over, Creoles totally unrelated to one another showed the same rules, the same kinds of grammatical structure.

If this was simply a monograph on Creoles, I could fill a book with examples of these similarities (indeed I did—it's called *Roots of Language*). Here, a single example must suffice, but it's a telling one.

Take two Creoles many thousands of miles apart. Saramaccan (we'll meet this again in Chapters 9 and 11) is a language spoken by the descendants of maroons in the interior of Suriname, South America, with a vocabulary drawn mainly from English. Fa d'Ambu is a language spoken by the inhabitants of Annobón, a small island in the Bight of Benin off the coast of West Central

Africa, with a vocabulary drawn mainly from Portuguese. Here are the TMA systems of Saramaccan and Fa d'Ambu, and note that this isn't my analysis, but that of three Dutch linguists, Peter Bakker, Marike Post, and Hein van der Voort (note that here "anterior" is equivalent to what I've called "past-before-past," "irrealis" refers to events that haven't actually happened—futures and conditionals—while "punctual" refers to actions occurring at a single point in time; pluses and minuses indicate the presence or absence of these factors, so that "-punctual," for instance, means any action prolonged or repeated):

	Saramaccan	Fa d'Ambu
−anterior	zero	zero
+anterior	bi	bi
+irrealis	o	ske
−punctual	ta	xa
+anterior+irrealis	bi-o	bi-ske
+anterior−punctual	bi-ta	bi-xa
+irrealis−punctual	o-ta	ske-xa
+anterior+irrealis−punctual	bi-o-ta	bi-ske-xa

(The last example, "+anterior+irrealis-punctual," corresponds, very roughly, to "would have been doing" something or other.) Now compare this with the system of Guyanese Creole described in Chapter 3 and the slightly less developed, but very similar, system I found in Hawaii, described in Chapter 6.

How could grammars so similar (and different from the grammars of any of the languages around at their birth) have come into existence in so many different parts of the world?

When you've ruled out the impossible, Sherlock Holmes said, then whatever is left, however improbable, must be the answer.

Around the middle of the last century, almost all linguists held as an article of faith that children were born with their minds a blank slate and that language had to be learned from scratch, like any other skill. It followed that language was purely a cultural construct and there were no limits, biological or other, on what a language could be like. One leader of the field went so far as to opine that if some hitherto unknown language were to be discovered tomorrow, it could be totally different from any human language hitherto known.

Then Chomsky appeared with the claim that human language formed part of human biology, and that somehow the fundamental principles of human language were latent in the brains of all normal human infants. Children did not learn language the way they learned times tables, or riding a bike, or tying their shoelaces—language was more like walking, or getting second teeth. Not exactly like, of course. Your teeth would come anyway, and they'd be the same regardless of whether you grew up in Kansas or Kazakhstan, but your language wouldn't. If you were raised by wolves and never heard any language as a child, you might never talk. However, children acquired language without conscious effort, fluently, in a relatively short space of time, and up to a universally similar level of competence, regardless of the apparent "ease" or "difficulty" of the language concerned. Whereas in contrast, grown-ups seeking to acquire a second language often applied immense effort (not to mention expense), hardly ever became fluent, and often, even after years of struggle, arrived at a shocking level of incompetence. And this, when you considered the relative mental powers of adults and small children, looked like the reverse of what it should be.

Chomsky held that each child must be born with a language acquisition device, usually shortened to LAD (some linguists, terrified of looking sexist, suggested instead a language acquisition support system—LASS!). This LAD was a black-box mechanism that somehow enabled children to learn any language they were exposed to. But suppose that what they were exposed to wasn't a real language—was a chaotic mishmash like pidgin in Hawaii?

If Creoles were produced by children from pidgin input, and if they were substantially similar wherever they were produced, it could be that the LAD contained (or even consisted of) a biologically based program, or "bioprogram" for short—something that would enable children receiving confused and/or inadequate linguistic input to still create a full human language.

I wrote up this idea and presented it at the Creole conference we held in Hawaii in 1975. Everyone in Creole studies immediately rejected it.

Why?

There were a number of reasons. One was that Chomsky's theories were still violently contested by many linguists (and are, even today, for that matter); relatively few creolists were followers of Chomsky. Those who were suffered from the NIH syndrome: not invented here. If one of the faithful had made the proposal, I'm sure they would have treated it with the greatest respect. But I'd never paid my obligatory visit to MIT, never sat at the feet of the master. And new ideas are supposed to travel from Massachusetts to Hawaii, not vice versa.

Some of the critics showed sheer scientific ignorance. Their tacit assumption seemed to be that if there was a biological program for something, its instructions had to be mandatory and inescapable. Therefore, if they could find a Creole that lacked any of the features I described, the theory was automatically refuted.

That was nonsense, of course. No biological program exists in a vacuum. Every biological program has to interact with the environment, and its expression will be modified by that environment in a variety of ways. You only have to think how Japanese born and raised in the United States are on average bigger than Japanese born and raised in Japan. Their genes are the same but the environment is different: a different diet, for one thing. So obviously— at least I thought it was obvious, until I saw the responses—a language bioprogram would be modified by the environment just like any other genetic program.

For the bioprogram to cause the same results everywhere, the input would have had to be exactly the same in every place where a Creole arose. How likely was that? Since in every such place the population consisted of a different mix of ethnic groups, with different percentages of dominant-language speakers not only in each place but even in the same place at different periods, the input would be richer in some places, less rich in others. All the bioprogram did was make sure that any deficiencies in the input would be filled—that whatever was needed for a full human language would be available. And it did this by providing not a smorgasbord of choices, but a simple list of preferred options.

Another argument assumed something I had never claimed: that for the bioprogram to work, the pidgin had to be the only linguistic input the first Creole generation received. I never said anything of the kind. To the contrary, the final report on my National Science Foundation project contained details of all the languages spoken by subjects in our survey: all of the older Creole speakers spoke at least one other language, sometimes two.

Careless reading and poor scholarship aside, I can see where this misunderstanding came from. My critics assumed, on no empirical basis whatsoever, that if children developing a Creole from a pidgin were at the same time acquiring a preexisting language, they would use that language to make up for any deficiencies in the pidgin. They'd simply transfer to the pidgin rules and structures from their parents' language or languages. And this belief fit perfectly with one of the existing major theories of Creole genesis, substratism—the theory that any differences between the Creole and the dominant language came from the substrate, the languages spoken by the parents of the first Creole generation and by at least some of that generation as well.

However, the Hawaii data showed beyond a doubt that substrate influence affected pidgin speakers more than it affected Creole speakers. Besides, if Creole speakers were taking rules from their own ancestral languages, then you'd expect to find not one Creole, but several—a Chinese-influenced Creole, a Portuguese-influenced Creole, a Filipino-influenced Creole, and so on. But Hawaiian Creole, while it might vary according to the degree of English influence, showed no differences on any other dimension. There was no way you could tell what the ancestral languages of any Creole speaker had been (and as I would later find, things had been like that from the very beginning).

In Creoles that had been around for two or three hundred years, you could claim there might have been a process known as "leveling," in which two or more varieties influence one another and gradually converge on a common norm. But Creole in Hawaii had been around for less than a century, far too little time for leveling to take place. If, on the other hand, the earliest speakers had taken one rule from Chinese, one from Hawaiian, one from Japanese, and so on and so forth, how had they managed to choose the precise selection of rules that yielded a grammar similar to those of Creoles with entirely different substrate languages? Besides, the vast majority of substrate rules never made it into Creole. If something was forcing you to choose one specific handful of rules from the substrate, what was the difference between that and claiming a specific biological program for language?

I've never disputed that there's substrate influence in the sounds of Creoles, in the words, even in the idioms—look at things like *hard-ears* or *eye-turn* in Guyana, things that are calques, literal translations of substrate expressions. You can't say "How pretty it is!" in Hawaiian Creole, you must say *Oh da pretty!*, and you can't say "How tasty it is!," you have to say *Broke da mouth!*; both of these are literal translations from the Hawaiian language. Even in the grammar you find occasional substrate constructions—look at the Bantu-type sentence-final negative in Palenquero, described in Chapter 4.

But such things are very rare, very obvious when they occur, and, just like substrate effects in sounds and vocabulary, result in differences between Creoles. The grammatical features I've been describing in this book all involve similarities between Creoles. And that's just what you'd expect. Words and how they're pronounced differ from language to language and have to be learned. Grammar doesn't. Words are unconstrained by anything except human creativity, but grammar depends on principles that all languages share—principles that derive, in ways still mysterious but by no means undiscoverable, from the working of the human brain.

All these arguments fell on deaf ears. Up until then, I guess, I had assumed, as most of us do, that folk in academia were more knowledgeable and more intelligent than the average person. Now I began to realize that most of them just knew more dogma, sported a fancier vocabulary, and had more confidence in their own opinions than the rest of us.

It was around this time that I first came into contact with Tom Givon.

Tom, who began life as Talmy, was born in Israel and raised on a kibbutz. He was a lieutenant in the Israeli army and fought in the Suez War of 1956, but being fond of Arabs he became disillusioned by Israeli policy and finally wound up as a linguistics prof at UCLA. Now he was interested in language change and wanted to know what Creoles could tell him about it.

Tom is far from your standard prof, which of course was why we got on so well. He is in love with the American West. He owns the entire oeuvre of Louis L'Amour. He plays lead fiddle in the Cat Creek band. He ran for sheriff in Archuleta County, Colorado (but lost). He turned up once at a linguistics conference in Santa Barbara in a poncho and sombrero with a Winchester in the gun rack of his pickup—with his shaggy mustache he looked like the bad guy in a spaghetti Western.

He came to visit us, and he, Yvonne, and I spent a few days together on the island of Lanai. Lanai is really upmarket these days—Bill Gates got married there—but back then there was nothing but pineapple fields and space. You could rent a genuine World War II jeep for eight dollars a day. We went everywhere, regardless of whether there were roads or not. Over an open fire in the lee of Mount Lanaihale, smoking some of Hawaii's most profitable crop, we discussed how we might test my theory empirically.

Suppose we found an uninhabited island. Suppose we brought in speakers of six different, unrelated, mutually unintelligible languages, together with their children. Suppose we gave them a starter language, a vocabulary of a few hundred words, just words, without any grammar, so that they could communicate with one another. And suppose they stayed there for three years or so. What would happen?

My prediction was that the adults would create a pidgin, and the children would convert it into a Creole.

We looked at one another in the firelight.

"Shall we go for it?"

"Yeah, let's do it!"

8

THE FORBIDDEN EXPERIMENT

———

- 2 Tri-Ex crank-up radio towers model T-652
- 2 Mosley TA-33 beam antennae
- 2 T-Tower guying kits model T-652K
- 2 Cornell Dubilier Ham II beam rotors
- 2 Yaesu solid-state transceivers model FT-301D
- 1 Sears 1,400-watt generator
- 2 Sony video cameras model AVC-3400
- 2 Sony Betamax cassette portable video recorders
- 2 Ac-1,000 A/C adaptors
- 2 16-foot camera extension cables
- 6 AKG electret condenser microphones model 113
- 6 Vega transmitters model 77
- 6 Vega receivers model 58
- 1 26-foot wooden boat hull (ex Palau)
- 2 85-hp Johnson outboard engines

And that's just part of the equipment in our proposal budget, some of the things we would need for what already had its own acronym—ECOANL: Experimental Creation of a New Language—but was more informally known as the Island Experiment.

A few weeks before, I wouldn't have known a T-Tower guying kit or a solid-state transceiver from a hole in the ground. Over our campfire in Lanai, our pakalolo-induced visions had not included anything as mundane as hardware. But Tom and I were both serious players; once we were committed we would take it anywhere it had to be taken. We would be responsible for the lives of thirty-odd people, experimental subjects and grad students. That meant we had to be able to stay in contact with someplace that had emergency services, hospitals, helicopters, search-and-rescue teams. And we had to have a fast boat, nothing fancy, just an overpowered shell that would get us from A to B in a minimum of time. Plus all that was said and done on the island had to be recorded, aurally and visually. I spent weeks poring over brochures, struggling with technospeak, finding out what was state-of-the-art then, in the late seventies.

But first, find your island.

Logically, it had to be in the Pacific somewhere. The Pacific has more desert islands than any other ocean and Hawaii was right in the middle of it. As I was already there, Tom left the pick to me. I consulted atlases, experts on the region. My basic choice, I was told, was between an atoll and a high island.

High islands don't have to be high. The real difference is that high islands are made of volcanic rock, atolls of coral. High islands range from a couple of dozen feet above sea level to the thirteen-thousand-plus of the Big Island's Mauna Loa and Mauna Kea. Atolls are roughly donut-shaped rings with lagoons in the middle, just a few feet above sea level. Much more global warming and there'll be no more atolls.

Finding that you can use the residues of a National Science Foundation grant to prepare for the next one, I decided to search personally in two archipelagoes, Palau and the Marshall Islands. Palau is located just east of the Philippines and north of New Guinea. It consists mostly of what are technically high islands, although the highest rises only to about seven hundred feet. Although it's less than three times the size of Washington, D.C., it contains over three hundred islands with a coastline of nearly a thousand miles. Most of the islands are uninhabited. The Marshalls are a few hundred miles west of Hawaii. They mostly consist of atolls, twenty-nine of them, but many are broken into segments, yielding (at least according to Lonely Planet) over a thousand separate islands, some no more than sandbars. The total area is only slightly larger than Washington, D.C., but the population is triple that of Palau.

Palau looked a better bet, so I went there first.

My contact in Palau was Kathy Kesolei, an ex-girlfriend of Don Topping, my boss in the University of Hawaii's Social Sciences Research Center. It was lucky Kathy came to the airport to meet me, because like an idiot I had written "research" in the "purpose of visit" slot on my immigration form. Haole researchers are cordially loathed through much of the Pacific as vampires who suck the cultural lifeblood of innocent islanders and bring trouble wherever they go. The immigration guy started telling me I couldn't land, I'd have to get back on the plane. I was in frantic argument with him when Kathy showed; she and the immigration guy had been in high school together, it's that small a place. "Don't be stupid," she told the guy, "I know him, he's okay, just let him in."

Never, ever write "research" on an immigration form. No matter what you're doing, just write "tourist."

Palauans are among the nicest people I've met. Physically they're more varied than any group I've encountered, because the world's seamen have left their semen there. In a bar one afternoon I nearly had a fight with a guy who looked exactly like a Welsh rugby forward, and then as soon as our misunderstanding was sorted out I got the sunniest of smiles and a sincere apology. But despite their physical differences they're very much together as a people, more so than many more homogeneous peoples; they all speak their native tongue (Palauan), which is almost as horrendous as Hungarian, and yet they're also all fluent in English, enough so to make jokes, and quick-witted enough to ensure that the jokes are really funny.

Go out with them in one of their twin-engined launches from the ramshackle capital, Koror. They'll gun the boat up to fifty and head straight for a high tree-hung cliff. Just as you start thinking disaster is imminent, they'll give you a malicious grin and swing the boat ninety degrees into a channel you can't see until you're right on top of it. It's only yards wide, canyon-walled. Then you burst out into the lagoon.

The great lagoon of Palau measures twenty miles by ten, reef-enclosed, water like glass until the keels of the powerboats cut it.

It's studded with tiny islands, knobs of limestone shaggy with vege-
tation, their bases sometimes narrower than their tops—bases
gnawed away by tide action and a local brand of mollusk so they
look like giant mushrooms. Scimitars of white sand curl away from
the tails of some of them; you can beach your boat, swim, picnic,
be king of your own castle for the day. On the return, if two
launches meet they race each other, twin outboards on full throt-
tle, each crossing the other's tracks as they jostle for position,
drenching each other with spray from their wakes.

At the far end of the lagoon lies the island of Ngemelis.

I'd picked Ngemelis on the advice of the locals. The island of the
Island Experiment had to be uninhabited (yes), several miles from
the nearest habitation (yes), large enough to support three dozen
people without undue crowding (yes), have a source of freshwater
(locals thought there should be a spring somewhere), and have an
area that could be used to grow crops, partly because the devil finds
work for idle hands, and partly because doing agricultural work together would oblige our subjects to interact, and consequently try
to talk to one another. To check the last two points, personal in-
spection was a must.

It also seemed a good idea to find out what threats the island
might pose for future inhabitants. I figured that if I had myself marooned and spent thirty hours or so alone there I could get a fair
idea of any actual or potential risks.

And that's how I got to the point where this book started.

When I landed, I had a loaf of bread, some cheese, some fruit, a water bottle and a moth-eaten old blanket I'd borrowed from Kathy. I
walked southeastward along the shore with the coconut grove to
my left and the lagoon on my right, just a narrow strip of it because
a few hundred feet out lay the encompassing reef and a precipitous
drop-off thousands of feet deep, Mecca nowadays, I hear, for serious
scuba divers. Here the island was a broad strip of sand only a few
feet above sea level. Among the coconut palms I made out the island's sole building, a rusting, half-collapsed Quonset hut left over

from World War II. I went on, and the land rose maybe forty or fifty feet, all spiky rock covered in thornbushes, virtually unnavigable. I tried navigating it anyway, but soon gave up, returning to the beach, where cliffs forced me into the water. I waded, scrambled over rocks, waded again, along a coast that was like a mini-Riviera, cut up into a succession of cliffs and inlets.

Ngemelis is not a single island but consists of a large one with a string of islets at its tail, the first one separated from the main island by a channel about twenty yards wide, through which water was pouring at the speed of a millrace. The tide was going out, the great lagoon emptying into the ocean.

It looked dodgy. If I tried to cross it and got swept over the reef, it was open to question whether I'd ever make it back. But, hell, I was here to test for dangers, wasn't I?

I swam hard at an angle against the current. Even so I only just made it—I wound up right where the second island curved away from the channel. And it was hardly worth the risk. The next island was no more than rock and scrub, ditto the one after that, and they got smaller and smaller. I turned back, but this time I waited for slack tide.

I returned along the east side of the island, and here the rocks retreated and suddenly I saw about an acre of swamp. I gazed at it, fascinated. There had to be freshwater in there. I tasted it, and it was brackish. Uh-oh, what was happening here?

Well, the swamp was separated from the beach by a low, narrow rib of rock, and through this rock the mollusks that undermined all the lagoon islands had chewed a hole two or three feet in diameter. When the tide rose, saltwater entered the swamp; when it went down it went out, but not before mixing with the fresh. The plants in the swamp had to be salt tolerant.

One stick of dynamite, I thought. With a single stick I could seal up the hole, then pump the swamp dry and convert it into a rich vegetable garden, enough to feed the whole project. I'd been a truck farmer in another avatar; I knew how to grow veggies. I could almost feel rich dirt under my nails again.

Bickerton, Destroyer of Wetlands! my conscience yelled at me. Shut up, I said, it's all for science.

Night fell. I repaired to the Quonset hut. A full moon shining

through the holes in it made spooky shadows, and I could hear
noises like rats in the rubbish that filled one end of it, so I took my
blanket out on the sand under the moon-drenched sky, and tried to
sleep, and did in spells.

The next day was uneventful. I looked again for the spring
but couldn't locate it; it must have been under the surface of the
swamp somewhere, or maybe there was just general seepage. If
there was no spring and well water was too salty, we could still collect rainwater (an annual sixty to eighty inches). If worse came to
worst, we could always ship freshwater in containers from reliable
springs in Peleliu, only five miles away.

The only out-of-the-ordinary thing that happened was that
while I was standing thigh-deep in the sea off the west coast, there
came rushing toward me an arrow of motion in the calm water and
something shot between my legs, followed immediately by a larger
something. Clear though the water was, they moved far too fast for
me to register, but the pursuer was some kind of long slender thing,
and could have been a small barracuda. We'd have to review the
marine life to see what it contained that could be lethal.

Three o'clock came around, and three-thirty. I was beginning to
wonder if I was marooned for real when in the distance I heard the
faint mutter of the outboards.

In addition to finding an island, I needed permission from the local
authorities—both the official ones, represented by Thomas Re-
mengesau, district administrator for the Pacific Trust Territory of
Palau, and the unofficial ones, represented by the High Chief
Ibedul, the traditional leader of the southern half of Palau, who
had the improbable name of Yutaka Gibbons.

I'd been told that Gibbons was at a meeting of the Koror city
council, and called a cab to get me there.

The driver shook his head gloomily.

"You won't find him there," he predicted.

"How come? He's supposed to be there."

"He never goes to meetings if he can help it."

We drove to City Hall anyway, and the driver was right.

"Now what do we do?"

"Check the bars. He'll be in a bar somewhere."

It was Barranquilla all over again; cabdrivers know everything. In the third bar, sure enough, there he was, standing by himself with a can of Bud in his left hand and a pool cue in his right, lining up his next shot—a man after my own heart. I figured any guy smart enough to drink and shoot pool rather than go to some boring meeting would quickly grasp my project, and I was right. A couple of drinks and a handshake and I had the Ibedul's blessing— subject of course to approval by his council of elders, to whom he promised to pitch the scheme in favorable terms.

I still went to check if there was a better site in the Marshall Islands, but right away I knew there wasn't. It was the first time I'd been on an atoll, and it felt claustrophobic—lagoon to the left of me, ocean to the right, stuck in the middle on a narrow sandbank with a bunch of coconut palms and the detritus of too many underprivileged people.

The fishing was great, quantity- if not quality-wise. Take a boat out in the lagoon, bait a hook, drop a handline, pull in a fish, repeat ad nauseam. I've never seen fish so eager to commit suicide. But the ambience sucked. In a bar one night there were a couple of guys who'd originally come from Bikini, isle of atomic testing. "Wow, look out," some other guys were saying. "He's radioactive! Don't go near him!" I couldn't believe my ears, such meanness. Within minutes violence erupted; it was the only bar fight I ever saw where the weapons of choice were folding metal chairs.

Palau would be our site, no contest.

Back at the ranch, everything was going more smoothly than I had expected. For one thing, I had braced for trouble with the university's Committee on Human Experimentation. No proposed experiment that involves human subjects can be sent for funding to any federal agency without a stamp of approval from the local human experimentation committee, guaranteeing that the experimental subjects will be provided with sufficient information for them to give informed consent and that they will receive fair and ethi-cal treatment in the course of the project. And that's as it should be—I might destroy a wetland for science, but people were another matter entirely.

I went before the committee and explained what we were do-ing. The risks as well as the benefits of participation would be thor-oughly explained to our subjects. In selecting them, cultural and psychological variables would be taken into account so that as far as possible we would avoid interpersonal tensions and conflicts. There would be a registered nurse in attendance throughout the experiment, a psychotherapist on site for the first month and subse-quently on call. We would be in constant touch with the outside world so that in the event of any emergency, people could be evac-uated in the minimum time.

In the first year of the project, during which suitable subjects would be selected—the experiment proper wouldn't start until year two—we would hire three graduate students, each of whom would be required to learn two of the subjects' languages, enough for basic communication at least, so that subjects could keep us informed of their concerns. In case of emergency, we would have a panel of skilled translators who could be contacted by radio, and subjects could request at any time to talk to family, friends, or advisers in their home countries. The subjects would have useful work to do and healthy activities for their free time. Any subjects who wished to leave before the termination of the project would be returned to their homeland immediately, at the project's expense. At the end of the project each couple would receive a sum of money that, if picayune by U.S. standards, would be sufficient for them to buy a house or start a small business in their own countries. But they'd get that only if they stayed the course.

The committee signed off on it.

I was amazed. Not because I felt that our safeguards were inade-quate in any way, but because university committees are notori-ously cautious and hidebound and I doubt they'd seen anything like it before. This committee, luckily, was far more open-minded than most.

As regards the project itself, this was simply a detailed version of what we'd thought out on Lanai. We'd take twelve adults, six married or common-law couples from six different areas. Selection of the areas was tough because they had to satisfy several criteria. We wanted to get as diverse a mixture of languages we could. Since there's still no way to compare the entire structures of any two languages in detail, we'd have to go with something simple, like preferred word order. Most of the world's languages fall into one of three groups—SVO (subject-verb-object) languages, like English, SOV languages, like Japanese, and VSO languages, like Hawaiian. Two languages should come from each of these three groups.

Within each pair we would try to ensure that there was no close historical relationship; otherwise cognates and/or shared structural tendencies might again skew the balance. This meant that as many as possible of the languages chosen should belong to different language families. We wanted whatever resulted from the experiment to be affected as little as possible by preexisting languages. Thus, we hoped, we would get a purer expression of whatever bases for language lay within the human mind.

We'd prefer monolingual subjects. But since monolinguals are rare in so-called underdeveloped nations—it's only in the developed West that the thought of speaking more than one language brings fear and horror—we'd have to settle for people with no exposure to "metropolitan" languages, particularly to English, which even in those days was racing through the world like some linguistic HIV. And since our subjects when onsite would be living a life similar to that of island subsistence farmers, it would help if they themselves happened to be island subsistence farmers. A townie might freak out from the scarcity of people; someone from wide open spaces might get rock fever.

After months of work we settled on the following six languages:

- Korean (SOV, Altaic—subjects would come from isolated islands off the south of the peninsula)

- Kagayanen (VSO, Austronesian—spoken by inhabitants of an outlying island in the Philippines)
- Land Dayak (SVO, Austronesian—subjects from the border between Indonesian and Malayan Borneo)
- Futunan (VSO, Polynesian—spoken on an island in the New Hebrides)
- Taiwanese Chinese (SVO, Sino-Tibetan—speakers of a dialect of Chinese distinct from mainland dialects)
- Kiwai (SOV, Papuan—spoken on an island in the mouth of the Fly River in Papua New Guinea)

We would choose from each of these areas a young couple who each had one or two children. The children should be as close as possible to two years of age. Children of that age are on the brink of syntax, and often go from utterances of two or three words max to complex sentences within a matter of weeks rather than months. Stephen Crain of Macquarie University in Australia has performed a series of ingenious experiments to show that many, if not all, complex structures in English are fully understood and, under appropriate conditions, can be produced by three-year-olds. Maybe by kids even younger, but below three their attention spans were so short that Crain couldn't carry out his experiments. But at two they control so little of their native tongue that when they started acquiring the new language, no first language was likely to bias their behavior. Or if it did, we would soon see that it did.

As for the new language itself, to get them to create their own words would take too long and leave unanswered our main research question: How do children acquire grammar? For this reason we prepared a starter vocabulary expressing over two hundred concepts, those we thought would be of most use in the experimental setting; they included names of body parts such as "head" and "belly," names of foods ("rice," "beans"), living creatures ("bird," "fish"), actions ("swim," "run"), "psychological" verbs ("want," "know"), as well as more abstract things ("now," "far," "same," and so on). For these concepts we would create our own words, using sounds common to all the subjects' languages—words of one or two syllables only, for maximal ease of learning and remembering.

Anything outside of the list they could describe by periphrasis. We saw at the beginning of the last chapter how creative pidgin speakers can be in using several words for one they don't know. (There's also the famous New Guinea pidgin speaker who called a piano "big box you fight him he cry"—some idiot actually published this in a dictionary as the pidgin for "piano," but it was obviously what is known as a nonce form, something used maybe one time only.) We expected that at least some of our subjects would create compounds out of words in the starter vocabulary, like "belly-run" if they were suffering from diarrhea, and that these would not constitute nonce forms but would be picked up and used by everyone. You find lots of two-word compounds in Creoles, like the question words I discussed in Chapter 3: "what-place" for "where," and so on, but who invented them, Creole speakers or pidgin speakers? It's hard to see how anyone could get by without "who, what, where," but short of watching a pidgin-Creole cycle in real time, how could you ever know what really happened?

The experiment was scheduled to run for three years; the first year would be entirely taken up with subject selection, site preparation, purchase and deployment of equipment, and other nonlinguistic tasks, and the third with analyzing the mass of data we would hopefully have accumulated and writing up the results. This meant that the island would be occupied for one year only. Could we realistically hope to compress into a single year processes that in the real world would take a minimum of fifteen to twenty?

There were of course very practical reasons for our choice. How long could you expect people to stay in what was, let's face it, a totally novel situation? How long could you expect a federal agency to fund a totally novel kind of experiment? Of course, as we argued in the proposal, the kind of pressure cooker in which our subjects would have to interact would surely step up the pace of linguistic evolution. We would have preferred three years, but we figured that in one year any processes operative in that kind of situation should have gotten going, and if we had positive results and no blowbacks, a longer experiment might follow.

But there was another argument I didn't see at first. I'd originally conceived the project as "starting our own Creole." But I
eventually realized this wasn't what we were doing at all. Creole
languages were born under certain social conditions—slavery, or at
best indentured labor—that could hardly be replicated nowadays,
and even if they could, neither Tom nor I were up for a Simon
Legree shtick. Basically what we were doing was comparing, under
controlled conditions, the language-creating capacities of adults
with those of children.

And (perhaps most important of all) since we controlled the input, we would be able to determine whether either children or
adults were capable of inventing grammatical structures, ways of
forming sentences that were not modeled on anything they'd ever
heard. In other words, we were looking for an empirical answer to
the question that had divided the cognitive sciences for decades,
and that still continues to do so: how much of our language capacity is owed to experience, and how much is innate?

Had we thought of everything? Probably not—who could? We sent
draft versions of the proposal to dozens of linguists, anthropologists,
and experts in other fields whose input might help. We knew too
that for a project so unprecedented to succeed we needed the support or at least the goodwill of the general academic community.

Somewhat to my surprise, most of the responses were favorable,
some extravagantly so. My old ally Dave DeCamp, after starting
out with "At first glance, this proposal seems so wild that one takes
it as a joke," called it "the most fundamental of basic research
projects ever proposed." Bill Labov wrote that "the experiment is
brilliantly and economically planned, and should be far more
rewarding than many research projects with larger budgets." I also
tested the water with Paul Chapin, the linguistics officer at the
NSF, who "read [my] proposal with astonished admiration" but
feared that "the bureaucracy will be scared to fund this."

And indeed there were a few negatives, like this one, from John
Lynch, professor of language at the University of Papua New
Guinea:

"The project is unethical, racist and exploitative, particularly given the fact that the subjects are to be from areas with little or no contact with the Western world, it seems that there is no way in which the ramifications of the project can be made known to them, no way in which any real counseling can take place on site, and thus no way in which the experimentees' rehabilitation can be ensured. One staff member summed it up very succinctly: the Pacific is not a cultural zoo."

No, and I never thought it was, and I'll never know the kind of distorted reasoning that could lead anyone to assume that I thought it was. But that's so-called liberal progressives for you. Professing to be the protectors of underdogs, all too often they secretly (perhaps unconsciously) despise them. Oh, those poor schmucks, they're far too dumb to understand us hypercivilized Westerners! Well, I've worked closely for years with illiterate and underprivileged people who've had little or no contact with the Western world, and I'd back their judgment and grasp of reality against that of coddled members of academe any day of the week.

Lynch included a bunch of letters from members of his faculty in the same vein. I can imagine what must have preceded the writing of them. Have you ever been in a room with a bunch of well-meaning but experientially challenged PC folk when they're working themselves up into a mega-tizzy of self-righteous indignation over some supposed injustice? If not, lucky you. One of them, fancying himself a wit, referred to my prospective subjects as "New-Guinea pigs," thus inadvertently showing what he really felt about them.

At last there came a time when we couldn't think of anything to add to our proposal, so we sent it off to the National Science Foundation, crossed our fingers, and waited. After anxious months, the answer came.

The panel of experts convened by the NSF to review our project had approved it.

Not without a few qualms and caveats, however. Full approval was contingent on certain changes, the most important of which was that we must recruit an advisory board. The board would be made up of six experts from a variety of fields relevant to the enterprise, of which the most important were psychology, anthropology, and isolation studies.

One of our psychologists was Harry Triandis of the University of Illinois, a genial and warmhearted man with whom I felt comfortable right away. Our isolationist was Bob Helmreich of the University of Texas, less outgoing than Harry but probably more like me. He had studied isolation in the crews of those giant tankers that load and discharge their cargoes at sea, and that may not see land for eighteen months on end; I was surprised to learn that these monsters need only four or five men to run them. Bob was also a consultant for NASA on the possible interpersonal downsides of long space missions. One of our anthropologists was Ward Goodenough of the University of Pennsylvania. Enough of him for now; more later.

One paragraph of the panel's report read as follows:

"However, the panel all agreed that this interdisciplinary group should be under the control of PI's [principal investigators, i.e. Tom and me]. The main interest of the proposal is linguistics. PI's need to take socio-psychological concerns into account, but should design a program to suit themselves primarily."

If only!

All that now stood between us and our experiment was for the NSF to officially sign off on the project. Just a matter of weeks, we were told, and a mere formality. The NSF never, ever went against a unanimous recommendation from one of its panels.

I was due a year's sabbatical leave and expected to spend a fair part of that year traveling from island to island around the Western Pacific, interviewing prospective subjects and negotiating all the bureaucratic hurdles I would surely encounter. There was however a complicating factor. Our daughter Julie, then fifteen, had just won a scholarship to the school run by the American Ballet Theatre in New York. There was no way Yvonne and I were going to let a fifteen-year-old girl go there on her own. The boys were old enough to look after themselves by now, but we would have to go to New York with her. We got ourselves a sublet on the Upper

West Side for the first month, to give us time to find a more permanent base.

We had just arrived in New York when the blow fell.

Tom and I both received letters from the deputy director of the National Science Foundation, informing us that due to concerns over the safety and psychological well-being of our subjects, the process of reviewing our application was suspended until further notice.

9

AFTER THE ISLAND

———

The NSF's decision—or rather their failure to decide, for every two or three weeks I'd get a letter saying they would make a final decision in two or three weeks—had serious financial consequences for me and my family.

Sabbatical years are on half pay. In the proposal I'd budgeted for the other half, as I was fully entitled to do. Now we were committed to a year in New York, for which six months' salary was totally inadequate. We had to move fast. Yvonne, who'd had to give up her job with Hawaii's Child Protective Services, got another at a psychiatric clinic on the Lower East Side, and I wrote the synopsis and first chapter of a science fiction novel about a man who went to live with dolphins, called *King of the Sea*. With a hubris that now astounds me I sent it off to Random House.

By an incredible stroke of luck—perhaps fate had decided to compensate me for the loss of my project—it landed on the desk of a sympathetic editor, Barbara Hammer, who promptly accepted it and got me a $5,000 advance. It may well have been the very last over-the-transom sale in the history of publishing. I'd like to be able to say it was a great book, but at least it kept the wolf from the door. Immediately $2,000 went to buy the furniture of an old man who was the tenant of a rent-controlled apartment on West Twenty-fifth Street but was going into a home. In return for this cash payment we took over his apartment and the ridiculously low rent that went with it. Illegal? Sure, but this was New York. And

Yvonne was able to walk to work through the Bowery, stepping carefully over the bodies of drunks still clutching their empty bottles of Thunderbird.

Both Tom and I were immigrants, and fairly recent ones at that. We still didn't quite know how America worked. We didn't know, for instance, that the NSF has a mechanism for appealing its decisions. We didn't know that, since the project would bring a nonnegligible amount of money into the state of Hawaii, we could appeal to Hawaii's representatives on Capitol Hill to lobby for us—nothing scares bureaucrats like a senator scorned.

We didn't even know that, with a project so controversial, we could invoke the power of the media and see which way public opinion could be tilted. In fact, the most amazing thing about the Island Experiment was that everything happened under the radar. The only published reference to it I've ever seen was totally garbled, part of a footnote in an article on classical and medieval experiments to discover the first human language (more on these in the last chapter). After referring to such experiments as "barbarous," the authors, one in Scotland, one in Australia, state: "At the time of writing [c. 1980] we have received news of an attempt by a Californian group to obtain funds (and presumably permission) for such an experiment in the remote southern seas . . ."

It couldn't happen nowadays; the bloggers would be all over us like a rug.

Finally in November the NSF got off the pot.

Before we could proceed with our experiment, we would have to meet with our advisory board and work out with them a way of carrying out the experiment that would satisfy any objections members of the board might raise. In other words, the NSF panel's stipulation was reversed; instead of our being in charge of the advisory board, the advisory board was now in charge of us. I was advised to sit down and write another proposal, this time for us to thoroughly explore with the board all the issues involved, for which I could budget not more than $25,000.

I did so. I included two months' salary for myself. The NSF accepted the proposal but refused the salary, saying rather snottily that they "didn't pay people for writing proposals." I pointed out that I was not being paid to write a proposal but rather for what could well turn out to be several months of research to find alternative subjects, locations, or conditions that the board might require, not to mention the substantial portion of the two months that would be taken up by actual meetings with the board. I further reminded them that I had already written a proposal, for which I had naturally not been paid, that that proposal had already passed an NSF panel, and that the only reason I was writing the current proposal, for which I was not being paid either, was because the NSF was now countermanding their own panel's decision by refusing to fund the first proposal.

They took the point, and I got my two months.

We arranged for our meetings to take place in Colorado, partly because of its central location, but mostly because Tom was in tight with the Southern Utes; he had spent several years working on their language, helping them preserve it, writing a dictionary and a grammar. Consequently he was able to get us good rates at the motel-restaurant owned and operated by the Utes on their reservation in Ignacio, near the Four Corners. It was an excellent motel, though board members from coastal states were mystified by the menu. Was "chicken fried steak" chicken fried like steak or steak fried like chicken? If you put "antipasta" on a plate with spaghetti Bolognese, would they annihilate one another, like matter and antimatter?

Pointless to describe our two week-long sessions, separated by two months in which we imagined we had met all the objections of the board, only to find ourselves faced with an entirely different set of objections. I sensed someone on the board was determined that the experiment should not be carried out in any shape or form, and rightly or wrongly I identified that person as Ward Goodenough, the anthropologist. In hindsight I wonder how much of my sense of betrayal was linked to the fact that he was the only member with any credentials in linguistics, and I therefore felt he should have been more supportive. Anyway, when it was all over I wrote him a bitter and angry letter, to which he replied with a long and apologetic one seeking to justify his fears for the safety of our subjects.

Whether he turned the board against us, whether it was someone else, or whether board members individually changed their
minds, I guess I'll never know. At the end of the discussion we were
left with the following situation. We could do our experiment provided that:

1. We used only subjects from developed countries.
2. They could only be adults—no children involved.
3. The experiment could last no longer than three months.
4. It had to take place within the continental U.S.

Tom and I came independently to the same conclusion: screw it.
The whole point of the experiment was to compare the language-
building capacities of children and adults. The proposed substitute
would tell us nothing that we didn't already know.

Today I'm far from sure that this was the right decision. We had
made a serious tactical error, going off the deep end, so to speak,
into a kind of human experimentation unprecedented in modern
science. Yvonne tells me that in psychotherapy there's a technique
called "successive approximation." Suppose a client complains of a
fear of heights. Have her look out of a first-floor window: no problem. Have her imagine looking out of a second-floor window; then
have her look out of one for real. Now have her imagine . . . well,
you get the idea. Eventually you can take her up to the thirtieth
floor and your problem will be stopping her from flying over the
balustrade.

What we had in mind needed the same treatment. Start with
something quite innocuous, proceed to something slightly less so,
and in ten years or so we might have gotten people to where they'd
accept the original experiment. Who knows how it would have
gone? But we were both far too burned out by the two years of setting the thing up and the year of fruitless struggle we had just gone
through to even consider it.

At the end of my sabbatical year, Yvonne and I still had the
dilemma of either leaving a now sixteen-year-old to live alone in
New York or finding some alternative solution. Luckily I was able

to work an exchange with a colleague at the State University of New York at Stony Brook. He took my job and salary for the fall semester and I took his; guess who got the better deal. I managed to have all my classes scheduled on two days a week, so twice a week I made the sixty-mile commute from Manhattan across Long Island. And Long Island, as a linguist once noted, is a very long island, especially if you're on a train that's like one out of the previous century.

During that fall, I made the acquaintance of an Italian linguist, Antonio Gnierre, who was working in Brazil. He was one of the organizers of a linguistics summer school (their summer, our winter) scheduled to take place in Campinas, a nowheresville a couple hours drive north of São Paulo, and he invited me to teach there. That was for two months, and after that I got myself a two-month gig at the Pontifícia Universidade Católica in São Paulo, known to Paulistas as "Pooky," and à further two months at the Federal University in Rio de Janeiro. I didn't like leaving Yvonne, but I'd already had one New York winter.

For me, Brazil was a bit of a disappointment. Brazilians have this reputation of being go-go extroverts. In fact, until you know them, they're a lot less outgoing than, say, Costa Ricans. Get on a bus in Costa Rica and within ten minutes everyone knows everyone else and a good chunk of their life history. But in Brazil I've ridden intercity buses for ten hours at a stretch and nobody so much as cracked word one. And Brazilians are supposed to be far less racist than Americans. True, they recognize several dozen shades between black and white, as opposed to our none—they have a whole special vocabulary for that. But walking by a Campinas auto dealer one morning I couldn't fail to note that the salesmen lounging around chatting and drinking *cafezinhos* as they waited for customers were all lily-white, while the two guys fitting the new sliding doors and chipping holes in the concrete for the bolts to go in were both jet-black. And if you go through the alleys behind Rio's fanciest restaurants around three in the morning, you'll see that most if not all the dumpster divers are black too.

As for their brand of Portuguese, and its peculiar speech sounds, all chuches and slushes, I couldn't stand it. I found my knowledge of Spanish a hindrance rather than a help; the languages are so close, in grammar and vocabulary if not sound, that it's almost impossible, for me at least, to keep from mixing them up (in the popular sense of "linguist," I'm nowhere near as good as Yvonne). Fortunately this is exactly how some people speak in the southern provinces of Brazil bordering Paraguay and Uruguay—there's even a name for it, Portiñol—so my students understood me perfectly, even if they had to hide superior smiles.

It could have been interesting from a Creole perspective. There had been a very large slave population; indeed Brazil was the last country in the world to officially abolish slavery (1888). You can still get into an argument over whether some differences between Brazilian and metropolitan Portuguese are residues of prior creolization. But one thing known for sure is that Brazil hosted the biggest-ever *palenque* in the Americas, the maroon settlement in the northeast known as Palmares.

Palmares kept Dutch and then Portuguese armies at bay for almost a century and at the height of its power may have had as many as thirty thousand inhabitants. What did they speak? Nobody knows, but the Portuguese had to use interpreters in their negotiations. Was it an African language, or a koine (a kind of lowest common denominator) of several African languages, or a Creole too deep to be mutually intelligible with Portuguese? We may never know, for in 1694 Palmares fell, and those of its inhabitants who were not killed in the fighting or executed after it were scattered to the four winds.

And maybe they took their language with them.

All the time I was in Brazil, stories kept surfacing about "funny languages" spoken in various parts of the country. Gnierre and his colleagues claimed to have discovered fossilized remnants of some sort of Afro-Portuguese right there in the outskirts of São Paulo. There was said to be a town on the Bolivian border where everyone, black, white, and the fifty-two varieties between, spoke some kind of Creole as a secret language. There was allegedly a village high in the Serra do Mar where linguistic researchers had been driven off by men with shotguns. I counted as many as sixteen such stories, but my teaching load prevented me from investigating any of them. And to the best of my knowledge, no one's investigated them since.

After a couple of months, Yvonne flew out to join me; Julie had just turned seventeen and now had older friends who would share the apartment with her, and since she had graduated into American Ballet Theatre's junior company she'd be on tour a lot of the time anyway. We made some good friends in São Paulo, in particular Mary Kato, who was chair of linguistics at Pooky and whose husband, who'd built the São Paulo subway, made the best caipirinhas in the state. In Rio, we rented a ratty little apartment in the great wall of high-rises that hangs over the beach at Copacabana, and if you leaned far enough out over our tiny balcony early in the morning you could see the beams of the rising sun touch the crown of the Sugarloaf. But linguistically speaking I was spinning my wheels, and wasn't sorry when the six months came to an end and we took off for another summer school, this time the Linguistic Society of America's biennial six-week institute that took place that year in Albuquerque.

In Albuquerque we had a big house with a soundproof basement where you could party hard all night without the neighbors complaining. Staying with us were two very beautiful grad students from Pooky who were attending the institute. Mary had asked us to keep an eye on them, but that would have taken some doing. Laura, the sexier of the two, was deep in a torrid affair with a well-known psycholinguist when the latter's current main squeeze blew into town. He dropped Laura like the proverbial hot potato, and at that precise instant Tom Markey arrived for a visit.

Markey would play a crucial role in my career. He was a historical linguist at the University of Michigan in Ann Arbor who, like the other Tom, wanted to know what Creoles could tell him about linguistic change. I'd known him a couple of years; we got on well because, again like the other Tom, he wasn't your standard-issue prof. He was full of old folk-sayings like this, which he claimed was the Midwestern farmers' response to the advent of canned milk:

No teats to pull, no hay to pitch,
Just punch two holes in the son-of-a-bitch.

One time he and a friend bought an apartment block and suddenly found themselves flat broke with the closing costs still to pay. So they advertised in the papers, took a month's rent in advance and a month's security deposit from each prospective tenant, and paid off the closing costs with minutes to spare. In those days he'd been an alcoholic; now he'd kicked the sauce completely, yet was as much fun on Virgin Marys at one in the morning as the rest of us were on the Bloody kind (a lot more coherent too). Tired of dealing with publishers, he had just started his own publishing firm, Karoma Press, aimed, he said, at giving a fair shake to his colleagues in linguistics.

He caught Laura on the rebound, or vice versa. The first morning when he came down to breakfast he looked in such bad shape that I offered him two matchsticks to keep his eyelids open. "I feel like I've been attacked by the Brazilian army," he complained.

Still, he wasn't too exhausted to get down to business. Would I help him launch Karoma by writing a book for it—needn't be that big, just a quickie about variation and change and all that sort of thing, just to get him started. Sure, I said, what are friends for? I didn't give it a great deal of thought, and indeed I postponed thinking about it at all until I got back to Hawaii. I did not have the slightest idea what would eventually come of it.

At the time I was much more interested in what I could do with the help of one of my students at the institute, Frank Byrne.

Frank was atypical, too, and for a variety of reasons. I first spotted him because of the company he kept. You don't find too many Irish Americans hanging with a couple of black guys, in this case Vince Cooper from the Virgin Islands and a Nigerian who'd been an army officer over there and told scarifying stories about the Biafran war. Soon all three became regulars at our house. They were lots of fun. One of us found out that llamas vomit on you if you upset them, so we invented the Llama School of Literary Criticism, in which reviewers, instead of dissing books they disliked, puked all over them, and their authors too, if possible.

Frank had been a Marine, and the training stuck. Hair trimmed, neat and conservative in dress, he stood out a mile from the run of sloppy, unkempt linguistics students (and linguists, whether students or profs, are quite possibly the scruffiest in all the academic disciplines). Currently A.B.D. at the University of Arizona, he was now teaching at a university in Cumaná, Venezuela. But what really got to me was what he wanted to write his dissertation on: Saramaccan.

Saramaccan, as I mentioned a couple of chapters ago, is a language spoken in the interior of Suriname by maroons who took off from Dutch and Jewish plantations in the last decade 'of the seventeenth century; we'll be going there in Chapter 11. At the time, no one had ever done a full-length study of the language. But it's almost certainly the most radical of all Creoles, by which I mean it's the one that differs most dramatically from the slave-owner languages, English, Portuguese, and Dutch, that contributed to its vocabulary. As such, and because 'of its large number' of African words—50 percent, one author claims—substratists have held it up as the clearest proof of their theory, not just like Haitian Creole ("an African language with French words"), but an African language that had nowhere near finished exchanging its words.

However, if my theory was correct, Saramaccan would tell a very different story. It would simply be the deepest and purest of the Creoles, the one that most clearly expressed the inborn capacity for language that all of humanity shared.

That was why it was so important for me that Frank complete his mission. Unfortunately the Venezuelans didn't pay much for a teacher with no Ph.D., and he had a family to support, so there was no way he could afford the many months in the South American rain forests that his project would entail. So I taught him how to write a proposal for an NSF dissertation grant and offered him every assistance along the way; since no one at Arizona knew much about Creoles, I even got myself appointed as an outside member of his dissertation committee.

That was for the future; it would take years for him to get the grant, do the research and analysis, and write it all up. Back in Hawaii, I had a book to write, real quick.

But did I really want to write a book about variation and change? Been there, done that. Many academics seem to have no trouble recycling the same book under different titles. I get bored far too easily. For me, a book is a journey of discovery, or it is nothing. For as the old adage has it, "How can I know what I think until I see what I say?"

No, I decided, I'd write a book about Creoles and the bioprogram, and Markey could take it or leave it.

When I began my academic career, John Spencer told me that the royal road to success was to publish papers and more papers. That's only partly true. Once in a blue moon you may hit the jackpot and write a paper that gets cited all over, but for the most part people read them and pass on, and the main function of scholarly papers (apart from what you were about to suggest) is to stuff your CV if you're up for promotion or tenure or grant money. Even if you publish in peer-reviewed journals (that's supposed to be a guarantee of quality, but merely means your colleagues get to trash your submission if they don't like you or bless it if you're a good buddy and/or can be useful to them), a paper doesn't carry a fraction of the weight a book does. People in academe still respect books; if you've gone to all that trouble, they think, there must be something in it.

So a book seemed the best way to sell the bioprogram. If my theory was correct, it followed logically that three things not normally thought of together must be intimately connected: the origin of Creoles, the acquisition of language by children, and the original emergence of language in the human species. For if a shapeless pidgin could be turned into a full human language in a single generation, surely such a development could tell us something about how language got going in the first place. So the book, *Roots of Language*, would set out to answer three questions:

1. How did Creole languages originate?
2. How do children acquire language?
3. How did human language originate?

I began by looking at the profound gulf that, in Hawaii, divided pidgin speakers from Creole speakers. How could that be, unless Creole was created by the children of pidgin-speaking parents going far beyond what was licensed by the input those parents gave them? From there I moved to an account of the features of Hawaiian Creole and a comparison of these with the many similar features found in other Creoles worldwide. Similarities of such breadth and depth were extraordinary, given the lack of contact between the languages concerned and the very different mixes of languages that had preceded their births. Not one of the languages spoken by immigrants to Hawaii was spoken by immigrants to the Caribbean, for instance, and the mix in the islands of the Indian Ocean, Mauritius and the Seychelles, was different again.

How could children learn things they had never heard? That raised a broader question that still awaited its definitive answer: How do children learn things they have heard? The commonsense answer is, "Well, it's simple—they just imitate their parents." But if that's all they're doing, how do you explain all those funny sayings parents love to quote, things kids could never have heard because grown-ups never say them? The more I looked into the acquisition literature, the oftener I noticed that these "mistakes" wouldn't have been mistakes if the child had been acquiring a Creole.

For instance, there was the child who said, "Nobody don't like me." His father corrected him: "No, it's 'Nobody likes me.'" (Some linguist self-righteously complained that in such circumstances no decent parent would correct the child's grammar; they'd be too busy reassuring him, "That's not true, dear—everybody likes you!") The child went on saying, "Nobody don't like me"—children are amazingly resistant to grammatical correction—until finally after about the eighth round he got half of it and said, "Nobody don't likes me."

Now this doesn't happen in any dialect of English. So-called "double negatives" always involve negative concord of verb and object ("They *don't* know *nothing*," "I *never* told that to *nobody*"), and never negative concord of verb and subject, as in "*Nobody don't* like me." But negative concord of verb and subject is found in many Creoles; in Guyana, for instance, you can't say, "A dog didn't bite me" or "No dog bit me"; you have to say:

None dog na bite me.

Another example was produced by Seth, the son of one of my students. At around two and a half, Seth produced several sentences like this:

Take pencil write it, Daddy.

Now you might well think that this was just shorthand for "Take a pencil and write it"—which it probably would have been, if his father hadn't already had the pencil in his hand. Also you need to know that Seth hadn't yet learned the word "with"; what he actually intended was "Write it with the pencil," but instead he produced an instrumental serial construction. (These constructions will constitute crucial evidence in Chapter 12; they are, again, typical of Creoles worldwide.) Within three weeks he had learned "with" and other prepositions, and his serial constructions disappeared. Note that the monthly sampling that's typical of so-called longitudinal studies would probably have missed this altogether.

These are just two out of the many cases where children's expressions that are quite ungrammatical in the languages they are supposed to be learning would be fully grammatical if what they were learning was a Creole. Which made me think: How do children know what they are learning? How could they tell if what they were exposed to was a pidgin, a Creole, or a fully developed language? How, with zero experience of any language, could they possibly do any of this?

Obviously they couldn't.

But suppose they were born with some kind of mental template for language. Perhaps it was a set of basic principles, perhaps just a consequence of the ways in which the human brain worked—who could tell, without a whole lot of research that's still to be done? But if they had such a template, they had no need of a LAD or a LASS, no need for any kind of specialized mechanism for working out the rules of whichever of the six thousand human languages fate had destined them to learn. Nor would they have any need, contrary to substratists' claims, to make up deficits in the pidgin by borrowing grammatical rules from their parents' native tongues. To do that would mean waiting until they'd thoroughly acquired their parents' language (or languages), and they needed' language now, not five years from now.

So they would just forge ahead, taking the words they picked up from whatever language they encountered—pidgin, Creole, established language with millennia of history behind it, it made no difference—and putting those words together to make sense in ways that were natural to them. If the language they were acquiring already did things that way, fine—they were home free. If it didn't, they would note the discrepancy, as Seth did when he found out about "with" and learned that English doesn't have serial verbs. They would then adjust their speech accordingly, because nobody likes to talk funny and perturb the people around them.

But if there was a template for language, where had it come from? Unless you believe in Creationism or Intelligent Design, it can only have come from evolution, like our bipedalism or our opposable thumbs or the whites of our eyes—all of the traits that distinguish us from the rest of the primate species. The question of how language evolved had been on my back burner for over a decade, ever since Yvonne, at the University of Guyana, had taken Harry Drayton's social biology course and reported back to me on its content. How I handled it in *Roots of Language* was pretty naïve; I still knew next to no biology and no paleoanthropology or primatology whatsoever. I would eventually remedy those defects, and language evolution would usurp Creoles as the main focus of my research. But that was still a decade or more ahead.

Markey wasn't the least fazed by my change of topic. He figured that something that was, whatever its faults, pretty original would surely serve to launch Karoma, and he was right, beyond anything that either of us dreamed.

The media picked up on it. There was a review several pages long by Jerome Bruner and Carol Feldman in *The New York Review of Books*, which noted how unusual it was for a "little-known linguist" to produce a book that "even if [it] were wrong in its major details (which is probably not the case) . . . would still be an original and important contribution." (I was a bit miffed by that "little-known"—surely most people in the language sciences knew who I was by then!) *The New York Times*, too, reviewed it favorably. I got a full page in *Newsweek*, titled "The Fossils of Language."

Roots was also reviewed extensively, sometimes skeptically but for the most part favorably, in a wide spectrum of professional journals. Condensed versions of its take on Creoles began to appear in textbooks and books of general linguistics. Favorable mentions cropped up in the most unexpected places, in essays by Lewis Thomas, Stephen Jay Gould, Oliver Sacks, Jared Diamond. And years afterward in Budapest the philosopher John Searle told me it had convinced Willard Quine, doyen of American philosophy in his day, that Chomsky was right about an innate universal grammar, even though none of Chomsky's own arguments had convinced him. "Did he write that down anywhere?" I asked eagerly. "Not that I know of," Searle, to my disappointment, replied.

Meanwhile Markey, under the strain of simultaneously running business and professional careers, had fallen off the wagon. My success seemed to have gone to his head; he kept ringing me up at three in the morning, announcing in slurred tones the most improbable apotheoses: "I've got you booked on *The Dick Cavett Show*," or "on *The Tonight Show*," stuff like that. Luckily 3:00 a.m. in Ann Arbor is only 10:00 or 11:00 p.m. in Hawaii (no Daylight Saving Time there). He did have one great comeback. A book distributor refused to deal with him because, their representative said, "You're only a one-book publisher." Quick as a flash, Markey asked him, "Who was Darwin's publisher?" and of course the guy couldn't tell him. Whether that got him the deal I can't say; I'd already given up believing anything he told me.

I try to live my life by the great maxims of folk wisdom: what goes around comes around; if it ain't broke, don't fix it. The one I should have remembered here was, never do business with friends. I don't believe I ever even got a royalty statement from Markey. Indeed, I hardly got any money at all until Yvonne, furious, did a woman-to-woman thing with Markey's wife, Patty, as a result of which he reluctantly disgorged a couple of thousand bucks. I later learned I was not alone. A number of my colleagues were similarly stiffed; not only that, he'd gotten some of them to put money up front for publicity, too. I could have taken him to court and probably bankrupted him, but I didn't need the aggravation. I had more interesting things to do with my life.

As a result of *Roots*, I got invited to give lectures or courses or to speak at conferences all over the place: Japan, Venezuela, Israel, even Texas. But the weirdest gig was in Provo, Utah.

Provo, home of Brigham Young University, is of course the true Mormon capital, high (both morally and geographically) above sinful, secular Salt Lake City. When my commuter plane droned into the valley where Provo lies, I thought, "My God! The American Shangri-la!" It was almost April, but the surrounding mountains were deep in virgin (naturally) snow.

The thing that struck me most about Mormons was their relationship with liquor. They didn't have any, but how they missed it! The revolving restaurant atop a tower was called High in the Sky, and its signature drink was called High in the Sky, too; it was a mix of seven nonalcoholic beverages whose specific gravity was such that they lay on top of one another in a rainbow spectrum of nauseating colors. At a party, my host offered me a Coke and with a leer that in another country might have accompanied the offer of his sister, asked, "Would you like a dash of Sprite to spritz that up a bit?"

I've no idea why they invited me. They didn't seem to know too much about Creoles or about modern linguistics either. I can only imagine that something I wrote in *Roots* accidentally resonated with something in Mormon doctrine, but I'll probably never know.

On my way to Japan I decided to stop off at Zamboanga, in the Philippines, and take a look at a Fort Creole. I didn't think there'd be much there for me, but Creoles can be quite different from their descriptions, as we'll see in Chapter 12.

Creoles can be divided into Plantation Creoles and Fort Creoles. Fort Creoles came into existence around the forts that Europeans set up on the coasts of Asia and Africa to protect their traders. There was a lot of miscegenation, naturally, and in many places there sprang up communities as mixed in language as they were in parentage. These typically spoke a Creole of which most could be accounted for by the respective influences of superstrate and substrate. You might find a small subset of the features typical of Plantation Creoles, but for the most part the founders of these languages had had better access than plantation slaves to both substrate and superstrate—Daddy spoke the superstrate, and the substrate languages remained all around them. (In Plantation Creoles, the superstrate speaker was on a horse and the substrate was thousands of miles away.) Consequently, the deficit that the bioprogram had to fill was much smaller around the forts than on the plantations.

Zamboangueño seemed pretty typical of a Fort Creole. Although the Philippines were nominally a Spanish colony, the Spanish presence there had never been large, and no plantation industry had ever established itself. The Spanish hung out mostly in a few towns, and around each of these the folk who depended on them commercially had developed a mixed language. After the Spanish left, Zamboangueño was said to be dying, but one should always treat reports of language death with some skepticism. Languages are tough beasts and die hard.

When we landed at Zamboanga airport, the Marcos dictatorship was in its final throes and Filipino society was coming apart at the seams. In Zamboanga Province there were two separate insurgencies, one Communist, one Islamist. Zamboanga City itself was riddled with "motorcycle diablos" (probably members of the security forces moonlighting as hit men) and "sparrow teams" (Communist three-man urban guerrilla units specializing in assassination). The "City of Flowers" averaged three murders a night while we were there. Everyone had guns, but nobody seemed to have had a lick of gun training—they'd bounce the butts of their assault rifles on the pavement while they chatted on street corners. Supermarket guards had the firepower of Green Berets. While we were there, somebody spat on one and the guy loosed off a burst from his AK-47 that missed the perp but wounded three innocents in the checkout line.

On City Hall there was a fund-raising thermometer, like they have on American city halls for the March of Dimes. But instead of charitable contributions, this one tallied the number of murder victims since the start of Mayor Climaco's incumbency. During our visit the total stood in the nine hundreds. Shortly afterward, the mayor himself became a statistic on his own thermometer.

Yet for all the mayhem, Zamboanga had a relaxed feel to it; Filipinos accentuate the positive, no matter what. The only time I even got near to being scared was one night in the casino when all the lights went out. Everyone had had to check their weapons at the door, so we were defenseless. A wave of silent but almost palpable terror swept the place—in the next few seconds, would Reds or Moslems or just plain criminals rake the place with gunfire? But it was only Zamboanga's ailing power plant on the blink again.

Linguistically there were no surprises. Zamboangueño was a blend of Spanish and Philippine VSO languages, and, other than a form of accusative case marking that seemed to be developing (a very un-Creole development, that) there was little in it that didn't spring from those two sources. All it did for me was to confirm that Plantation Creoles were the real scene.

Indeed, part of the problem I faced was that the languages labeled as Creoles did not form a true natural class. Just about any language that showed substantial mixture was called a Creole. There were even people who claimed that Ancient Egyptian and Middle English were Creoles. The term "creoloid" started to be flung about. Even if you discounted these fringe cases, ignored Fort Creoles, and dealt only with Plantation Creoles, there were clear differences in the grammatical distance between any given Creole and the metropolitan language that supplied most of its words. Take English Creoles, for example. There was Sranan, spoken in Suriname, which is totally incomprehensible to the naïve English speaker, and Bajan, spoken in Barbados, which is quite comprehensible even with no previous exposure. Strung out between these are Guyanese, Jamaican Creole, Krio (in Sierra Leone), and all the other English-related Creoles. And there's an identical range in French Creoles, from Haitian, opaque to French speakers, to Réunionais, spoken in the island of Réunion in the Indian Ocean, but far more transparent than the other Indian Ocean Creoles.

In fact, the situation of Creoles in general precisely mirrored the situation I'd explored in Guyana—a continuum of varieties from something remote from the dominant language at one end to something hardly distinguishable from it at the other. I should have spotted this resemblance far sooner. But my training, such as it was, had taught me to regard languages as one thing, dialects or sociolects as something quite different. And when you're trained to see things a certain way, it's amazing how blind you can be to the obvious. To really get to the heart of something, you can't have too little training.

My real concern lay with the Creoles at the far end of the continuum, for if there was a natural human capacity for language, it was there that this capacity would be most clearly expressed. But in *Roots* I had made a tactical blunder: instead of invoking a continuum, I tried to isolate the Creoles I was most interested in with an arbitrary stipulation. I proposed that the term "Creole" should be limited to languages in areas where no more than 20 percent of the population spoke the superstrate natively and where 80 percent or more spoke several different substrate languages.

This seemed logical enough. The lower the percentage of dominant-language speakers in a population, the less access the oppressed majority would have to that dominant language. Consequently, where there were fewer superstrate speakers, pidgins would be more variable and more impoverished, increasing the deficit between what children could get from the pidgin and what they needed for a full human language. That deficit would be made up by the bioprogram; the more that was missing, the more it would have to provide.

But naturally my critics claimed that my 20 percent stipulation was just a device to get rid of counterexamples to my theory. I tried to back up my claim with something I called a "creolization index," a figure based on the actual proportions of dominant to nondominant speakers in each population that would correlate with the deepness or what I called the "radicalness" of the Creole. As John Singler of New York University pointed out, this just wouldn't work. That proportion varied over time in any given colony, and it was by no means the only variable that had to be taken into account.

I realized that if I was ever to understand in detail how Creoles emerged and what determined their distance from the dominant language, I would have to look at all the social, historical, and economic forces that shaped Creole colonies, and understand creolization as an ongoing process—a movie in real time, rather than a succession of snapshots.

10

THE INFERNAL MACHINE

W hat finally got me started on thinking about creolization as a historical process was a book that Markey published the year after *Roots of Language*—*Isle de France Creole*, by Philip Baker and Chris Corne. As often happens, what looks at first sight like a petty squabble over some boring triviality turns out to have far-reaching consequences, if you only follow them up.

"Isle de France Creole" was a cover term adopted for the several French Creoles spoken on islands in the Indian Ocean. (Under French occupation, Mauritius, scene of the novel *Paul et Virginie* and of one of Baudelaire's loveliest poems, was known as "Isle de France.") Philip, a maker of documentary movies as well as a cre-olist, and Chris, who before his untimely death was a no-nonsense New Zealander and connoisseur of microbrews, had gotten into an argument with Robert Chaudenson, always an unwise thing to do. ("*Mais tu es complètement fou*, Derek" was his most frequent re-mark in arguments with me—"But you're totally crazy!") In Creole studies, Robert was France's undisputed champion—he'd probably knock you down if you disputed it—and he had declared it as es-tablished fact that people from the island of Réunion, the first one to be settled by the French, had populated all the others: Mauritius, Rodrigues, and the archipelago of the Seychelles.

Chris and Philip thought about this and it didn't make much sense. The Creole of Réunion was much closer to French than any of the other Isle de France Creoles; indeed nowadays people from

Réunion can hardly understand these others. But if the other Creoles had been started by Réunion folk, how could this be? The islands were settled less than three centuries ago, far too short a time for languages to diverge so dramatically.

Philip, who has more *Sitzfleisch* than me or Chris, dug into the historical records and found that in fact very few people from Réunion were involved in the settling of Mauritius, and almost all of them soon left. In other words, the Creoles of Réunion and Mauritius had developed independently. Since the other islands were mostly settled from Mauritius, his picture fit far better with the current state of the languages than Robert's, since Réunion was the odd man out and the Creoles of Mauritius, Rodrigues, and the Seychelles closely resembled one another. But Robert was livid—since Philip and Chris were Anglos, this was also a turf war—and some of the remarks exchanged were, well, unusual in academic discourse.

But what amazed me about the book was that it was possible to reconstruct the early history of Creole colonies, even down to names and details of individual settlers. More important, it revealed for the first time a pattern of Creole-colony settlement that, as I later learned, was not limited to Mauritius. It was true for all Creole colonies. And better still, it was true not by chance but by necessity. When the infernal machine of plantation slavery began to grind its wheels, iron laws of economics came into play, laws that would lead to immeasurable suffering but would also, and equally inevitably, produce new languages all over the world—languages that ironically, in the very midst of man's inhumanity to man, demonstrated the essential unity of humanity.

It took me several years, on and off, in the midst of other things, to figure out in full detail how the machine worked, and I wouldn't be sure I had it right until another hero of the stacks, Sarah Roberts, uncovered the hidden history of Hawaii. Rather than drag you through all my hesitant steps, I'm going to depart from strict chronology in this chapter and lay the whole thing out: the social and economic forces that drove creolization and the consequences they had for language.

Most of the Creoles we're concerned with formed on islands. Why islands? Because islands are ideal for plantation monoculture; they're universes unto themselves; you can control them and all that goes on in them. You can turn them into machines whose sole object is to produce sugar and money. Mainlands are too big and messy; there are too many other things going on: large-scale white immigration, different trades and industries, expanding frontiers. That's why Creoles could only flourish in odd, isolated corners of the Americas: French Louisiana, the Sea Islands of South Carolina and Georgia, the coast of the Guianas, Belize. Yet in the Caribbean there's hardly an island that doesn't have its own Creole.

In the beginning, some Caribbean islands—Barbados, for example—were uninhabited (as were all the islands in the Indian Ocean). Others that were inhabited could be depopulated pretty fast. The Caribs, who had wiped out the Arawaks, were in their turn mostly wiped out by Europeans; they fought with suicidal courage, outnumbered and outgunned. You can never have a truly blank social slate—people have to come from somewhere and bring baggage with them—but sugar plantation islands came as close to blank slates as anywhere in human history.

Most of these islands were not intended as slave colonies. One of Robert Chaudenson's most useful contributions to Creole studies is his distinction between *sociétés d'habitation* (residential societies) and *sociétés de plantation* (plantation societies). In the first phase, islands were seen as places for homesteading by the surplus populations of France and Britain. Barbados was first settled in 1627; within a dozen years it had as many as forty thousand whites, mostly homesteaders or indentured laborers, but very few Africans. In addition to subsistence crops, they raised cash crops, cotton and tobacco as well as sugar. The Portuguese were the first to develop the plantation society, on islands off the west coast of Africa: Annobón, Príncipe, Fernando Póo. They carried the system to Brazil, where the Dutch discovered it during their ill-fated attempt to take over that country, and their engineers took the *ingenho*, the Portuguese-invented sugar mill, north to the Caribbean. In the opinion of many economic historians, it was the sugar mill, with its unprecedented demand for heavy machinery—gears, levers, axles, and huge cast-iron wheels—that kick-started the Industrial Revo-

lution, ultimately giving birth to the technological society we
know today.

What I had not previously realized about Creole colonies was
the shift over time in the balance of whites and nonwhites. If there
is one crucially important factor in the formation of Creoles, it is
this shift.

In residential societies there were more whites than nonwhites.
Even in later colonies that began as plantation societies, there were
at first more whites than nonwhites. There had to be. You couldn't
just jump from an empty island to a full-blown plantation society.
We're talking cutting-edge technology here—well, seventeenth-
century cutting-edge. The sugar mill was far more advanced than
anything in Europe, where the most complex piece of industrial
machinery was the handloom. But Europe was more technologi-
cally advanced than Africa. You couldn't set up a sugar mill, or
even the stone warehouses you'd need to store the sugar, or the
stone jetties you'd need to moor the ships while you loaded it, using African slave labor. You had to have European artisans and indentured laborers with the appropriate skills. And since European
navies were constantly fighting one another, you needed soldiers
too, in case some other nation tried to take over your island.

In other words, in the early days of any Creole colony, speakers of a European language would outnumber speakers of non-
European languages.

I asked myself what linguistic consequences this would have.
Until then I don't think many creolists had thought about those
earliest days; I know I hadn't. I guess they'd all assumed, as I had,
that some kind of pidgin existed from the moment of contact. But
how could that be, if for every non-European there were several
Europeans to serve as models? That situation was not so different
from the situation that faced German or Italian or Scandinavian
immigrants to America in the nineteenth century. Did they produce a pidgin? No way: what they learned was some kind of English, good, bad, or indifferent, easily recognizable as foreigner talk,
but nothing like pidgin in Hawaii.

Of course slavery was a complicating factor. But there is every
reason to believe that the social distance between Europeans and

others was far less in the earliest days of slave colonies than it was a few decades later. The total population of each colony began in the low hundreds; everyone faced similar hardships and similar dangers; on some islands, there were serious food shortages due to lack of settlers experienced in tropical agriculture. Under such circumstances it is not easy to maintain social distinctions. Moreover, the lot of many white indentured laborers was little better than that of slaves. For a brief period, there were even white maroons alongside black ones in Barbados. Mixing on such terms, slaves could hardly have failed to learn something not too far distant from English.

So how had there developed Creoles that in many cases could not be understood by English speakers?

I still wasn't clear about that, but one surprising thing followed inevitably.

Creole continuums must have been formed backward.

I should have seen it sooner. There had been at least two major clues. One of them came from Mervyn Alleyne.

Mervyn worked at the University of the West Indies in Jamaica, where our first Creole conference was held. Once when I finished a presentation there, on how varieties in the continuum related to one another, he walked across the floor to the podium and congratulated me. I've never forgotten that, because this was at the height of the Black Power movement and Mervyn was a big Black Power man, so it was pretty gutsy of him to publicly shake a white guy's hand. But Mervyn always has been an independent thinker.

Since he's also a dyed-in-the-wool substratist, we've disagreed on quite a few things over the years, but in one thing at least he turned out to be right. He's an expert on Haitian, and he'd pointed out how many Haitian words have French definite articles and other bits of French grammar stuck to them. For instance, "sea" is *lamer*, so "the sea" is *lamer-a* (definite articles follow the noun in Haitian). To a French speaker this might suggest you're saying "the sea the," but not to a Haitian, of course. In the same way, "water" is *dlo* (from French *de l'eau*, "some water"), "friend" is *zami* (from French *les amis*, "the friends"), "smoke" is *lafime* (from French *la fumée*, "the smoke"), and so on. Mervyn also noted that in Jamaican and other English Creoles, a number of verbs took their basic form not from the English infinitive ("to break/lose/leave"), as is usually the case, but from the irregular past participle: "break" becomes *brok*, "lose" becomes *los*, "leave" becomes *lef*.

This shows that somewhere along the line, immigrants must have failed to analyze things like *la mer* as "article + noun." Perhaps because their own language didn't have articles, they assumed the whole thing was a noun. Kids make this kind of mistake all the time when they're learning their first language—allegedly, many have interpreted a verse from "The Star-Spangled Banner" as "By the donzerly light"—so it's not surprising that adults acquiring a second language without benefit of instruction should do likewise. But that's not the point here. What these cases show is that native speakers of French and English must for at least part of the time have been using more or less their normal speech when conversing with African slaves.

Now people usually simplify their language when they talk to foreigners who can't speak it or who speak very little. They certainly miss out things like definite articles and use the bare infinitives of verbs. The fact that we find fossilized articles and participial forms in Creoles shows that Europeans couldn't have been doing this, or at least couldn't have been doing it consistently. They must at some stage have used these forms in talking to slaves, fully expecting to be understood. And they must have been understood, or they would have quickly stopped using those forms. What Mervyn failed to suggest was that the time during which they used straight French or English might not have been all that long, that it might have been a behavior limited to a particular stage in the evolution of the plantation system.

The other clue as to what happened in first contact lay in the simple words "does" and "did."

Remember the Guyanese continuum and especially the varieties between the Creole and English extremes. These were not formed by simply popping in fully fledged English words and constructions to replace Creole ones. There were intermediate forms in the intermediate varieties, forms that were not exactly Creole and not exactly English. As you moved across the continuum in the direction of English, you got progressions like these:

me bin say → ah did say → I said
dem a wok → dem does work → they work

It was easy, all too easy, to conclude that this reflected an ongoing development over time. At the beginning, everyone said *a* and *bin*; then as they got more exposed to English (which wouldn't have happened until slavery was over) some of them started to make their speech sound more English but didn't quite get it right. I had even published an ingenious, well-documented, and completely misguided paper to show that, in at least one case, they couldn't have progressed directly from Creole to English; they had to take a circuitous route.

There was one big flaw in this notion to which I turned a blind eye.

The behavior of *does* and *did* in Guyana was totally different from their behavior in English. In the first place, English habitual present contrasts third-person singular "does" with "do" for all other persons—but there's no *do* in Guyana outside the varieties closest to English. In the second place, although it's possible to use English "did" in affirmative sentences, this always carries heavy stress and is generally used to contradict a previous statement ("But I DID send you a check!"). However, *did* in Guyana was always very lightly stressed, just like any other verbal auxiliary. In the third place, "does" and "did" can be used in abbreviated answer forms ("Does she play tennis?" "Yes, she does") or abbreviated conjunctions ("Mary thought that was a great movie, and I did too"). Things like these are totally impossible in Guyanese.

Most important of all, the distribution of these words wasn't just different; they were in what linguists call "complementary distribution" with one another. That's to say that where English uses "does" and "did," Guyanese doesn't, and where Guyanese does use them, English doesn't. English uses "does" and "did" in negatives and interrogatives, but not (except for the emphatic form noted above) in affirmatives. Guyanese uses *does* and *did* in regular (non-emphatic) affirmatives but not in negatives or interrogatives. Here's the negative "progression," for example:

me na bin say → ah never say → I didn't say
dem naa wok → dem en work → they don't work

How could they have got the words right and their distribution so wrong? One good answer was, "Well, when they originally learned them, that was the right distribution."

Fast-rewind to Shakespeare's day. In seventeenth-century English there was something called "periphrastic do," the distribution of which was much closer to the Guyanese distribution. In Hamlet, for instance, we find:

If you *do* meet Horatio and Marcellus
He *does* confess he feels himself distracted
But wilt thou hear me how I *did* proceed

In other words, "does" and "did" were used as low-stress verbal auxiliaries in affirmative sentences, just as they are today by many middle-of-the-continuum speakers in Guyana. The conclusion was inescapable. *Does* and *did* had been acquired, not by upwardly mobile children of recently freed slaves in the mid-nineteenth century, as I had supposed, but by the very earliest slave arrivals in the New World.

This discovery had important, and pretty negative, consequences for some of my earlier work. But before we look at those consequences, we really need to understand exactly how plantation societies developed.

The history of sugar planting in the Caribbean falls into three clearly distinct phases.

First comes the establishment phase.

In this phase, a plantation system has to be started from scratch.

Infrastructure must be put in: houses and roads, docks, wharfs, warehouses, sugar mills. Skilled and experienced craftsmen imported from Europe must organize this work and carry it out with the help of indentured laborers who have signed away their freedom for five or seven years in return for a paid passage to the colony and a bonus, in land or cash, on completion of their term. Meanwhile the clearance of land begins, and here the unskilled work is given to less-skilled indentured laborers and increasingly to the first slaves as they become available. During this first phase, those who have bought land or who have invested in the development of the island have laid out substantial sums of money on which, at this stage, there is very little return. Many, sensing the prospect of riches to come, have borrowed heavily and are deeply in debt. If the enterprise fails they face bankruptcy and an ignominious return home.

Since throughout this phase there is at worst a rough equality of numbers between whites and nonwhites, and in many cases a preponderance of whites, any African slave had a reasonable chance of acquiring a working second-language version of whatever European language was spoken in the island. It was during this phase that a contact language much closer to the dominant language than the subsequent Creole briefly established itself. This language would become the lingua franca of the few hundred or a thousand or two individuals who, at the end of the establishment phase, constituted the total population of the colony.

Second comes the expansion phase.

In this phase, the planters and entrepreneurs who have invested in the colony seek to recoup their expenses, maximize their profits, and amass substantial sums that would enable the more fortunate or ruthless to return to their homeland and live in luxury. This could be done only by expanding landholdings as quickly as possible and producing the largest possible quantity of sugar. To do this, the planters had to acquire large numbers of slaves as quickly as possible, if possible before payments on their loans fell due. Within a few years, the importation of slaves, a mere trickle in the first phase, became a torrent. Supply could hardly keep pace with demand; planters mobbed the auction blocks, bid against one another, cleared each slave cargo within days if not hours of its arrival. In a few years the colony's population tripled, quadrupled, and kept on climbing.

The expansion phase radically changed the demography of the sugar colonies. The numbers of whites did not change dramatically; in most cases their numbers grew only slightly and gradually. The places of some of the artisans who left were now filled by managers, accountants, and shopkeepers ministering to the needs of a newly prosperous society. It didn't take large numbers of whites to run a plantation society. Indeed, in those colonies that had been set up as residential societies, the white population sometimes fell, as homesteaders, bought out by sugar growers, either returned, defeated, to the homeland or headed for the wide open spaces of what was still a century away from becoming the United States of America.

At the same time, the nonwhite population was ballooning as the Moloch of sugar cried out for more and more bodies. The white to black ratio soared from near parity to 1:5, 1:10—even, in at least one case, as high as 1:30. That was in the Dutch colony of Berbice (now a region of Guyana) and it was dangerously high, for in 1763 the Akan slave "Cuffy" (Kofi) revolted, drove out the Dutch, and held the colony for the best part of a year before the Dutch could regroup and take it back. Needless to say, they then quickly lowered the ratio by encouraging white immigrants from Barbados and other Caribbean islands. But a dangerously high ratio of Africans to Europeans still persisted in most places throughout the history of the plantation colonies.

Inevitably, with such a disproportion, the nature of the society changed. It became highly stratified, with layer upon layer of classes buffering those in power from the *Lumpenproletariat* hacking sugarcane in the fields. Beneath the owners were the managers, beneath the managers the accountants and clerks and field supervisors. (Only the success of his first book of poems saved Robert Burns, that great apostle of liberty, from becoming a field supervisor in Jamaica—it's fascinating to think how he might have turned out if he had.) Beneath these white layers lay the black layers of the social pyramid: the skilled artisans who handled the technicalities of the sugar mill and the transportation, often by boat, of sugar to the port, and the coopers who made the barrels for the rum that was a high-value by-product of sugar-making; the house slaves, with their own internal hierarchy; the foremen, or drivers as they were called, who directly supervised each gang of workers in the field; and finally the lowest and by far the largest layer, the field slaves.

It was a paranoid society, one that believed it could persist only by imposing draconian punishment on any deviation from its arbitrary norms. It had created its own monsters, the maroons, who would steal into a plantation by night, kill any European they found (can you blame them?), and hopefully add some recruits, female where possible, to their bands. It lived in terror of slave revolts, while creating ideal conditions for revolt by lethal working conditions. (Many slave owners thought it was cheaper to work slaves to death and buy new ones than to breed from existing stock.) It was a society in which "Get Rich or Die Tryin' " was no mere slogan but a way of life.

But what happened to language in all of this?

Everyone had always assumed that once a contact language of any kind was established, it would be handed on, like an Olympic torch, to each succeeding cohort of immigrants. This idea of the persistence of languages is deeply rooted in Creole studies. Substratists believe that African languages persist in Creoles. Superstratists believe that European languages persist in Creoles. Monogeneticists believe that an original Creole (or pidgin; they tend not to commit themselves on this) persisted all over the world, through all manner of metamorphoses. So obviously, once a contact language had formed, it too would persist.

But it hadn't. Or, at best, something had grown up alongside it. And no one had any clear idea how that happened. The only suggestion that seemed to hold any water was that the contact language, passed from cohort to cohort of new immigrants, had gradually degraded with each transmission, until finally it was whittled down to the shape of a Creole. Everyone assumed that the first cohort of slaves, the ones who arrived when races were near parity, would use their contact language with the next cohort, and that cohort would understand it, more or less, and pass on something similar, if a little reduced and simplified, to the cohort after that.

But this didn't make any sense. Persistence is a feature of established languages, not of contact languages. (We saw in Chapter 1 how Catalan speakers reacted when Franco tried to destroy their language.) People have loyalty to their birth language, the tongue they acquired at their mother's knee. They have no loyalty whatsoever to any kind of contact language—that's a purely instrumental thing, what you need to get by, to make money, or to survive in a new situation. A situation had given birth to it and a different situation could kill it, almost overnight.

On top of this, you have to take into account the fact, known not merely to linguists but to every man and woman in the street, that people simplify even their native languages when faced with people who don't understand them. And I had heard with my own ears how Creole speakers in Hawaii repidginized their speech in order to communicate with their pidgin-speaking parents. Well, a contact language close enough to English to contain *does*, *did*, *broke*, *lost*, and all the rest of these nonreduced, nonsimplified items would have been as opaque as Standard English to any African fresh off the boat.

Now on top of all that, consider the work situation. What did the old hands, the earlier slave cohorts, have to do with the new arrivals? They had to teach them how to work, how to do all the jobs required on a sugar plantation. They had to get it right and get it right fast, because there was always a driver with a whip hovering in the background and if they screwed up it would be their hides rather than those of the new hands that would suffer.

Under these conditions they were not about to give language lessons and hope that the newcomers would quickly pick up the old contact language. They would take the shortest, most reliable route. They would pidginize their contact language just as my Hawaii informants had pidginized their Creole. They would get down to the basics: words, simple predications, string things together as best you can and to hell with rules of grammar.

What's so beautiful about these processes is their inevitability. Nothing happened by chance. Details varied, naturally, from colony to colony, but the overall pattern remained everywhere the same, because simple laws of economics and of language dictated that pattern.

There had to be something near racial parity in the early stages because setting up the infernal machine required at least as many Europeans as Africans.

Consequently, the original contact language had to be not too far from the language of the slave owners. Because at this stage Europeans were teaching Africans what they had to do, the contact language had to be intelligible to native speakers of the European language. Because so many interactions were between Europeans and Africans, the latter would have much better access to that European language than at any later stage in plantation history. We should remember that Africans, unlike modern Americans, do not regard monolingualism as a natural state, but expect to have to use several languages in the course of their lives. (In Ghana, our houseboy, Atinga, spoke six languages—two European, four African—and this was nothing out of the ordinary.)

But as soon as the infrastructure was in place, the slave population of sugar colonies had to be increased both massively and very rapidly. If not, the plantation owners, who had invested significant amounts of capital, would have gone bankrupt and the economies of those colonies would have collapsed.

When the slave population ballooned in this way, new hands heavily outnumbered old hands. No longer did Europeans instruct Africans; now it was the older hands among the Africans instructing the new ones, and the vast majority of interactions were no longer European to African, they were African to African. Since this was the case, there was no longer any need for the contact language to remain mutually intelligible with the European language. Africans in positions of authority could become bilingual, using one language with Europeans, another with fellow Africans. The code-switching I found in Guyana, which I had assumed was a relatively recent development, had been there, like most other things, from the very beginning.

In any case, Africans in authority could not have gone on using the original contact language even if they'd wanted to. As we saw, it would have been as opaque to the new arrivals as undiluted

French or English. The old hands had to use a primitive pidgin to communicate with the new hands. And, needless to add, the new hands had to use a primitive pidgin to communicate with one another.

Since new hands now constituted a large majority of the total population, the primitive pidgin soon became the lingua franca of that population. A minority of relatively privileged slaves (house slaves and artisans) may have kept the original contact language alive among themselves, thus giving rise to the intermediate varieties in the continuum that confronted me when I first arrived in Guyana. (For reasons still unknown, this process seems to have happened more often in English than in French colonies.) But it was the primitive, unstructured pidgin that formed the input to the children of the expansion phase.

Therefore it was the children of the expansion phase—not the relatively few children of the establishment phase, the first locally born generation, as I had originally thought—who were the creators of the Creole. They were the ones who encountered the pidgin in its most basic and rudimentary form, and consequently they were the ones who had to draw most heavily on the inborn knowledge of language that formed as much a part of their biological heritage as wisdom teeth or prehensile hands.

All the serious business of language creation happened during the expansion phase. After that, nothing of much linguistic interest happened.

The expansion phase went on until all the good agricultural land, and even some marginal land, had been put into production. In Haiti, the expansion phase never reached this goal. Because Haiti is bigger than the other sugar colonies, planters were still opening up new land when the revolution came and the slaves took over. Elsewhere, most colonies arrived at the third phase, the plateau phase. All available land had been exploited, so there was no motive for further expanding the slave population. Thanks to negative population growth—many African mothers, very naturally, would avoid pregnancy, abort, or commit infanticide, rather than allow their children to become slaves, while death rates remained abnormally high—more slaves were always needed just to keep the population at its optimal (for slave owners) level, but the pace of immigration had slowed dramatically. The aim was simply to maintain the population at approximately the same level, so that the infernal machine, invulnerable until the abolitionists attacked it, could keep on churning out sugar and money.

And, never forget, that machine not only spearheaded the technology of the Industrial Revolution, but it also provided the capital accumulation that built all those dark satanic mills. And at the same time it developed an essential ingredient of our modern world, the work discipline and the system of organization that, replacing the whip with economic necessity, kept countless millions working at sterile and repetitive tasks throughout their lifetimes. Would the world we know today have come into existence without sugar and slavery? Think about it.

Hey, come on, this is not supposed to be a book about serious social and economic issues. We're talking about language, and, as a colleague once said to me, "Isn't it nice that what we do has no practical consequences?" So instead let's look at what consequences this new analysis of the creolization process had for some of my previous theories.

It's clear now that the continuum must have formed backward—backward from the way DeCamp and I had supposed, that is—with the varieties closer to English forming first, and those furthest from English at a later date. This new picture was consistent with what we were learning about the way in which the slave colonies were originally populated. Moreover, it became highly likely that the whole process, clearly a retreat from English rather than an advance toward it, had not stretched out over centuries, but had been compressed into a space of a few decades two or three centuries ago. Hence the middle part of the Guyanese continuum was formed not in the nineteenth century, as I had assumed, but much earlier, almost certainly before the "deep" or "radical" Creole, the variety furthest from English, had formed.

So *bang* went my beautiful theory that the continuum was living history, a record of three hundred years of linguistic change. But I wasn't in the least upset. What I had now found had much greater significance—another milestone on the road to answering the questions: What is language, really? How is it acquired? How in the world did it ever start?

Two places in the world seemed to me to be crucial in this quest, Hawaii and Suriname. Hawaii was the place where creolization had happened most recently, where it might still be possible to find historical records from which the process could be reconstructed. Suriname was the place where the most extreme Creoles had been born, the Creoles that looked least like European languages. Sranan, a.k.a. Takitaki, the language spoken by the descendants of plantation slaves, is already hardly recognizable as something that took most of its word stock from English. For instance, take the word *suma*. That's from English, and it means "who." How on earth could you get from "who" to *suma*?

But wait, there's worse. More opaque even than Sranan are the maroon Creoles, Aucans (a.k.a. Djuka), Boni, Paramaccan, Matuari, Kwinti. But most opaque of all is Saramaccan, oldest of the maroon tongues, the language of people who fought the Dutch for a century and finally won, not their freedom—they'd already taken that—but Dutch acceptance that they'd be free in perpetuity. Then the Dutch built the huge dam at Brokopondo and progress did what force of arms never could: drive the Saramaccan from their forest homes.

So see if you can guess what English words these Saramaccan words come from:

beee
buuu
feee

Here's a clue. The first two are English words of one syllable, and the third has two. In each Saramaccan word there are three syllables, with a high tone on the middle vowel and low tones on the first and last. But all three words come from common English words.

Promise me you'll try to figure this out before you go on to Chapter 11. I know you'll cheat and peep, but go on, promise me anyway.

11

SURINAM: THE CRUCIBLE

B y this time, Frank Byrne had gotten his NSF dissertation grant and had left for the interior of Surinam. (I'm going to stick to the old spelling here; since independence it's become Suriname, but when the stuff in this chapter happened, it was still known by its Dutch name of Surinam.) Soon Frank started sending me long handwritten letters with masses of Saramaccan data. I was especially fascinated by this three-way split:

Mi go a wosu go njan.
"I went home to eat [and did eat]."
Mi go a wosu fu njan.
"I went home to eat [at least it was my intention to eat,
    maybe I did, maybe not, it doesn't matter]."
Mi go a wosu bi-fu njan.
"I went home to eat [with the intention of eating, but for
    some reason I didn't eat]."

So Creoles are simplified languages, huh? Come on, you can't do that in English, or any other European language. English, of course, is spastic in this respect:

I managed to get one.
I failed to get one.

In both you intended to get one; in the first you succeeded and in the second you didn't, but the grammatical forms are identical in each case. If the main verb doesn't tell you the answer through its own meaning, as "manage" and "fail" do, you have to use some kind of circumlocution, just as I did above, to clarify the meanings of sentences like these.

But my main interest was the striking similarity between Saramaccan and Hawaiian Creole:

Morning we go over there *go* plant [and actually planted].
Morning we go over there *for* plant [intending to plant, but may or may not have actually done so].

All that's lacking in Hawaii is a form that means you didn't do what you meant to do. But as far as I know, that's unique to Saramaccan.

What is not unique, what is shared by all the Plantation Creoles I've studied, is the rest of this subsystem. The English ones all use something derived from "for"—might be *fu, fi, fe*—to indicate what traditional grammars ("steam grammars," we linguists call them) describe as "adverbial clauses of purpose." French and Portuguese Creoles do exactly the same, only of course they use their equivalent of "for": *pour* (in practice, this becomes *pu*) or *para*. Whatever the word, the meaning is always the same—someone intended to do something and may or may not have done it. (Remember the zero article form that means "maybe singular, maybe plural, it's not important or we don't know." Don't you wish your language had forms like these?) But if the intention was carried out and it's important that it was carried out, these same Creoles will indicate the fact either by using *go* or its local equivalent, or a zero form.

Wait a minute, you say. Weren't you going to tell us about *suma* and *beee/buuu/feee*?

We're getting there. Before we do, it's important to know why the Surinam Creoles are so far from the English that originally gave them birth. And that involves a substantial slice of history.

In 1650, Barbados, the biggest English slave colony in the West Indies, no longer had any space for would-be homesteaders. All arable land had been parceled out among sugar planters. The golden handshake for indentured laborers had shriveled from several acres of land to several hogsheads of rum (a hogshead is sixty-three gallons—whether the preferred option was to sell it or drink it is not recorded).

So there were lots of strong, healthy, would-be pioneers around. And the governor of Barbados, Lord Willoughby, thought of something for them to do. Why not start a new colony on the coast of South America? Neither the Spanish nor the Portuguese seemed to have much interest in the northeastern part of the continent between the mouths of the Orinoco and Amazon rivers. It looked ripe for the taking.

In fact, people had already had that idea. There had been several attempts to found colonies in Surinam—all had failed, sometimes with the deaths of everyone involved. However, a number of hardy individuals signed up for what had already been christened Willoughbyland, and soon there were two hundred settlers and two hundred slaves—the parity typical of a colony in its establishment phase.

The balance changed very slowly; it took another ten years for the black to white ratio to go from 1:1 to 2:1. In other words, there was still plenty of opportunity for slaves to pick up, if not the King's English, then something far closer to it than what would be spoken there a few decades later. Unless . . .

Unless whatever the slaves spoke had been carried in from elsewhere, and this language was already like, if not the same as, what later on were to become the Surinam Creoles.

Many creolists do indeed believe that contact languages are just as persistent as established languages, can be brought from one place to another, and can spread all over the world without changing their structure, even when those who spread them aren't native speakers. Those who believe this naturally oppose any theory, including the bioprogram, that sees Creoles as developing separately each in its own part of the world. Now nobody disputes that most if not all of the slaves who first settled Willoughbyland came from Barbados. So naturally those first arrivals wouldn't have acquired a new contact language there—they'd just have gone on using whatever they'd learned in Barbados. Which could have been much more like the eventual Surinam Creoles—or could it?

In fact, slaves in Barbados would have had an even better chance of picking up English than they did in Willoughbyland. Barbados had a ratio even more favorable for learning. In 1650 there were still more whites than blacks, and the whites weren't all homesteaders or planters by any means; plenty of them were indentured laborers. Especially on the smaller plantations, these whites worked side by side with slaves on the same tasks under similar working conditions; would they, or even could they, have failed to talk to one another? And we have actual figures for a representative sample of ten Barbadian plantations in the decade before 1650, showing 139 indentured against 234 enslaved. That's better than one native speaker of English for every two slaves.

Slaves brought to Willoughbyland from Barbados surely spoke what they had spoken in Barbados. But that would still have been something close to English.

Diffusionists do have an alternative. Maybe the Creole that would spawn the Surinam Creoles didn't start in Barbados, but was brought to Barbados. Maybe it actually started in West Africa.

So let's look at West Africa. A handful of intrepid Englishmen went native there as early as the 1550s—some even acquired tribal scars—so there's no doubt that some kind of English was spoken there. And a century later there were forts and trading posts operated by the English (not the British, as most people insist on saying—before 1707, there was no such thing as "Britain") along the West African coast. Unfortunately the mixed-race offspring of the intrepid Englishmen were in Guinea and the forts were on the Gold Coast, the best part of a thousand miles away. Some kind of contact language could have gotten from Guinea to the Gold Coast, but there's no evidence it ever did, or even any plausible way it could have. But let's just suppose that, somehow, it did.

If it did, say the diffusionists, it would have been used in the fort areas. And surely, whether it came from Guinea or not, some kind of contact language must have been used around the forts. But the vast majority of Africans who interacted with Europeans in fort areas weren't slaves; they were either independent traders or paid workers. Short of committing some heinous offense, there's no way any of these Africans would have become part of a slave cargo.

Maybe, say the diffusionists, but the forts typically contained dungeons in which slaves brought from the interior had to wait until a ship came for them—sometimes for several months. There they would interact with fort workers and in the course of such interaction would pick up the language that was the daddy of the Surinam Creoles and carry it to Barbados. But the idea that fort workers had long chats with slaves while they waited to be shipped is not just unlikely but irrelevant. In the years prior to 1650, almost all the slaves brought to Barbados came in Dutch ships that had sailed from Dutch forts in Africa, where there's no reason to believe that anything remotely connected with English was spoken. So it's almost certain that, until they arrived in Barbados, most if not all of those slaves didn't know a word of any English-related contact language.

But suppose that, despite all these formidable obstacles, a bunch of slaves speaking a radical English-based Creole that would ultimately sire the Sranan Creoles had actually made it into Barbados. What use would their language have been? Other slaves wouldn't have understood it—to them it would have been as opaque as English. Indentured laborers, green farm boys from Devon or Yorkshire fresh off the boat, with no previous experience of any foreign language, wouldn't have understood it—they'd probably have thought it was just another African language. Even if such a language had gotten there, it would have withered and died long before it could be transported to Surinam.

So the chances that any ancestor to the Surinam Creoles arrived in or was developed in Willoughbyland fall somewhere in the range between zero and none.

To the disgrace of British scholarship, there is still no complete history of Willoughbyland, and the information we have about it is scanty, sketchy, and far from reliable. With this caveat, what follows is as accurate an account as you're likely to get.

Those who first went to Willoughbyland did so in a glow of optimism not wholly attributable to Willoughby's skillful propaganda. Visitors (including Aphra Behn, England's first woman novelist and one of the first tropical tourists) brought home rapturous reports of an earthly paradise: the climate was mild and healthy, the soil fertile, the natives friendly. Nobody suspected that the little colony was in for the roughest of rough rides.

Sixteen years in, plague struck. Almost immediately, war broke out between English and Dutch. The Dutch raided the colony. The English raided it back. Since plantations had to be located alongside navigable rivers—with no roads, the only means to transport sugar to the port of Paramaribo was by boat—naval vessels could sail in and their crews could burn, plunder, rape, and kill with impunity. In the 1667 treaty that resolved the conflict, the English gave up Willoughbyland and took New York in exchange. And the Dutch were laughing—who'd not pick a potentially rich tropical colony in place of a nonproductive outpost with a climate featuring all of what Samuel Beckett described as "the rigors of the temperate zone"?

However, there were problems. The population, close to five thousand before plague struck, now barely topped three thousand. There were only a handful of Dutch on site, and if the English left before Dutch planters arrived, the jungle, not the Dutch, would take over the plantations.

So a deal was worked out whereby English planters would stay on until, but only until, Dutchmen could move in. Then they, together with all the slaves they had owned in 1667, would leave, mostly for Jamaica. In order to keep the plantations up and running, they might have to import additional slaves, but any imported after 1667 were Dutch property and would remain when the English left.

The year after the treaty, there were still nearly two thousand "old" (English) slaves left, but no "new" (Dutch) slaves had yet arrived. Three years later there were just over a thousand of each. Four years after that, only two hundred old slaves remained (far fewer, by some accounts) and there were eight times as many new slaves.

In terms of language, this sequence of events means that if any language was to be passed from old slaves to new slaves, the effective window of opportunity was less than eight years. At the beginning of this period, the close-to-English contact language of Willoughbyland would have been as opaque as English itself to the new slaves. For a year or two in the middle, with parity between old and new, the new slaves might have had a better shot at picking it up—that is, if the old hands hadn't had to repidginize it in order to communicate with newcomers, the most likely contingency.

There's no way of knowing how much the new hands could have learned in that time. Evidence that would later turn up in Hawaii suggests that people in an area of severe language flux can get by for eight years or longer on just a handful of words and phrases. And every day from then on the language-learning situation would get worse, as more and more old slaves left and more and more new ones arrived.

And then the kind, friendly natives turned on the colonists in a series of uprisings and massacred hundreds of them. In the confusion, many slaves escaped. By 1679 there were only nine hundred new slaves, plus a hundred (or maybe only fifty) old ones who would almost all be gone by the following year, leaving what was now Surinam without any source of English. So anything that came from English would have had to be learned by then.

The Dutch struggled to build up the colony.

Thanks to the Dutch historian Johannes Postma, we have a reasonably complete record of all shipments of slaves into Surinam from 1680 on. From 1680 to 1684 he records fewer than two thousand arrivals, probably an underestimate, since the slave population went from a thousand to over three thousand in that time and all slave colonies suffered negative growth rates. From 1684 to 1689 he records nearly seven thousand arrivals, and from 1690 to 1694, close to three thousand. In other words, the population of Surinam was increased by the addition of between nine and ten thousand slaves in ten years—nearly a thousand per year. But this was an expansion phase without any expansion. For at the end of those years, the net increase in the total population was just over a thousand slaves.

Where did the other eight thousand–plus go?

If they'd run away, they'd have greatly outnumbered the population of the colony and could have conquered it, as Cuffy conquered Berbice in 1763. The only possible conclusion is that most
of them died or were killed. I've found nothing in the literature—
though there may of course be something in Dutch sources; I don't
read Dutch—that shows even an awareness that anything out of
the ordinary had occurred. But hey, who cares? They were just poor
black folk. Nothing interesting's happening, come on now, move
along there.

So the colony had not one, not two, but at least four disastrous
population crashes:

- 1666, the plague
- 1667, Dutch and English raids
- 1674–78, Native American uprisings and massacres
- 16??, ?????

As a result of these crashes, it took thirty years—until 1695—for
Surinam to regain the population it had had in 1665. (In the same
period, the slave population of Barbados more than doubled, while
that of Jamaica tripled.) Since most of the slaves who came to Surinam must have died before they had time to learn anything, let
alone pass on what they'd learned to new arrivals, the chances of
any coherent language making it through this period are, again,
zero.

The crucible of Surinam brought about a linguistic meltdown
that may be without precedent in human history. The amazing
thing is that anything came through at all—that people didn't just
restart the pidgin-Creole cycle from scratch, this time in Dutch.

But some things came through. Some English words came
through. According to Norval Smith of the University of Amsterdam, an expert in this subject, around seven hundred English
words, basic vocabulary mostly, made it through all the catastro-
phes. These words formed just part of what must have been a "macaronic" jargon, a mishmash of words from African languages and
Native American languages as well as from English, Dutch, and

Portuguese. The Portuguese came from some two hundred Portuguese Jewish planters, who arrived a couple of years before the end of the English period (whether they brought with them slaves who already spoke a Portuguese Creole is still controversial, but immaterial, since even if they had, that language couldn't have survived the crashes either).

But a lot of words in this jargon wouldn't even have been recognized by the people whose language they came from.

Take *suma*, for instance. Here's how it came to mean "who."

Remember that in Creoles generally, question words from previous languages often don't survive, and have to be replaced by two-word expressions, the first of which translates roughly as "question" and the second of which tells you what kind of question it is. In Surinam, *who* came to mean just "question," so its original meaning had to be reconstituted by adding "someone." "Someone" soon lost its final consonant. John Stedman, a Scottish soldier of fortune who fought the maroons in the latter half of the eighteenth century, records a Sranan speaker calling out, *Who summa datty*, "Who's that?" In rapid speech this would become *usuma* or *osuma*, and then the initial vowel came to grief, a common fate, as we saw in Guyana, giving simply *suma*.

So what about *beee*, *buuu*, and *feee*? .

Before we can talk about these, we need to know how Saramaccan began.

Somewhere around 1690, the slaves on the plantation of Antonio Machado, a Portuguese Jew, revolted and took to the jungle en masse. Ironically, they adopted the name of their former master and became the Matjau, the oldest of the clans that make up the Saramaccan maroon population. For they were soon joined by others, and in a few years there was a thriving free community, firing pebbles and brass buttons from their looted muskets at the Dutch who came after them.

They had no shortage of recruits. Surinam had by now become notoriously the worst of all the slave colonies. Stedman, who respected the maroons he fought against more than the burghers he defended, gave us our most vivid picture of it. His book, illustrated by his friend the poet William Blake, describes a society in which greed, arrogance, and gross, vulgar luxury rode on a bed of unspeakable suffering. Violence begat violence; the brutal degradation of the slave gangs bred the retaliatory fury of the maroons, which terrified the Dutch, who in turn inflicted sadistic punishments (some starkly illustrated in Blake's engravings). So there was always new blood for the Saramaccan and other maroon communities that kept forming all through the eighteenth century.

If you were going to run for it, the first year was the best, while you still remembered what liberty was like and hadn't been broken, physically and mentally, by years of grueling toil. The longer you left it, the less the chances you'd be able to pluck up the courage and the strength to make your run.

Think what the consequences of that would have been in terms of language acquisition.

Most slaves who escaped could have had at best a year or so of exposure to what must already have become an unstructured jargon, an early-stage pidgin probably even more impoverished than the remnants I had found in Hawaii in the seventies. They would have come away with no more than a scattering of words, words drawn from a variety of languages, even if the core remained English. Because many, perhaps most, of the Saramaccan came from Portuguese-speaking plantations, they took with them more Portuguese words than the majority of those who failed to escape.

So, in the closing years of the seventeenth century and the first few years of the eighteenth, two Creoles developed side by side. Saramaccan grew up in the forest, and, as the colony stabilized with no further population crashes, Sranan grew up on the plantations. And their grammars are close to identical.

That was enough for most creolists. The two languages had to be from the same parent. Damn the historical evidence; there just had to have been a single stabilized Creole prior to 1690, or maybe two. Maybe the Creole had relexified on the Portuguese-speaking plantations but retained its original structure—two vocabularies, but the same grammar.

Now there are two quite distinct but mutually supporting reasons why this cannot be so. The first we've already reviewed: the chaotic social and political conditions that prevailed in Surinam through three decades, the statistics that show how the population must have turned over several times during those decades, making the transmission of any structured language virtually impossible. Language doesn't happen in a vacuum. It may be in the mind or the brain but it is deployed in the world, and therefore suffers the buffetings of fate in countless ways.

The second reason lies in the languages themselves.

Can you possibly imagine sharing a complex grammar and then selecting different sets of words to express the most crucial grammatical relations in it?

Of course not, but that's what would have had to happen if Saramaccan and Sranan were once a single language. Just look at this table:

	Sranan	Saramaccan
all	ala	hii
anterior marker	ben	bi
definite article	da	di
irrealis marker	sa	(g)o
nonpunctual marker	(d)e	ta
plural marker/they	den	de
where	pe	naase
who	suma	ambe
why	sanede	andimbei
you(sing.)	yu	i

None of the above examples has anything to do with the Portuguese-English split that's supposed to be responsible for most of the differences between Sranan and Saramaccan. Except perhaps one—you might think that *ta* is from Portuguese *estar*, "to be [temporarily]," which is just perfect for a nonpunctual marker. After all, you also find *ta* used as a nonpunctual marker in Palenquero, where it can only be from Spanish *estar*, with the same meaning as the Portuguese. For a long time I too thought the source for Saramaccan *ta* must be *estar*. But according to Norval Smith, and nobody knows more about Surinam Creole phonology and word derivations than Norval, *ta* is from English "stand." Indeed, in early texts we find *tan* instead of *ta*.

From this account it's obvious what was happening. The Saramaccan weren't replacing words that lay at the core of a language they already had; they were executing the instructions of the bioprogram, building a new language from scratch out of the scraps they'd shared on the plantation. But in order to execute those instructions, both they and those they'd left behind on the plantation, who were in exactly the same linguistic situation, had to pick, from the word-salad that was Surinam pidgin, words to express the grammatical categories that the bioprogram had given them.

The two lots made a different pick, that's all.

English Creoles typically form their definite article from "this" or "that." Sranan picked "that," transforming it to *da* (not many languages can handle "th"—for that matter, some English dialects can't handle it either, as you'll know if you've ever been to Brooklyn). Then in rapid speech the final consonant got lost. Saramaccan picked "this" and got *di*.

For an irrealis marker, Saramaccan picked "go" (optionally losing the initial consonant, depending on how fast you're speaking), which is boilerplate for both French and English Creoles. For Sranan *sa* there are two possible derivations: it is either from Portuguese *sabe*, which can mean "can" as well as "know," or from English "shall," simplified to *sal* and then dropping the final consonant.

For a plural marker, instead of -s, which quickly gets lost in pidginization, English Creoles typically use the third-person plural pronoun. But the third-person plural pronoun, in English, has two forms: nominative "they" and accusative "them." Sranan modeled its plural on the accusative form; Saramaccan preferred the nominative.

When it comes to finding a "where" marker, there are two likely candidates: "place" and (as we saw in Guyana) "side." Saramaccan chose "side," adding the locative *naa*, "to" or "at"; Sranan chose "place," reducing it to an easy-to-say, consonant-vowel syllable.

In English there are two ways of referring to an unknown or indefinite person: "someone" and "somebody." When it came to making the question word "who," Sranan picked the first, Saramaccan the second.

In seventeenth-century English, "you" and "ye" were in competition, slugging it out to see which would be our second-person singular. Exposed to both, Saramaccan picked the old champ, Sranan the young contender.

But maybe the most interesting of all is "why." The Sranan word means literally "thing-head," which sounds weird until you think about it (doesn't "why" simply mean "What thing in your head made you do it?"). The Saramaccan word means literally "what-makes," which is quite a bit more transparent. But what's truly bizarre is that the Guyanese version of "why" is identical: *wa mek*, in other words, "what-makes"!

Any linguist who saw the similarity between the Saramaccan and Guyanese forms for "why" would naturally label the Guyanese expression as a calque, or "loan-translation." It seems obvious that the Guyanese expression has literally translated the Saramaccan expression. However, to translate something you first have to know it. And although Surinam and Guyana are neighbors, there is no record of any contact between the Saramaccan and the Guyanese; the coast is one thing, the jungle another, seldom if ever do the twain meet, and to the best of my knowledge, this is the only case where a Guyanese form mimics a uniquely Saramaccan one. On the other hand, there may well have been contact between Sranan and Guyanese—archaic forms of Guyanese strongly suggest a connection—but if Sranan had served as the model, Guyanese for "why" would have been *ting-ed*, not *wa mek*.

In light of the bioprogram, however, the solution is clear. The human mind holds a set of meanings that have to be "grammaticized"—expressed in terms of grammatical forms like articles, auxiliaries, prepositions, and the like. The ways that can be chosen to express these meanings are quite few. Picking from such a limited menu, is it surprising that here and there people who have no contact with one another make the same pick? Not at all, if you accept bioprogram theory. If you don't, if you think there is no mental template and the only way you can acquire language is by having it

passed on to you by someone else, stuff like this is just plain inex-
plicable.

Anyway, the grammars for which Sranan and Saramaccan made
these choices are—at least as regards their core subsystems—not far
short of identical. The TMA system, for instance, is exactly the
same in both languages. It's the same system we've seen in Fa
d'Ambu and Guyanese Creole and, in a slightly abbreviated form,
in Hawaii (and you'll find it too, with minor additions, in Haiti,
Mauritius, and many more far-flung places that have never had
contact with one another). It's the same because the human brain
is the same, regardless of where you are or who you are or what you
are. And that same brain has the same resources everywhere, resources that enable children with no language in common to re-
constitute a full human language even in a linguistic crucible like
that of Surinam.

I said, "Not far short of identical" in their core subsystems. That's
only natural. If there is a biological blueprint, you'd hardly expect
it to provide all the peripheral details of a language. People need
differences between their languages to give them identity. "Part of
being an American," said the British linguist Raymond Firth, "is to
sound like one."

So of course there are some differences between Sranan and
Saramaccan, and not just in the words they chose to express grammatical categories. For instance, Saramaccan has distinctive tone,
Sranan doesn't (by distinctive tone, we mean two or more tones
capable of distinguishing a pair of words that in every other feature
are identical). Most Creoles don't have distinctive tone, or only
have it very occasionally—Hawaii has none at all, and Guyana has
it only in a handful of words, such as "bro-*ther*" (low tone, high
tone) meaning "male sibling" and "*bro*-ther" (high tone, low tone)
meaning "member of a religious order." Because Saramaccan, unlike Sranan, has it right across the vocabulary, and because many
West African languages have it too, substratists again assume that
tone must have come directly from speakers of tonal West African
languages.

There are a couple of problems here, though. First, where an African word has survived in Saramaccan, it seldom has the same tones, or the same distribution of tones, as it did in its original language. Second, the pattern of tones in English-derived words looks as if Saramaccan simply places high tone on what was the stressed syllable in the English word. And here, finally, at last (bet you thought we never would), we come to *beee, buuu,* and *feee.*

Beee is Saramaccan for "bread," *buuu* for "blood," *feee* for "afraid" (also "fear"). These are all words of three syllables, low on the first and third, high on the middle syllable.

To get some help here, let's look at the Sranan equivalents. These are respectively *brede, brudu,* and *frede.*

Now it's plain sailing, good old-fashioned reconstruction, a technique known for at least two centuries and originally used to piece together the Indo-European language family.

You take a pair of cognates in languages believed to be descended from the same parent, and figure out what was the original form in that parent language (protoform, it's called). Of course you have to be able to show that the sound changes involved are well motivated and well attested in other contexts. In citing a protoform, an asterisk doesn't mean ungrammatical, it means unattested but plausibly conjectured.

Well-established patterns of sound change are indeed involved here. We know that many languages do not tolerate consonant clusters (indeed, the commonest syllable pattern in the world's languages is CV, consonant-vowel, like "do" or "pa" or "be." If you're a native speaker of a CV language and encounter a language with words that have clusters, the usual strategy is to insert what's called an epenthetic vowel, which because of something called "vowel harmony" will more than likely be the same as a vowel already in the word. So you would get *bered, *bulud, *fered.*

But such languages also don't tolerate final consonants (except, sometimes, /n/). So the speakers of CV languages have to add another epenthetic vowel, again harmonizing, giving you *berede, *buludu, *ferede.*

These had to have been the forms in Surinam pidgin. But once children started to acquire language, the two languages went different ways. Sranan, perhaps because it was spoken on the plantations alóngside Dutch, a pretty clusterful language, grew more tolerant of clusters and dropped the first epenthetic vowel. Saramaccan, perhaps because it was under no such influence and could go wherever its speakers wanted to take it, weakened the stop consonants by turning a firm tongue-touch to just a flap—*berere, *bululu, *ferere—then reduced the liquids, the /l/s and /r/s, to the point of extinction and thus arrived at the modern forms.

Changes like that make words easier to say quickly, but the downside is that words "fall together," as they say; that is, they become almost indistinguishable from one another. For instance, while "bread" became beee, "belly" became bee. My suspicion is (and I confess I've never actually flown this one past Norval) that tone in Saramaccan is not a West African retention but an innovation designed to distinguish from one another words that Saramaccan sound changes have made too much alike. It can't be coincidence that high tone always falls on the vowel that was there in the original English word, never on the epenthetic vowels that were inserted by pidgin speakers.

So now we can see why Saramaccan developed tone—it was an innovation, rather than an African retention. In Saramaccan, phonological changes unique to that language removed many consonants that had served as syllable boundaries. But since Saramaccan, like most languages (though unlike English), doesn't feature contrastive stress, tone was about the only means left for keeping syllables separate and distinct from one another.

I didn't learn what I've summarized above all at once, but over the years—some of it from Frank Byrne, some from my own reading and talking with colleagues, but some also when Yvonne and I went to Amsterdam to meet Surinam Creole speakers in the flesh.

I was due for another sabbatical, and where better to spend it than Amsterdam, where many Surinamese lived, having headed, like Jamaicans in London, to the capital of the old empire of which their land had once formed part? We took with us a student of mine, Sabine Iatridou.

Sabine, my research assistant, was well qualified for the job. A native of Greece, she'd lived for years in the Netherlands and

spoke Dutch natively, as well as English and French. She's the only
student I ever had who knew more syntax than I did. Eventually I
performed for her the college teacher's ultimate act of self-sacrifice:
I told her not to waste her time doing her dissertation under me but
to apply to MIT. Normally their doctoral program won't accept
graduate students anyone else has taught—they might have
learned things that were not in the True Gospel—but in her case
they made an exception, and she's now tenured faculty there.

I was making up my half-salary by teaching courses at the University of Amsterdam under the aegis of Pieter Muysken, a fellow
creolist, the kind of genial, laissez-faire Dutchman who makes you
wonder how Surinam could possibly have happened. Most of the
Surinamese, he told me, like nonwhite immigrants anywhere, were
poor and underprivileged, and they lived in a working-class district
called Bijlmermeer. He asked me how I proposed to do my research.

"Oh," I said, "you know, the usual. Just hang out in bars and get
talking to people."

He gave me a funny look. "There are no bars in Bijlmermeer."

"You're putting me on," I said—who'd ever heard of a working-
class district without bars? But he was right.

Bijlmermeer isn't actually in Amsterdam, but it's linked to it by
a commuter train line that traverses a couple of miles of flat, gray,
colorless fields—only in the Netherlands can fields be gray and colorless at the same time—stopping at a deserted, skeletal station
that, at first sight, looks like it's in the middle of nowhere. Then
through the enveloping gloom, in the middle distance, you make
out the familiar stark rectangular shapes of your classic housing
project.

And that's exactly what it was—piss-stained, used-condom-
strewn hallways, graffiti-covered staircases, broken, boarded-up
windows, here and there a blackened hole where an apartment
seemed to have been burned out. Block after block it stretched,
lightened only by the occasional forlorn-looking tree, with not
only no bars, but also no restaurants, no stores, no theaters, no
cafés, not a single place where people could meet and talk and try
to have a normal life together. I hear it's been gussied up since, that

it now has Amsterdam's biggest mall and even a community center, but twenty years ago it was like somewhere in Bed-Stuy or the Bronx, but without the street life.

I assumed that the place had been purpose-built as an immigrant ghetto by some fascistic government determined to isolate the starvelings of the earth where they could easily be mown down with machine-gun fire if they ever arose from their slumbers and challenged the regime. I was quite wrong, my Dutch friends informed me. It had been built by a socialistic government, with the very best of intentions. Instead of boozing away their wages, Mr. and Mrs. Immigrant could go quietly home together and listen to Mozart sonatas. Not the government's fault if the frustrated tenants ripped out all the trees for firewood.

I was a little shocked but not, I admit, all that surprised. A progressive never asks people what they want—why should he, when he already knows what's good for them?

One of the things Sabine's and my research focused on was a discovery Frank had made that was unexpected, indeed unprecedented.

We've already met the constructions known as serial verbs, where two or more verbs and their appendages get smooshed together under the same intonation contour; things like saying, instead of "He cut the bread with a knife," *He took knife cut bread.* Now in all Creoles so far described, you could mark tense and/or mood and/or aspect on the first verb in a series but not on any of the others. But Frank claimed to have found a dialect of Saramaccan in which you could mark all the verbs with tense, mood, and aspect, provided you used the same marker for all of them. Indeed some of his informants would accept sentences where a second or third verb was marked but not the first.

Now Frank, ex-Marine that he is, does things by the book; he wasn't likely to be making stuff up, or even (this can happen with inexperienced researchers) leaning on informants to get the answers he wanted. But this was not an answer anyone would have wanted, and to make things worse the Amsterdam Saramaccaners weren't accepting his sentences—you'll see one likely reason why in the next chapter.

So Sabine and I spent (or wasted, depending on how you look at it) a lot of time trying to figure out how serial verbs really worked; currently, there were almost as many analyses as there were researchers. Sabine being Sabine, that meant I had to get force-fed with all the latest convoluted syntactic analyses from the Chomsky bunch. And I've wondered since if I wouldn't have been better off learning to read Dutch and trying to find out more about what happened in Surinam. Ah, well, water under the bridge.

We did try to learn Dutch, Yvonne and I. During our first few weeks in Amsterdam, we went to Dutch class three mornings a week. Dutch is a bitch to learn if your native language is English— there are so many similarities and then suddenly there's a yawning gulf and you're totally lost. Better if you're a Scot. Norval Smith is, and when he first landed at Schiphol airport he exclaimed, "My God, they speak my language!" Because the Dutch exit sign reads *Uitgang*, and in Scots, "to go out" is *gang oot*.

The trouble is, learning Dutch in the Netherlands is, for conversational purposes, a losing game. In a year I met only two Dutch people who couldn't speak English. And most of them speak it fluently, albeit with that quaint, just-a-few-centimeters-off accent; their educational system could sure teach Americans a thing or two.

The crunch came one day when a Dutchman stopped Yvonne in the street and asked her, in Dutch, the way to the post office. By some serendipitous fluke, the topic of that morning's class had been "Going to the Post Office." So Yvonne explained it to him in perfect Dutch, at the end of which he exclaimed, "Ah so! You are English," and proceeded to address her in English for the rest of the conversation.

After that we gave up.

Anyway, serial verbs give us a nice segue to the next chapter, for there we're going to delve into their mysteries and slot in another piece of the puzzle, something else that shows conclusively how substrate theories of Creole genesis can't account for facts that the bioprogram can.

What got me into this next episode were, strangely enough, financial considerations.

Back then, IRS regulations allowed you to shelter $70,000 of income from federal taxes if you stayed out of the country for more than a year. If I went back to Hawaii, I'd be taxed at the normal rate. But if, instead, I took a year's unpaid leave and availed myself of an offer by Robert Chaudenson of a visiting professorship in Aix-en-Provence . . .

No contest. We'd already bought another camper van. In the last throes of a Dutch so-called summer, we loaded it with our worldly goods, hit the autoroute, and headed south.

12

SEYCHELLES AND SERIALS

———

In Aix, city of fountains and plane-tree-shaded boulevards, it was still high summer. The city's northeastern side ends abruptly with a row of what Yeats called "grey eighteenth-century houses" and beyond that is nothing but lush Provençal countryside. In Amsterdam we'd lived over a methadone clinic in a block that was Gestapo headquarters in World War II, but in Aix we rented a *mas*, a marginally modernized eighteenth-century hunting lodge with a walled courtyard in several acres of olive trees in that same countryside a few kilometers northeast of the city. It was owned by a retired opera singer in Marseilles, whose eccentricities would fill this chapter if I'd let them. Our neighbors included a Dutch physicist, the irrepressible *mais-tu-es-complètement-fou* Chaudenson, and a colonel who detested cats. Indeed, eccentrics were everywhere. In the gym where I worked out, one guy did nothing but facial exercises in front of a mirror, while another, forced to attend by his wife, sat glumly on a bench till she came to collect him. We could have written *A Year in Provence*, but for one crippling handicap: we speak French.

As regards Creoles, there were two goals I could pursue in Aix.

Aix is the home of the Centre des Archives D'Outre-Mer ("Overseas"), where most of the records of the French colonies are stored. As you know by now, I'm not an archive man, unless there's some narrowly focused target—the source of the Guyanese

TMA system, or, as here, the numbers of children in slave colonies.

One of the arguments advanced against the bioprogram was that Creoles couldn't have been created by children—there were never enough children in slave colonies to create a new language. Nobody ever suggested a number that might, in principle, have been sufficient. The idea seemed to be that, if there were too few kids, grown-ups would simply ignore them and get on with the job of relexifying their language by swapping most of their African words for European ones. By the time enough kids had grown up to influence the situation, the Creole would be a done deal. Naturally, none of the people who pushed this idea had been to Hawaii and seen parents learning (or oftener, failing to learn) the Creole from their own children.

I and everyone else knew that birthrates in slave colonies were below normal, and that this factor as much as high mortality rates caused the negative growth that characterized all slave populations. But just how low were those rates? According to Claire Lefebvre of the University of Montreal, in Haiti at least they were so low that there simply could not have been enough children to create a Creole. And as Claire had worked for years on Haitian, generously funded by the Canadian government, you'd assume she'd have checked her facts.

Or would she? Never assume, always check.

I checked. There had indeed been several censuses in the early years in Haiti, some local but some islandwide, and there in the archives they all were. At no time in the history of Haiti had the proportion of children in the slave population fallen below 15 percent. Most of the time it was around 25 percent. If that wasn't enough to start a Creole, what was?

But this finding was relatively minor. My main goal was to discover whether there were any serial verb constructions in the Creoles of the Seychelles and Mauritius.

Now, it was almost universally accepted by creolists that there were no serials in these languages. There were several published descriptions of each language, none of which showed any serials, and the only person to suspect there might be was Chris Corne. Walking along a road one night in the island of La Digue, he'd overheard a woman call out:

> Rod diven amene.
> Search wine bring.
> "Fetch some wine!"

Unfortunately he hadn't checked at the time. When he tried this and similar sentences on expatriate Seychellois, they unanimously rejected them. However, he concluded that the situation "clearly needs to be further examined."

Well, I'd further examine it, for an issue of some importance turned on it.

The absence of serial verbs formed a crucial part of the substratist case. On the face of things, there was a beautiful correlation. Caribbean Creoles had lots of serial constructions and a West African substrate; the substrate languages had serial verbs. Indian Ocean Creoles had no serial constructions and an East African and Malagasy substrate; the substrate languages had no serial verbs. Consequently, the West African substrate must cause the presence of serials in the Caribbean, while the absence of a West African substrate led to the absence of serials in the Indian Ocean.

Without that correlation a sizable chunk of the substratist case would collapse.

But what exactly are serial verb constructions, anyway?

I've mentioned them several times in passing, but we need to know a little more about them here. The first and most important thing is that they're a pretheoretical category. That simply means they're one of the many ill-defined notions, like "passive voice," "subjunctive," "adverbial clause," and so on, that were used in the study of language before linguistics tried to turn that study into something more scientific. Linguists still use some of these terms, because they're convenient when you want to refer to a general area rather than a precise one, but we all are, or should be, very cautious in the way we use them. Since these terms existed before there was anything you could call a theory of grammar, they don't fit well into any systematic analysis of language.

With this caveat let's say that for anything to be a serial construction, it has to be a sentence with at least two verbs, neither of which is clearly subordinated to the other but which are not linked by a conjunction ("and," "or," "but" . . .); it should be uttered under a single intonation contour with no kind of pause anywhere. All the verbs should have the same subject, and until the events described in this chapter, everyone would have said that once that subject has been stated, it can't be repeated, no matter how many verbs the construction may have. Certainly, if the first or any other verb has an object, that definitely can't be repeated—it's "understood," as traditional grammars used to say, meaning we know what it is even if we don't see it or hear it. For instance if I say in Saramaccan:

Mi suti Amba kii.
I shoot Amba kill.

it's clear that I killed Amba as well as shot him and that it was I who did it. Curiously, English can do something similar the other way around—instead of saying "I shot Amba and killed him," I can say "I shot and killed Amba," hiding the first object, not the second, but that's not a serial (because of the conjunction) and indeed serials are quite foreign to the way English does things.

What really fascinated me about serials were precisely these unstated subjects and objects, or "empty categories" as linguists call them. I already knew that "empty categories" posed the biggest challenge to those who still thought children "learned" language the way they learned to play checkers or do their times tables. How could you learn a "nothing"? And if you couldn't learn one, how could you invent one? And what would guarantee that your "nothings" would always come in the same places, with the same meanings, whether what you were creating was Saramaccan, or Haitian, or—as I'd soon find out—the Creoles of the Indian Ocean?

In Aix there is a large community of immigrants from Mauritius. They live on the south side of the city, where there are huge barrack blocks of public housing, not quite as dire as Bijlmermeer but just as soulless. I had written up a bunch of hypothetical sentences, sentences with Mauritian words but modeled on Saramaccan serial structures, and I trudged from apartment to apartment, interviewing Mauritian expatriates and asking them if these sentences were possible in their language.

No, they all said unanimously. Serial verb constructions were definitely ungrammatical.

Fortunately, in the department at Aix there were two young and very charming native speakers of Mauritian Creole, Daniel Veronique and Didier de Robillard, so I tried my sentences on them. Daniel rejected most of them, was dubious about the others. But for Didier, several of them were just fine.

At first sight this didn't make sense. Since serial verbs are about as far from French as you can get, you would expect, if they were accepted at all, they would be accepted by working-class speakers, people who were the least influenced by French. But Daniel came from a modest middle-class background, while Didier was a *grand blanc*, son of a white plantation owner (whites in Mauritius are divided into two classes, "big whites" and "little whites"). How come a member of the highest class had the more proletarian grammar?

Then the penny dropped.

Who does the son of the plantation owner play with? The sons of plantation workers, of course—out in the country, there's no one else to play with. While Daniel was attending an urban school with kids of his own class, Didier was growing up bilingual, speaking perfect French at home, rock-bottom Morisyen (the people's own name for Mauritian Creole) in the street.

I knew then I had to go to the Indian Ocean.

We were actually happy to be leaving Aix in midwinter. People think Provence has a Mediterranean climate, which is true if you happen to live within five miles of the Mediterranean. Elsewhere, winters are bleak and rainy, and our main means of heating was a coal fire that filled the place with smoke, despite the hole that our landlady personally drove through the three-foot-thick wall of the kitchen.

We took off on New Year's Eve. We saw 1988 in at Djibouti airport, where we were corralled in a dark little hall under the menacing gaze of gun-toting soldiers while the plane refueled. Three hours later, back on board, a steward shook me awake and thrust a glass of champagne into my hand.

"Eet eez ze New Year in Paris," he explained.

Those French! If it didn't happen in Paris, it didn't happen.

Mauritius and the Seychelles have very similar histories. Both were settled and developed by the French in the eighteenth century; both were taken by the British in the Napoleonic Wars, and remained British colonies until they became independent in 1968 and 1976 respectively. In both, the British presence was minimal and left few traces—the Creole remained clearly affiliated with French, and not many English words got into it. And yet as countries they were strikingly different.

In the Seychelles, with its dozens of tiny islands, sugar was never a big deal; in Mauritius it was everything. Thus, when slavery ended, Mauritius, like Guyana and Trinidad and Fiji, imported large numbers of indentured laborers from India to keep the plantations going; the Seychelles didn't. In consequence, Indians now outnumber those of African descent (known locally as "Creoles") and all other races combined.

Mauritius is anarchic. When we rented a house by the beach for a month, we asked our landlord what day the garbage was picked up. He looked at us in bewilderment. "There's no garbage collection."

"Well, what do we do with our garbage?"

"Oh, just throw it over the fence."

There appeared to be no emission controls, so driving behind grossly overloaded trucks on the winding hilly roads was like a cross between a nineteenth-century London fog and a World War I gas attack. There were no controls, or no enforcement of them, on dynamite fishing, so when we swam off our beach, all we saw was a gray, blasted underseascape, where the only living things were giant sea urchins and huge, revolting worms. There were, however, private controls; hotels could privatize large sections of beach and keep out anyone who wasn't a guest. To one small island with public as well as private beaches, the hotel ran the only boat service, and its security guards ransacked the bags of passengers, confiscating any food they found, to ensure that if you ate at all you ate in a hotel facility.

Ah well, free enterprise in action.

On the plus side, Mauritius was fun. The people were outgoing; there were lots of parties. The Seychelles were not as much fun. The people there are polite but reserved, a bit dour, even. The government, while we were there, was a relatively benign socialist dictatorship. It kept its oceans pure, and consequently had some of the best snorkeling we'd seen anywhere. It kept its buildings small and discreet; you couldn't build anything taller than a palm tree. All beaches were public, as for that matter were the hotels; we met a tourist family staying in some cheapo boardinghouse who'd walked into the best hotel, spread their mats by the pool and eaten their picnic lunch right there without anyone bothering them.

In the Seychelles, I took a Seselwa teacher (Seselwa is the locals' own name for their language); he was the twelve-year-old son of a sous-chef and a chambermaid, and he was good. I also made the acquaintance of Marcel Rosalie, assistant director of the National Archives of the Seychelles, and it was he who introduced me to the oral histories.

These were recordings, made several years before, of Seychelles residents in their seventies and up telling their life histories in Seselwa. All the recordings were transcribed, so I read along with the tapes until the following sentence leapt out at me:

Zot pran balye koko bat Kazer.
They take broom coconut beat Kaiser.
"They beat the Kaiser with a coconut broom."

Elina Charles, seventy-four, was describing a bizarre scene she had witnessed in her childhood. At the start of World War I, the British high commissioner came down to the beach where a straw

effigy of the German Kaiser Wilhelm had been erected. After a pa-
triotic speech, the commissioner and his aides ritually beat Kaiser
Wilhelm with the aforesaid broom and then set fire to him.

This sentence was, of course, an instrumental serial, one of a
type common in the Caribbean. I ran the tape over and over, to
check that the transcriber hadn't missed or altered anything (with
the best will in the world, this is easy to do when transcribing
recorded speech) and if the sentence had no internal pause, however slight, and fell under a single intonation contour. Sure
enough, right words, no pause, and a contour that rose in pitch on
the second word and declined gracefully thereafter. I knew right
away I'd hit pay dirt—there's no feeling quite like it.

Sure enough, I found many more serial constructions in Mme.
Charles's and others' oral histories. In addition to instrumentals,
there were benefactive serials like:

Mon frer tir larzan donn mwa.
My brother pull money give me.
"My brother withdrew money for me."

There were serials of motion, like

Prezan seren i tonbe vini.
Then weaverbird TNS fall come.
"Then the weaverbirds descended (on the rice crop)."

There were "dual-action" serials, where you have first to take hold
of something before you can do something to it:

Li pran sa de ti lisyen tuye.
He take the two small dog kill.
"He killed the two little dogs."

What's significant here is that you can't repeat the object, even as
a pronoun; you can't say:

*Li pran sa de ti lisyen tuy zot.
"He took the two little dogs [and] killed them."

(Note that verbs lose their final *e* when an overt object directly follows them.) There were, more rarely, several serial verbs strung together, incorporating more than one type:

Lulu n pran papa n ale n manze.
Wolf ASP take daddy ASP go ASP eat.
"Wolf's gone and eaten daddy!"

Or:

Zot amene vin zet isi donn bann blan isi.
They bring come put here give PL white here.
"They brought [the slaves] here for the whites."

In fact, the range of types was almost as wide as in the "deepest" among the Caribbean Creoles, and wider than in several "shallower" ones.

Now I didn't have to rely on my made-up sentences; I could test informants on sentences actually uttered by native speakers of Seselwa.

The results were intriguing. In every case, the lower the socioeconomic status of my informants, the likelier they were to accept the sentences. But this was skewed by the fact that, if all the verbs were tensed, middle-class informants would accept just about anything—anything but the last of the sentences above, which nobody accepted, period.

Well, that sentence had been produced by a woman of ninety-six, so it represented a century-old grammar. Just as Creoles get deeper as you go down the classes, they also get deeper as you go back in time.

Or if you're a cynic, you could say, "Oh well, she was past it." I don't think so. The content of her tape showed she had all her wits about her.

Anyway, it seemed I'd been right in thinking that, despite a population of barely sixty thousand, the Seychelles had two class dialects. When I put this idea to Marcel Rosalie, he nodded as if I'd just found out something everyone knew. He himself was from La Digue, where Chris Corne had heard his solitary serial, and La

Digue, being a small outer island, housed people poorer and less
privileged than those of the main island, Mahe. But kids had to go
to Mahe if they wanted to go to high school. "And there," Marcel
said, "they used to get beaten for speaking bad French. Nowadays
they get beaten for speaking bad Creole."

As the old Cockney song has it,

> It's the sime the 'ole world over,
> It's the poor wot gets the blame.

What had happened was this. In order to demonstrate its independence from the West, the government had decided to teach
Creole (and teach in Creole) alongside the former official languages, English and French. But Seselwa, like Creoles everywhere
(and like every other language, if it comes to that) is full of variation. Now if you're going to teach something, you have to have a
fixed standard form for it, or so they tell me. (At all costs, you must
stop the slobs from saying "ain't"!) So a committee was formed to
determine what was the right kind of Creole, and naturally this
committee, like committees everywhere, was made up of educated
middle-class people. So the standard form of Seselwa was fixed, not
as the deepest form of the Creole, as it would have been if I'd been
on the committee, but as the kind that middle-class people spoke.

But one difference between middle- and working-class varieties
did not, as is usually the case, come from their relative distance
from the metropolitan language. It turned on whether or not you
had to put overt tense markers in serial constructions (as a rough
generalization—there were always exceptions—middle-class speakers did, working-class ones didn't). And these tensed serials shed
light on something that had been bothering me for quite a while.

Remember how Frank Byrne found a variety of Saramaccan
with tensed serials, how skeptical everyone had been (including
even me), and how expatriates in Amsterdam had rejected them?
But there was nothing in universal grammar that dictated whether
subordinate clauses should be finite, nonfinite, or both. It was one
of the options the bioprogram left open, so there was nothing to
stop serial verbs from being all finite, or all nonfinite, or a bit of

each. But expatriates, folk out of touch with their home language and all its natural variation, seem to have a narrower, less permissive concept of its grammar, whether they lived in Amsterdam or Aix. And especially in Aix, where they were surrounded by French speakers to whom a serial construction was as exotic as . . . I almost said a dish of snails; okay, as a hamburger.

We stayed a month on Mahe and another month in Mauritius, where I confirmed that, at least as far as serial verbs were concerned, Mauritius and the Seychelles were no different. Our last month was spent mostly in La Digue.

La Digue could be reached only by boat, two hours of wrenching nausea as the little tub pitched in the huge Indian Ocean rollers. Now it has nine hotels, but then it had only one, and the hotel station wagon was one of its four motor vehicles. The island is weirdly beautiful, its granite rocks eroded into grotesque shapes, its beaches blinding white. It's inhabited by giant 'bats, giant turtles, and sorcerers. The turtles have backs as big as dining tables; you can ride them, if you don't mind the glacial pace. The bats are fruit bats, not vampires, but big enough to look scary when you first see one crossing a full moon. The most notorious of the sorcerers became my informant. (I didn't find that out until I'd started working with him.) He was a charming old guy, but he could raise goose bumps when he told you about the things that moved by night along the *grande route*—the main road in La Digue, no more than a sandy cart track a few feet wide—whose presence you could hear and feel but never actually see.

Visiting with some of his friends one afternoon, I found something else that wasn't supposed to happen outside the Caribbean— verb-fronting, a.k.a. "predicate clefting."

English is challenged when it comes to emphasizing a verb. You must either put heavy stress on it ("I TOLD you she was coming") or use some clumsy periphrasis ("Told you she was coming, that's what I did") that involves dragging the whole predicate along after the verb. But all around the Caribbean there's this neat little construction that just moves a copy of the verb to the beginning of the sentence:

A tell me tell you se shi a come.

Another piece of the West African heritage, supposedly, but here it was in La Digue:

Li mon li en kantite me ekri mon pa ekri.
Read I read in quantity but write I not write.
"I can *read* a lot but I can't *write!*"

And it came out beautifully, just like every linguist hopes for—not elicited by dogged questioning, which always makes you worry a little that you might have pushed the speaker too hard, but in the natural flow of spontaneous conversation.

So where could verb-fronting and serials come from?

A serious substratist might have argued that they just might have come from West Africa after all.

In the first few years in Mauritius, according to Philip Baker, four shiploads of slaves from West Africa made the long and difficult voyage. Between 1729 and 1735, these slaves amounted to between one-third and one-half of the total slave population. Could not these slaves have placed their stamp on the languages that followed (for Seselwa, starting some forty years after Morisyen, clearly began as an offshoot of it)?

Well, no. In the first place, we need to get a little more specific about where in Africa serial constructions are found. They're found, not throughout West Africa, but mostly among the Kwa languages, which stretch roughly from Ghana to Nigeria. But of the four shipments, only one was from the Kwa-speaking port of Juda; the others were all from Goree, in Guinea, where the local languages don't have serial constructions.

For a few months in 1729–30, when the total slave population was less than five hundred, slaves from Juda represented over a third of the population, a proportion that shrank to just over 10 percent by 1735. Thereafter, they were lost in the masses that came in as soon as the expansion phase began.

In other parts of the Creole world, substratists based their argument on the large number of Kwa speakers in the population. Haitian, for example, was claimed to have close to an absolute majority of Kwa speakers. It would be hard to argue that a majority in one place and a tiny minority in another would have identical linguistic effects (unless you believe in magic). And even if anyone did argue it, they would have to contend with the unlikelihood that a stable Creole could be formed in less than the first decade of a colony's development, and the equal unlikelihood that any language formed so early could have survived the expansion phase.

So if we can rule out substrate influence, what's left? Only the bioprogram, the universal plan for constructing a language that every normal child in the world is born with.

As you might guess, my findings, when published in the *Journal of Pidgin and Creole Languages*, did not go unchallenged.

Pieter Seuren, of the University of Nijmegen in the Netherlands, interviewed a Seychellois couple that had lived in Holland for the previous three years "as political refugees." That right away stamped them as conservatives, and since both had also been teachers in the Seychelles, they were clearly at risk for SPS (severe prescriptivism syndrome), an affliction that causes its victims to pour scorn on any "nonstandard" (i.e. not utterly formal) kind of language.

Well, to no one's surprise, they unanimously rejected all the sentences I had cited. They assumed those sentences were meant to be coordinated, but with the conjunctions left out, and they obligingly supplied them:

Lulu n pran papa n ale e n manze.
Wolf ASP take daddy ASP go and ASP eat.
"Wolf has taken daddy, gone, and eaten him."

Note how stilted and implausible this sounds alongside "Wolf's gone and eaten daddy!"

The original form of the sentence met another major criterion for serial constructions, that is, there was no repetition of the object *papa* after *manze*—not even a pronoun. In any true serial construction, no object noun can appear overtly more than once. You can't refer to it via a pronoun even if it's the logical object of a subsequent verb in the construction. Conversely, in a conjoined (coordinate) sentence, you can't leave objects out, even though you can leave subjects out (think, "*I saw Bill and spoke to"). So if you insert or omit the relevant pronoun (*li*, "him") in the wrong places you can get the two following very bad sentences:

> *Lulu n pran papa n ale n manz li. (bad serial)
> *Lulu n pran papa n ale e n manze. (bad conjunction)

Yet Seuren's informants "repaired" another sentence by adding both a conjunction and a pronoun:

> I pran sa de ti lisyen e tuy zot.
> "He took the two little dogs and killed them."

And of course once you've converted a serial into a conjoined sentence, it's okay to include pronouns—but not before.

In my reply I pointed out that my original sentences showed all the characteristics of what, when they occurred in the Caribbean, had for several decades been unquestioningly accepted as serial verb constructions. Indeed, many sentences in Seselwa could be translated almost literally, word by word, into similar sentences in the most radical of Creoles, Saramaccan:

> Zot pran balye bat li. (Seselwa)
> De tei basoo fon en. (Saramaccan)
> They take broom beat him. (both)
> "They beat him with a broom." (both)

The title of my reply was, "If it quacks like a duck . . ."

Seuren, though, was far from alone. Not surprisingly, other critics were, like Seuren, people who'd previously worked on one or other of the Indian Ocean Creoles, and may well have been upset that

I'd discovered things they'd missed. The most serious contender was Chris Corne, who wrote a paper with two of his students; both their names began with "C" too, so I was able to refer to them, without irony, as C3.

C3 also had their expatriate informants, three persons who they claimed were "basilectal" speakers (speakers of the most different-from-French variety) belonging to "the urban working class." Hardly typical members, insofar as they were pursuing tertiary education in a first-world country (New Zealand), and perhaps not wholly unbiased judges, insofar as they'd been staying in Chris's home for two years, but let that pass; I'd never disguised the fact that there were Seychellois who found many if not all serial constructions ungrammatical.

C3 repeated the claim that serials were really conjoined sentences without overt conjunctions. They claimed that the sentences without conjunctions were "in free variation" with the sentences that had them.

Now "free variation" is a technical term with a very precise meaning. It means that two forms can be exchanged in any conceivable context with no change in meaning. It's hardly ever used except in referring to speech sounds. For example, the /nch/ in "French" or "branch" can be uttered as /nsh/ or /nch/ in the phrases "French dressing," "Bourbon and branch," "French letter," "branch out," or any other context, so /sh/ and /ch/ are in "free variation" between /n/ and a word break. But pairs of sentences had never previously been described as being in free variation with one another; no criteria were offered by which you could determine this condition, and it wasn't even clear what, in the case of sentences, "free variation" would mean.

But C3 claimed that what I called serials were actually "derived" from conjoined sentences. Again, "derived" is a technical term with a very precise meaning. Nobody ever, even in the wild and woolly early days of generative grammar, "derived" one surface sentence from another surface sentence. The technical meaning of "derive" is to construct a precise, principled relationship between a surface sentence (anything you might speak or write) and an abstract formal structure (a labeled syntactic tree) that is hypothesized as underlying that sentence.

I began my reply by pointing out that none of the writers who had declared Seselwa serials to be conjunctions had taken a second look at the Caribbean Creoles to see if perhaps they too were conjunctions. After all, on the surface at least the constructions were identical, so how could you be sure that everything hitherto described as a serial wasn't really a conjunction, unless you reexamined them with at least as much care as my critics had taken with Seselwa serials? I had my tongue in my cheek, naturally, but it was still a valid point.

Then I laid out the differences between serial constructions and conjoined sentences. In addition to those I've mentioned so far, there are two big ones. The first is that in conjoined sentences the verb can change tense from one conjunct to another without any restriction whatsoever:

Mon ti dir sa, mon pe dir li otrefwa e mon ava dir li tuzur.
I TNS say that, I ASP say it again and I MOD say it
  always.
"I said that, I'm saying it again, and I'll always say it."

However, this is impossible in Seselwa serials:

*Lulu ti pran papa n ale pe manze.
Wolf TNS take daddy ASP go ASP eat.

This would mean, if you could say it, "Wolf had taken daddy, has gone and is eating (him)." Either all markers of tense, mood, or aspect in the sentence must be the same, or no markers can appear.

While the first difference has to do with changing tense, the second has to do with changing subjects. In conjoined sentences, you can do this freely:

Li n al lakaz e zot n salye li.
He ASP go house and they ASP greet him.
"He went to the house and they greeted him."

But you can't change subjects in serial sentences.

Indeed, until the discovery of tensed serials in Seselwa and

Morisyen, people would have said that serials couldn't even have a second overt subject. They thought that verbs subsequent to the subject could only have an empty or "implicit" subject. That's simply because (except for Frank Byrne's Saramaccan examples) all the serial constructions hitherto analyzed had been nonfinite—they couldn't take a tensed verb.

It's easy to show that the differences between finite and nonfinite sentences extend beyond Seselwa, beyond serials (whether there or in the Caribbean), indeed across all languages. You can say:

I expected that I would see you. (finite)

Or:

I expected to see you. (nonfinite)

But not

*I expected I to see you. (nonfinite)

The reason serials in other Creoles did not repeat the same subject was not because they were serials but because they were nonfinite. Universal grammar predicts that if a sentence is finite (has a tensed verb), it can, in every case (and must, as in most English sentences) overtly express its subject.

The important thing about serials is that they can have only one subject. Whether, after its first occurrence, that subject can be repeated overtly or must be represented by an empty category is simply a function of whether the sentence is tensed or not. (There's a technical explanation for this, involving what are called "governed" and "ungoverned" positions; anyone who really wants to know about that can easily follow it up in the literature.) So it's okay to say:

Zot ti pran balye koko zot ti bat Kazer.

just as it's okay to say:

Li ti pran balye koko e zot ti bat Kazer.

("He took a coconut broom and they beat the Kaiser") but it's definitely not okay to say:

*Li ti pran balye koko zot ti bat Kazer.

without the conjunction *e* between *koko* and *zot*.

Alas, Chris was never able to respond to my arguments. He drove his car into the back of a truck on a lonely New Zealand highway, joining the all-too-long list of my creolist colleagues who met untimely deaths.

So what does this all boil down to?

It boils down to the simple fact that one can, if one insists, claim that Seselwa and Morisyen have a special type of conjoined sentence that just happens to have all the properties that serial verb constructions have in other Creoles but none of the properties that conjoined sentences have anywhere. There's only one reason why anyone would even want to make such a claim, and that's to preserve at whatever cost the good old correlation:

- Creoles with Kwa substrates have serial constructions.
- Creoles without Kwa substrates have no serial constructions.

However, there can be no doubt whatsoever that Seselwa and Morisyen have exactly the same kinds of serial constructions that Caribbean Creoles do, so the correlation no longer holds.

If a particular construction is present in two languages, one of which has that construction in its substrate while the other doesn't, it would be absurd to say that this construction comes from the substrate in one case and from a universal biological program for language in the other. It must surely come from the bioprogram in both cases. The fact that one of the two substrates happens to have that same construction is simply coincidental—which does not, of course, rule out the possibility that its presence in the substrate may have a reinforcing effect in the Creole.

The year after my first article on Seselwa, my book *Language and Species* came out. After that, the main thrust of my research turned away from the bastard tongues that, for more than two decades, had been central to my work and instead focused on the original evolution of language. The challenge was just too great to resist. Creoles, however much they could tell us about the power of language re-creation that all humans shared, could not tell us how language was first created. They could point out directions and they did; they took me a long way on my new quest, but they couldn't take me all the way.

The quest for the original source of human language is the topic of my next book, so I'll say no more about language evolution here. In Creoles, I still had one last thing to explore, and that was right where I lived and worked, in Hawaii.

13

HAWAII'S HIDDEN HISTORY

History's mostly written by white folk. It's not so much that they're racist as it is that they naturally tend to see things through the spectacles of their own culture, and it requires a constant effort to get past this.

The history of language is no exception. Accordingly, when people think about pidgins they immediately think of Pidgin English, Pidgin French, Pidgin of some European language or other. The idea of the big white guy on top, and all the little nonwhite guys under him struggling to cope with the sophisticated complexities of his language, is so firmly fixed in our minds that the idea of a pidgin based on a language of nonwhites, clumsily and haltingly spoken by members of the master race, seems almost inconceivable.

That's one reason why, throughout Hawaii's history, Pidgin Hawaiian was Hawaii's best-kept secret. It didn't fit the prevailing picture, scholarly as well as popular, of how people with different skins were supposed to behave linguistically when they were brought together. Remember John Reinecke, whose version of Hawaii's linguistic history I described in Chapter 6. His "hapa-haole" had an admixture of Hawaiian words, but it was basically a local form of Pidgin English, and he along with everyone else assumed that this kind of language was what Hawaiians, and later the immigrant peoples, spoke to haoles and to one another.

People conveniently forgot that the social dynamic of Hawaii, especially before sugar came along, was nothing like the social dynamic of European colonies. Hawaii was an independent kingdom and Europeans were there on sufferance. And when you enter somebody else's country, you don't get far if you try to make them talk your language. You have to try to speak theirs.

Plus there were more concrete clues. Don't forget that Hawaii became literate very early on. Newspapers and books written in Hawaiian go far back into the nineteenth century. And in one of these books, published in 1854, the author complained that "there has long prevailed, between natives and foreigners, a corrupted tongue, which the former use only to the latter, but never among themselves." But then, not many people can read Hawaiian.

And do you remember the guy who thought Pidgin English was real English? ("Wassamatta dis *haole*? He no can speak *haole*!") Well, as early as 1810 there was an Englishman called Archibald Campbell who lived in Hawaii for at least a year, but still thought Pidgin Hawaiian was real Hawaiian, and even published it as such. Here's one sample:

CAMPBELL: Eree te motoo mukee-mukee tooai nooee te poa.
              chief the ship like/want buy many the pig.
HAWAIIAN: Ua makemake ke ali'i o ka moku e ku'ai i na
              pua'a he nui.
              TNS like/want the chief of the ship to buy CM
              the-pl. pig a many. (CM = case marker)
              "The captain wishes to purchase a great many
              pigs."

Forget the differences in spelling, and the *t/k* and *l/r* substitutions that may simply reflect the difference between the Hawaiian of today and that of two centuries ago. What matters is that almost all grammatical words have been stripped off—tense markers, case markers, prepositions, and indefinite articles—and that the word order has been radically changed. Hawaiian is a VSO language, but Pidgin Hawaiian is SVO like almost all pidgins that have any kind of prevailing word order.

I'd suspected from my first year in Hawaii that Hawaiian had played a much larger part in Hawaii's history than had been supposed, but my reluctance to dive into the stacks ("Library research? Our students will do that for us!") had prevented me from following up. It was indeed a student of mine, Bill Wilson, who discovered the first solid source.

Everyone knows the story of how leprosy was brought to Hawaii by Chinese immigrants and how Father Damien selflessly sacrificed his life to care for lepers in the colony on Molokai. Not everyone knows that you didn't get a choice about going there; if you caught leprosy, the police took you. And still fewer people know that some Hawaiians resisted with armed force.

In the 1890s, the sheriff of Waimea, in the island of Kauai, was a German called Luis Stolz. Stolz tried to arrest a Hawaiian leper, Kaluaiko'olau, and Kaluaiko'olau shot and killed him, then fled into the mountains, where he evaded capture until his death. A few years later, a part-Hawaiian called John Sheldon wrote a novel about him in Hawaiian, and in reading it Bill Wilson quickly noticed that conversations in which Stolz took part were written in a quite different kind of Hawaiian from the rest of the book, a kind with all the features I pointed out in the Campbell extract above.

Bill also found old people on three different islands who remembered hearing Pidgin Hawaiian spoken, and what they described—particularly the mixing of languages—was strikingly similar to what I'd observed in the last surviving speakers of Pidgin English; there was an old Chinese cook, for instance, whose output was "one Hawaiian word and the rest Chinese." Again, all the features these people remembered matched those in Campbell's memoir and Sheldon's novel. Bill's final coup was to discover what I'd never expected to find—probably the last surviving speaker of Pidgin Hawaiian.

Tomas Quihano arrived from the Philippines in 1923, married a Hawaiian, and lived in an area of the Big Island that had a substantial proportion of Hawaiians. Again he showed all the features noted so far. Here are some examples:

PIDGIN: Wau no ku'ai kela kapiki.
I no sell that cabbage.

HAWAIIAN: 'A'ole au e ku'ai aku i ke kapiki.
Not I TNS sell thither CM the cabbage.
"I won't sell the cabbage."
PIDGIN: Aole makana kela.
Not gift that.
HAWAIIAN: 'A'ole ha'awi aku i kela.
Not give thither CM that.
"Don't give that away."

Three things are worth noting here. First is the use of "that" instead of a definite article; we've seen how Creoles often use "this" or "that" to make articles, and Tomas's sentence suggests this choice may be made at the pidgin stage. The second is the way Pidgin Hawaiian often selects the "wrong" Hawaiian word. *Makana* is a noun meaning "gift," but it's chosen instead of *ha'awi*, "to give," probably because the latter is more difficult to pronounce (the apostrophe indicates a glottal stop, unknown in most immigrant languages and in English outside of London's East End). Again this shows pidgin roots for a common Creole feature, the turning of nouns into verbs (remember Caribbean *teef* for "steal"). The third is the "no" inserted in the first example instead of the Hawaiian negative *'a'ole*. All pidgins incorporate words from diverse languages; Pidgin Hawaiian was no exception.

So we had a perfect fit between historical records, personal recollections, and a live speaker. What we didn't know, what we couldn't know without a far longer and deeper dive into history, was just how widespread, in its heyday, Pidgin Hawaiian had been.

In the early nineties I was teaching an undergraduate course on language in Hawaii, and of course I included a section on Pidgin Hawaiian. The two brightest students in the class wrote term papers on it that turned up stuff I hadn't known about. One had interests elsewhere, but the other, Sarah Roberts, was ready to pick it up and run with it. Oprah Winfrey says if you wish for something hard enough, the law of attraction will bring it to you. I'm not too sure about that, but in one case at least it worked—it had finally brought me my person with *Sitzfleisch*.

I was so impressed by the stream of data that Sarah kept churning out that I felt the project should be put on a more formal footing—one that would incidentally provide support for her through her postgraduate career. So I turned once again to the National Science Foundation and wrote up a proposal for a study of the use of non-European languages, in particular Hawaiian, as contact languages, not just in Hawaii but in the rest of the Pacific.

The Pacific end of it never really got off the ground, in part because the Hawaii stream became a torrent. The Reinecke-Tsuzaki bibliography I mentioned in Chapter 6 had had just three pre-1900 items, all of them simply comments on the language situation, with no citations of actual speech. But in two or three years Sarah collected over a thousand citations from this period, most of which contained what were, or were claimed to have been, actual words spoken in Pidgin English or Pidgin Hawaiian or some mixture of English and Hawaiian words.

How far can we trust such citations, given that untrained observers with cultural blinkers are recording from memory whatever they thought they heard?

The answer is, quite a long way. Without a tape recorder, naïve observers, people with no preformed ideas about language, are at least as likely to give you what was actually said as people who have been trained in what to expect. Impressionistic spelling seldom leaves doubts about what the sounds were. But the best testimony comes from sheer bulk.

If citations mutually support and reinforce one another, if they are consistent with one another in their sounds, words, and grammatical (or ungrammatical) structures, then you can be pretty sure they are accurate. Some will surely be faked for comic effect, but these will stand out from the rest. And there's no way you could have a conspiracy of hundreds of strangers spread out over more than a century.

In one way, though, cultural blinkers worked with stunning effect.

It soon became obvious why people had thought that the dominant contact language in early Hawaii was some kind of English. The citations from English sources almost all consisted of English words, occasionally with a few words of Hawaiian thrown in.

But when we turned to the Hawaiian sources, there was an equal imbalance; here Hawaiian expressions predominated, and English was the rarity. Obviously people were recording only what they best understood, and ignoring the rest. And though we did not find in either the Hawaiian or the English sources sentences that were predominantly Japanese or Chinese or Portuguese, when we got to the few newspapers published in these languages (yes, newspapers in at least five languages were published in Hawaii, which had the first literate sugar workers in history) a handful of these turned up as well.

An anonymous reviewer of my proposal had assumed that we'd find most of our data in the university's Hamilton Library, which has in its Hawaiian section what is almost certainly the world's largest collection of works on the islands. He (or she) was wrong. Sarah found it in court records.

Hawaii's European-style system of justice had been set up long before the demise of the free Hawaiian state. Records went back to the mid-nineteenth century, a little patchy in the first few years, quickly becoming more copious. And nobody before Sarah had thought of looking at court records, in Hawaii or anywhere else, so this was a vast and virgin territory.

Court records beat other sources in at least two very important ways.

In the first place, it's essential in court proceedings to record accurately any remarks relevant to the case, whether uttered at the scene or during police investigation. Suppose there was a dispute among witnesses as to whether the accused had said *me hakaka you* or *me hanamake you*. If it was the first, meaning "I fight you," the case is at worst one of assault; if the second, meaning "I kill you" (literally "I make you dead"), the charge could be attempted murder. So exact words must be given, preferably in whatever language, or mix of language, was actually used. (Sometimes interpreters had to be used, but this arrangement was always made clear in the records.) Often the official report includes extensive questioning of witnesses to determine just how much of which languages they could actually speak or understand; results of such questioning provide us with an invaluable picture of the very limited linguistic resources that many witnesses possessed.

In the second place, court records are neutral. They're not biased in the direction of English or Hawaiían or any other language. They're not constrained, as casual observers are, by their own linguistic preconceptions. Thus it's possible, from an examination of court records, to determine what was the most frequently used form of communication. While these records yielded many more examples of mixed English and Hawaiian than the Hawaiian or English sources had, the overall balance was quite clear: up until 1890 in Honolulu, and later in many country districts, Pidgin Hawaiian was spoken much more frequently than Pidgin English.

In conversations that included native speakers of English, Pidgin English was the likeliest medium for immigrants to use. But in conversations with native Hawaiians, or in conversations between people whose native language was neither English nor Hawaiian, Hawaiian was almost always used. And this was just what common sense, as opposed to linguistic stereotypes, would have predicted: there were far more Hawaiian speakers than English speakers, so most immigrants interacted with Hawaiians far more than they did with English or Americans.

From court records, newspapers, books, and unpublished manuscripts, Sarah built a rich picture of the use of Pidgin Hawaiian.

In 1791, an American on board a ship was warned by a Hawaiian about a treacherous chief:

Enoo, nooe nooe poo, make kanaka.
Bad many many gun kill men.
"He's bad, he has many guns [to] kill people [with]."

In the same year, several decades ahead of the first Portuguese immigrant, the Portuguese word *pequenino*, "very small," was incorporated into Pidgin Hawaii in the form *pikinini*. How it got there nobody knows; it couldn't have come from Caribbean Creole *pikni* or American "piccaninny" because both of these mean "child," whereas in Hawaii it meant just "small." Portuguese *sabe*, "know," arrived around the same time, and as mysteriously.

In 1818, another foreigner, the German Adelbert von Chamisso, mistook Pidgin Hawaiian for real Hawaiian. "The language of the Sandwich Isles [the first European name for Hawaii] really did seem much more childish to us . . . We have discovered only two pronouns in it . . . and only two adverbs for determining the time of an action."

In 1835, Pidgin Hawaiian turned up in, of all places, San Diego, and was recorded by Richard Henry Dana in *Two Years Before the Mast*, where he reported hearing, in a conversation with the Hawaiian sailor Mr. Manini, the phrase *Maikai, hana hana nui!* ("Good, work plenty").

In 1856, a clergyman reported overhearing "Canton men" and "Amoy men"—speakers of mutually incomprehensible Chinese dialects—talking to one another in some kind of Hawaiian.

In 1881, a doctor vaccinating children in a rural area was hidden by Hawaiians from a group of armed Portuguese who were pursuing him because they hadn't given him permission to stick needles in their kids. During this time he heard the Portuguese and Hawaiians "in animated discussion." This and a number of similar cases (such as a Portuguese policeman accusing one Chinese man of selling liquor to another—*Oe kuai lama hela pake?*, "You sell liquor that Chinaman?") flatly contradict the widespread belief that the Portuguese used only some form of English as a contact language.

By 1887, many people in Hawaii were speaking a pidgin that mixed Hawaiian and English words indiscriminately:

Mi ko kaonu polo Kukuihale, kaukau bia, mi nuinui sahio.
,Me go town large Kukuihale, drink beer, me plenty-plenty
    drunk.·
"I went to the big town Kukuihale, drank beer, and got
    very drunk."

In 1892 a Japanese laborer, Tokake Jinju, was beaten by a haole foreman, Henry Wramp, and died of his injuries. Wramp said to Jinju, *Pehea oe moloa? Wikiwiki!* ("Why you lazy? Quick!") before knocking him down and kicking him (according to one witness) "in the scrotum and left side." Jinju lay down and said, *Pilikia opu*

("Trouble stomach"). A German plantation owner, Otto Isenberg, came and asked him, *Pehea pilikia?* ("Where trouble?"—*pehea* could mean both "where?" and "why?"). Jinju answered, *Eha opu* ("Pain stomach").

By this time, pidgin had been reduced to a word-salad that combined words from a half-dozen languages. It became a macaronic pidgin, although I believe that to a greater or lesser extent all pidgins tend to be macaronic. Here's some typical examples, in which I've marked the different languages as follows: Chinese (C), English (E, only where it isn't obvious), Hawaiian (H), Japanese (J), Portuguese (P):

Pehea (H) you kaitai (C), you hanahana (H) all same lili
    (H/E) more me hanamake (H) you.
"Why, you bastard, you do [that] again I'll kill you!" (1898,
    Chinese plantation worker—*lili* may be from E. "little"
    or H. "li'ili'i.")
Luna (H) san (J), me danburo (E) fire de (J) mauka (H) ga
    (J) pilikia (H).
"Foreman, I have burning pains in my stomach and my
    head aches." (1900, Japanese plantation worker.
    Danburo = "down below." Note the Japanese case
    markers *ga* and *de* and the honorific *san*.)
Inu (J) shinda (J), pake (H) mejishin (E) koroshita (J).
"[My] dog died, Chinese medicine killed [him]." (1903,
    Hawaiian speaker addressing Japanese speaker.)
Apopo (H) I go tomorrow Wailuku manan' (P).
"Tomorrow I go tomorrow [to] Wailuku tomorrow." (1900,
    Portuguese speaker—note triple repetition of key word.)

As we shall see, it was during this linguistic meltdown that Creole was born.

So Pidgin Hawaiian described an arc through time. It began, alongside Pidgin English, as a makeshift jargon. It quickly established norms, while Pidgin English remained a continuum, stretching from the original jargon to second-language versions of English among a handful of speakers. In the 1860s and 1870s, there were signs that Pidgin Hawaiian might be moving from a stable to an expanded stage; complex sentences had begun to appear. Then came sugar and massive immigration of indentured laborers. Pidgin Hawaiian exploded under the pressure. Just as I had hypothesized for pre-Creole pidgins elsewhere, the sudden influx of new speakers totally destabilized the prior contact language, and its former speakers were forced into communicating any way they could.

It's clear from several contemporary accounts how this transition came about. Without a clear target, new immigrants were rudderless, adrift in a choppy sea of contending languages. Some stayed for years without picking up anything, leading to frequent use of interpreters in the courts. Others testified that they understood, or didn't understand, words uttered at crime scenes, because although they had been in Hawaii for eight years or more they spoke "only a little native [i.e. Hawaiian]," "some words of English," "a little English and a little Hawaiian," and so on. The prevailing strategy was to first use your own language in case the other person understood it; if not, use words from the other person's language if you knew any; if not, use words from any language you may happen to have picked up, and go from one language to another (like the Portuguese in the last of the four examples above, who said "tomorrow" in three languages) until, just as Rachel Kupepe had told me years before, you found a word they did understand.

But in any language, words come embedded in a grammar of some kind. Start plucking words at random from different languages, and any consistent grammatical structure disappears. That's not happenstance; it's a logical and inevitable consequence of macaronic speech.

Under these circumstances, it's hardly surprising that old hands picked up small vocabularies in each of several languages and used whichever one was appropriate for the occasion; the third example above is typical of this practice, as was the behavior of Joe Fern, a popular early-twentieth-century Honolulu mayor, who would campaign in whatever language his constituents spoke. Around 1905, Japanese accounted for nearly 50 percent of the total population, and in the 1970s I talked with several old-timers who could give pretty accurate imitations of pidgin as produced by Japanese.

Politics struck what was almost the final blow to Pidgin Hawaiian, and for that matter almost destroyed the Hawaiian language itself. The trauma of conversion from a free and independent country to a helpless haole dependency caused a sudden and tremendous loss of confidence among native Hawaiians, most of whom abandoned their language and culture. It's only in the last few decades that Hawaiians have rebuilt their pride and their language (two things that, after all, almost always go together). .

The target changed for children too. In the first years of immigration all children had ample access to Hawaiian; they could pick up something which, if the few surviving child citations are typical, was a lot closer to standard Hawaiian than what their parents spoke. But after the coup of 1893 (and still more after annexation) Hawaiian was no longer accessible. Hawaii was going American; everything would be English from then on.

But few non-haole children had access to English. At least, not in practice. In theory they did. Even before the coup, a majority of schools in Hawaii were officially teaching in English. And this fact is often brought up by those who insist that conditions in Hawaii were· very different from those in the Caribbean or the Indian Ocean—so different that no model of creolization based on Hawaii could apply elsewhere.

But how much English was actually taught? Outside of elite schools like Punahou, hardly any of the teachers were native speakers of English. Most were Hawaiians, and how much English they could actually speak—not to mention how much English they actually spoke in class—is open to question. Just imagine you're a Hawaiian teacher with a class of mostly Hawaiian children, and you're trying to teach them geometry. Some bureaucrat in Honolulu has told you that you have to teach it in English, but hardly any of the kids know any English. You start trying to explain the square of the hypotenuse and you watch their eyes glaze over. So what do you do? You're out in the boonies, there's not an inspector in sight. Do you persevere with English, or do you switch to Hawaiian? I mean, get real.

As late as 1899, a newspaper article complained, "In most schools of Hawaii there are children who speak at home from two to seven languages, yet none speak English—the language of the schools."

And at the turn of the century, native English speakers accounted for 5 percent or less of the general population, so there was no way most kids could pick up English informally. Consequently, by that time most of the words floating around were probably English words, that's all they were—words, not cemented together into any kind of regular structure.

If they wanted a language they could use among themselves, the kids just had to make one up for themselves.

One of the things Sarah Roberts decided to do was test the claim that similarities between Hawaiian Creole and other Creoles came about through diffusion—that what was found in Hawaii must have come from the Caribbean, somehow.

This claim had no evidence going for it but the similarities diffusion was supposed to explain—in other words, the whole thing was completely circular—yet it was widely, if not universally, believed. After all, it fitted perfectly with the conventional wisdom that if two languages resembled one another, it could only be because they shared a common ancestor. All of historical linguistics had been built on that belief.

But not only was there was no evidence, there was a striking anomaly that the claim had somehow to explain. My recordings in the 1970s showed that pidgin in Hawaii had never jelled, had never formed into any kind of system, let alone a system that bore even the faintest resemblance to that of the Caribbean Creoles. Indeed, the difference between pidgin and Hawaiian Creole was perhaps the single most striking fact I'd encountered. But if the diffusionist story was true, there shouldn't have been any significant differences.

So how did diffusionists deal with this? Well, they said, it must be that the pidgin I had recorded wasn't the real pidgin, the original pidgin. The real, original pidgin had been taken from the Atlantic to the Pacific, where it was enthusiastically adopted first by Hawaiians and then by the first immigrant groups, the Portuguese and the Chinese, evolving naturally into a Caribbean-like Creole. What I'd recorded was just a new pidgin, something that had been invented by the later immigrant groups, the Filipinos, Japanese, and Koreans. They must have gone back to square one and started pidginization all over again, from scratch.

Of course this made no sense whatsoever. The whole point of a pidgin is to serve as a contact language between different groups. If there had been any kind of stable, widely used contact language in Hawaii, then Japanese and Filipinos would have picked it up. It wasn't even as if the groups had come in separate blocks; they overlapped. Chinese were still coming in when Japanese started to come in. Japanese were still coming in when Filipinos started to come in. Koreans came in the middle of everything. Each group would have passed the contact language on to the next. Or did the diffusionists really think that Japanese, Koreans, and Filipinos were more stupid than Chinese and Portuguese?

The answer is, of course, that they didn't think.

The downside of higher education is that it gives you the confidence to maintain baseless fantasies in defiance of common sense. Ordinary folk are humble in the face of common sense; they have no agenda, and unlike academics, they know they don't know very much, so they act accordingly. But if you think you know a lot, and you've cemented that lot with a carapace of theory, you become immune to new facts and commonsense reasoning, and you have a knee-jerk negative reaction to anything that contradicts your agenda.

The only thing going for the diffusionist "explanation" had been the almost total lack of evidence for what people actually spoke in nineteenth-century Hawaii. What Sarah had found put an end to this blissful ignorance.

If the diffusion story had been correct, then the forms and structures that appeared in both Hawaii and the Caribbean would have had to appear in Hawaii at some time in the nineteenth century, and probably prior to the sugar boom that had been unleashed in 1876. There were at least two reasons for this conclusion. First, for

Chinese and Portuguese immigrants to have acquired this hypothetical language, it would have had to be there ready for them
when they arrived, or they would have acquired something else.
Second, the only people who could have brought anything from
the Caribbean were sailors. And Hawaii's first century of foreign
contact, from Captain Cook to sugar, was the heyday of sailors.
Honolulu, central point of the eastern Pacific, was visited by
countless sailors from all over the world. Their ships stopped there
to repair and refit, sometimes staying for weeks or even months; if
sailors had brought any language with them, then would have been
the time to distribute it.

But if they had, it would surely have been there, somewhere, in
Sarah's massive database. And it wasn't.

I know, I know—absence of evidence is not evidence of absence. But this hypothesized international contact language would
have had to be the stealth language of all time, passing under the
radar for the better part of a century only to erupt abruptly around
the late 1890s and affect everyone born in Hawaii from then on.
And while absence of evidence is one thing, massive evidence in
the opposite direction is something else again.

Some form of English had indeed been used, throughout the
first century of contact, alongside the Pidgin Hawaiian we've discussed so far. But all of it was one or the other of two things. For
most people, it was a highly primitive pidgin, just a few scraps of
words, and unlike the more widely used Pidgin Hawaiian, it never
stabilized, let alone expanded—it was an ad hoc thing that had to
be made up again every time it was used. For a minority, people
who had greater contact with English speakers, or were more
highly motivated for whatever reason, it was a second-language
learning continuum of the kind you'll find wherever any foreign
language is learned—some are content with a very modest competence, a few go on to almost native proficiency, and the rest are
strung out between.

Since the whole purpose of a contact language is contact, if a
ready-made contact language had ever made landfall in Hawaii you
can be sure everyone would have jumped on it and ridden with it.
But it hadn't. It was sink or swim, every man Jack and woman Jill
for their linguistic selves.

And then, after the 1893 coup, the kids took over.

One of the first people to spot what was happening was an astute journalist called Wallace Farrington, who went on to become the sixth governor of the Territory of Hawaii. In 1904 he wrote, "However pure the English, Chinese, Portuguese or Hawaiian [the newsboys] may speak in the school or homes, they have a complex pidgin English that is a universal language. They all meet on the 'I-bin-go' method of communication."

And indeed, *bin* was one of the commonest features of this new, more complex language. But it did not appear anywhere in the data before 1890. It was then used, though very rarely and sporadically, by one or two adult immigrants—only seven cases are on record between 1890 and 1910. However, it immediately became universal among the locally born; the probability that this difference between immigrants and locals results from chance was measured by Sarah and found to be less than 0.0001.

The nonpunctual *stay*, however (*us stay play*, "we are playing"), was clearly an innovation by children. As we saw in Chapter 7, it was derived from the locative copula (the equivalent of "be" in expressions stating location) *stay*; for example, *da book stay 'pon da table*. But in pidgin, the locative copula was not *stay* but *stop*. The word *stay* appeared in this context only after 1900, and the first attestations of its use as a nonpunctual preverbal marker (by children, naturally) date from 1921. And since it's unlikely to have been reported the moment it was first used, it probably first appeared earlier than that.

As for complexity, pidgin had been almost totally devoid of complex sentences. Now, people who were invariably identified as "children" or "young persons" or something of similar meaning began regularly to produce sentences like these:

That feller think he more smarter than me, but I never
'fraid for that thing he bin tell. (Child, 1909)
You been say go up on roof and paint him, but I no hear
you say come down. Why you not say when I bin
through come down? (Adolescent, 1913)

At the same time, adult immigrant speakers were still producing things like the following:

> I no afraid gun. Shoot, shoot me! I no care. Suppose I *make* [dead]. Plenty more Japanese stop. (Japanese adult, 1909)
> Oh missie, *wikiwiki*! Everything on fire! Too much smoke all over. Quick, quick! (Filipino adult, 1913)

But perhaps the most striking single feature of the Creole involved the replacement of nonfinite "to" clauses by finite "for" clauses. For example:

> CREOLE: I think more better [for I write that answer].
> ENGLISH: "I think it's better [for me to write that answer]."
> CREOLE: My mother tell [for I stop home].
> ENGLISH: "My mother told [me to stay home]."

In English, the subject of the subordinate (bracketed) clause, "me" in both cases, is accusative. At first sight this looks weird—aren't subjects supposed to have nominative case? Yes, but they can only get nominative case if the verb in the clause is finite, and in the English examples it isn't. But pronouns in English have to get case from somewhere, so here they get accusative case either from the preposition "for" (see translation of first sentence) or the preceding verb "tell" (see translation of second).

In Hawaiian Creole, on the other hand, the verb in the subordinate clause is finite, allowing it to assign nominative case to its subject. Two things about this structure are truly remarkable. First, the "for + tensed verb" construction is totally un-English and cannot in any way have been derived from English or any dialect thereof. (In and around the Ozarks you will find "for-to" constructions, but they're just as much nonfinite as the standard construction.) Second, the construction is typical of the more radical Creoles. Take Saramaccan, for example:

> Mi wani faa (fu a) go.
> I want for-he go.

"I want him to go."
*Mi wani fu en go.
I want for him go.

As this example shows, the correct Saramaccan construction is exactly analogous to the Hawaii one, while to use an accusative pronoun, though required in English, is flat ungrammatical in Saramaccan.

How was it possible for children in Hawaii to ignore all the English they were exposed to, in school and elsewhere, and acquire a Creole construction that they could never possibly have heard? Short of a desperate appeal to blind coincidence, there's only one possible explanation. The children were born with a grammar that obliged them to use finite constructions for clauses of purpose or intention, and that grammar was the same in Hawaii as it was in Suriname, despite the thousands of miles that separated them.

The most satisfying thing that can happen in science is when something you've claimed turns out to be right. That's prediction.

To the man in the street, prediction means foretelling something that hasn't happened yet. In science, it means making a claim on the basis of limited data (or on none at all, on pure theory, like Einstein with relativity) and then having your claim confirmed by facts nobody knew when the claim was made. It doesn't matter whether the facts are things that haven't happened yet or things that happened millions of years ago. As long as they weren't known to people, as long as they've only just been discovered, that's still prediction.

I had predicted that pidgin in Hawaii was made in Hawaii, and now we knew it was.

I had predicted that Pidgin English had always been as variable and as primitive as it was when I recorded it, and that's how it had been.

I had predicted that Creole was created by children, not adults, and any time after 1900 that a speaker was described as a child, a youth, or an adolescent, what he or she spoke was clearly Creole rather than pidgin—whereas when adults were quoted, what they spoke was either pidgin or, more rarely, some kind of second-language English.

I had predicted that Creole would emerge in a single generation and it had—not the first locally born generation, as I'd originally thought, because the target of that generation had still been Hawaiian and Hawaiian had still been an attainable goal, but the first locally born generation for whom pidgin was the only viable vehicle for intergroup communication.

I had predicted that this first-generation Creole would contain structures that were not present in any input its creators received, and it did. And, as we know, those structures are ones that are found in Creoles thousands of miles away, to which entirely different sets of both substrate and superstrate languages had contributed.

But, as you might guess, diffusionists who for decades had insisted on precisely these similarities now conveniently forgot about them, and began instead to search out differences. Their agenda clearly informed them that if the Creole hadn't come from the Caribbean, it couldn't really have the same features.

Old theories, alas, never die—they just change their clothes, primp up, and pop out again.

The final question was how far Hawaii was typical of the plantation colonies that had produced other Creoles. Could you generalize? Could you say, well, since this is how things went in Hawaii, this is how they must have gone in places for which we have no detailed record?

On the face of it, there are a number of differences, and, as you might guess, folk who had held the now-outdated picture of Hawaii's past were the quickest to point them out.

First there's the indigenous population. Nowhere but in Hawaii was there a sizable indigenous population with its own language and its own government. Then there is the status of the immigrant population. Everywhere but Hawaii the immigrants consisted mostly or entirely of slaves; in Hawaii, they consisted almost entirely of indentured laborers. Then there's the degree of access to the superstrate, English. In no other Creole society did children go to schools taught in the dominant language; for that matter, in no other Creole society did they go to school at all. Finally there's literacy. In Creole societies generally, literacy in the subject population was not just absent, but actively discouraged. We don't have accurate statistics on literacy among Hawaii's immigrants, but the fact that newspapers could be published in most of the immigrant languages, not to mention Hawaiian, suggests it was pretty widespread.

But the point is not whether there were differences or not. The point is, were there differences that made any real differences?

The existence of the Hawaiian state, culture, and language is an irrelevant confound. Its only consequence was to delay the onset of Creole by a decade or two. When political events suddenly and sharply reduced the influence of things Hawaiian, the predicted scenario promptly unfolded.

It is hard to see any way in which the status of workers could have affected linguistic development. They performed the same work in the cane fields as the slaves had done. They could not leave the plantation or even transfer to another plantation without encountering legal sanctions. They could be, and often were, mercilessly beaten by foremen and overseers; Henry Wramp was an extreme case, but he wasn't unique. About the only differences were that there was a limited term on their labor and they couldn't be tortured or murdered with legal impunity. I can't for the life of me see how such facts could have affected their language.

As for the other two differences, schooling and literacy, the only effect these could have had would have been to move Hawaiian Creole along the continuum of Creoles in the direction of English. And that's exactly what they did. Without knowing the first thing about the grammar of Hawaiian Creole, just from historical and sociological knowledge, you could have predicted that, while further from the dominant European language than Bajan or Réunionais, it would be closer to it than Guyanese Creole or Haitian, let alone Sranan or Saramaccan. Yet, as I've shown, some features typical of the last-named Creoles still came through.

But try a little alternative history. Let's suppose that around

1890, Hawaii had been seized by Germany. This scenario is by no means impossible; Germany was expanding its Pacific possessions throughout the latter part of the nineteenth century, and by 1900 its empire included a large portion of New Guinea, Bougainville, and other Solomon Islands, the Caroline Islands, Palau, Nauru, the Marianas (except for Guam), Western Samoa, and (getting real close now) the Marshall Islands. With Germans in control, the influence of English would have virtually ceased, just as the influence of Hawaiian did after the Anglophone takeover. (We've already seen how English influence was extinguished in Suriname when the Dutch took over.) And this process would have happened just at the point when pidgin was at its most chaotic and macaronic. The end result would almost certainly have been a Creole like those of Suriname with as mixed a vocabulary and as radical a grammar.

In short, none of the differences between Hawaii and other Creole societies are such that they could have influenced the development of Creole or made it different from its development elsewhere in any significant or unpredictable ways.

What matters here are not the differences but the similarities. Hawaii first went through a phase not unlike Robert Chaudenson's *société d'habitation*, in which a stable contact language developed among relatively small numbers of people. The fact that this language was derived from an indigenous rather than a European language is neither here nor there, because the infernal machine of sugar production ensured that it would disappear just as the early contact languages of other Creole societies had disappeared.

In the last quarter of the nineteenth century, Hawaii underwent the expansion stage of massive immigration, bringing together people who spoke different and mutually incomprehensible languages. The old hands and their prior contact language were swamped by a continuous inpouring of new labor, causing that contact language to disintegrate—a disintegration vividly and voluminously illustrated by Sarah Roberts's data. Since the children of these immigrants needed a language to talk to one another, and since children, by virtue of their innate language abilities, do not have to settle for a mishmash like the pidgin of the 1890s, the immediate and inevitable consequence was the creation of a new Creole language.

In short, although Hawaii had several points of difference from other Creole societies, the social dynamics I described in Chapter 10 applied as rigorously in Hawaii as they did anywhere else that large-scale plantation agriculture was practiced—as indeed they had to apply, given the laws of economics. And the linguistic consequences of those dynamics were also just what they had to be— what they had always been and always would be, whether in the Caribbean, the Indian Ocean, the Pacific, or even on some planet as yet unknown, if (God forbid!) we were ever to set up plantations there.

14

CODA

————

Once the research on Hawaii's history was completed, I concentrated more and more on the question of how language had originally evolved. That field was heating up rapidly as the findings of a dozen expanding disciplines narrowed the search space. Every year there were more books, more articles, more conferences. After all, it was one of the world's great questions, asked surely since the very dawn of language, yet still (a century and a half after Darwin) scandalously unanswered. And it offered almost limitless opportunities for finding out new things, not to mention making connections between new and old things that no one had made before.

How could I resist that?

But two things happened in the world of Creoles that, in their very different ways, were of great importance to me. And by an odd coincidence both came, directly or indirectly, out of political struggle and change, and both took place in Latin America, in areas only a few hundred miles apart.

Back in the 1970s, Nicaragua was controlled, and largely owned, by the infamous Somoza clan. It was a regime marked by the things it didn't do as much as by those it did, and among the objects of this unbenign neglect were the deaf. There were, in pre-Sandinista Nicaragua, no institutions that catered to the deaf—no special

schools, nothing. The deaf were isolated, each in his or her own
family and village. They had no language of their own. They got by .
on what is known in the trade as "home sign."

Home sign is what you or I would do if confronted by a deaf
person. (Don't, whatever you do, call them "deaf and dumb"—
that's like a white guy calling a black guy "nigger"; if they can't
speak it's only because they've never heard speech, and as for
"dumb" in its IQ sense, they're as smart as anyone.) In other words,
home sign consists of a handful of stereotyped gestures—putting
your fingers to your mouth to signify "eat," pointing to your eyes to
indicate "look" or "see," and so on. A home sign vocabulary is tiny,
featuring no more than a few dozen manual signs, and strictly
iconic, which means that the signs aren't arbitrary, abstract things
as most words are, but just mimic whatever thing or action is being
described. As for grammar—forget about it!

In other words, "home sign" is more impoverished than the
crudest, most basic form of pidgin.

So this was all that deaf children in Nicaragua received from
their hearing parents. And in Nicaragua, apparently, there was no
community like those of islands such as Martha's Vineyard or Prov-
idencia with a high percentage of hereditary deafness, so few of the
parents were deaf themselves. In consequence they couldn't communicate with their children any better than anyone else could.
But every human has an inalienable right to a form of communica- .
tion orders of magnitude richer than home sign. And in countries
where the deaf have any means of getting together, they have one.
ASL (American Sign Language) is, as its name indicates, what deaf
people in America use when communicating with one another, or
with hearing people who've taken the trouble to learn it. ASL is a
full human language just as much as any spoken language, with all
the inflectional tricks, the grammatical subtleties, that any language has; these are just transposed into a visual medium. And deaf
activists will fight like tigers, as they should, against any attempt to
make deaf people use anything else.

For ASL is a language, like a Creole, that developed independently among the deaf. But well-meaning idiots (the same folk who
brought you Bijlmermeer) never ask what people want; they al-

ready know what they ought to want. So they try to force the deaf to use some hybrid monstrosity, such as a thing called Signed English, because that will help them "transition into the speech community." But most deaf people don't want to transition into the speech community, thank you very much. They'd rather be fully functioning members of a deaf community than second-class citizens of a speech community.

Now you may well ask, if deaf Nicaraguan children received an impoverished pidginlike input, and if all humans have an innate language bioprogram that enables them to construct a new language out of such bits and pieces, why couldn't they have started a new language under the Somoza regime?

The answer is very simple. Biological capacities don't just emerge automatically, in the absence of any relevant experience. In order to function properly, any biological capacity has to be used, or it won't develop. But since most deaf children in Nicaragua were isolated from contact with other deaf children, there were none of their own kind with whom they could communicate. Earlier on, I mentioned the question of how many children it takes to start a Creole language. (Sounds like one of those light-bulb jokes, doesn't it?) I think the answer is "At least two"—one to speak, the other to understand and speak back. But if only two or three children start to develop a language (and this may well have happened, here and there in Nicaragua), that language will die with them unless they can inject it into a larger group. So the answer probably is "Two to start one, but quite a few more to keep it going."

Things changed in Nicaragua when the Sandinistas came to power, and for the deaf at least they changed in a positive way. For the first time, schools for the deaf were set up. At first the intake of such schools was limited to older children and adolescents. These students ignored the signed Spanish their teachers tried to instill, and developed among themselves what looks like an enriched or expanded pidgin—a language with regular structure, but without the detail and grammatical complexity of a full human language. This came to be known as Lenguaje de Señas Nicaragüense (LSN).

Then younger children were brought in, and they quickly developed a language that had the full range of complexity found in any spoken language. It came to be known as ISN, Idioma de Señas Nicaragüense. LSN and ISN are different ways of saying Nicaraguan Sign Language.

Several things are striking about ISN. In the first place, it's an even clearer case of spontaneous language creation than any Creole. Whenever Creoles were created, there were always other languages around. In preceding chapters I've given good reasons for discounting the importance of these languages, and for doubting that, except for the occasional borrowing of the odd feature, preexisting languages ever had any significant impact on Creole grammars. (Vocabularies and sound systems are another matter.) But whenever other languages are around, people can always say, well, you can't rule out the possibility of influence.

However, because we're dealing with a signed rather than a spoken language, here the possibility can be ruled out. No spoken language could have provided input, because deaf Nicaraguan children couldn't understand any spoken language, not even the Spanish that was spoken around them every day. No signed language could have provided input, because until those children invented one, there wasn't any kind of signed language in Nicaragua. As for the signed Spanish their teachers force-fed them with, they actively recoiled from that, and, to the chagrin of those teachers, wound up with something radically different from what they were supposed to be learning.

The next striking thing is the role played by age differences in the creation of ISN. Judy Kegl, of the University of Southern Maine (the first person to describe and analyze ISN) and some of her colleagues have argued that the earlier, pidginlike version was a necessary precursor for the Creole. But it's sheer happenstance that the first children to develop sign language were older rather than younger. To prove that an intermediate stage between home sign and full language is necessary rather than accidental, Judy would have to find a group of young children somewhere who had been exposed only to home sign and who consequently had been unable to develop a full, Creole-like language. But no such group is

known. It therefore seems likelier that the difference between the
two versions of Nicaraguan sign exists simply because (as we know
from independent evidence) the language-creating capacity fades
and degrades gracefully from say age six or so onward, finally disap-
pearing around puberty or thereabouts. If that's so, then ISN would
have arrived at its final form just as naturally if younger children
with only home sign as input had been brought together first, instead of older children and adolescents.

Now, let's exclude the one or two cases, like Tokpisin in New
Guinea, where a pidgin gradually built up almost to a full language
after several generations of mostly adult use. We are concerned
here only with what can be done in a single generation. We can
then make the following generalization about the agewise distribution of the language-creating capacity:

- Adults can't create a new language to save their lives.
- Older children can create a new language, but not a full
  one.
- Younger children can create a full human language out
  of ???

More about those question marks in a moment.

The last striking thing about Nicaraguan Sign Language involves what's been a recurrent topic through this book—serial verb
constructions. It turns out that ISN has them. Now wherever ISN
signers got them from, it couldn't have been the substrate, as substratists claim, because ISN doesn't have a substrate. Even if ISN
signers had access to their parents' (spoken) languages, there's no
language the parents of ISN signers speak that has serial verbs
(Spanish surely doesn't). So what I found in the Seychelles—that a
Creole can have serial verb constructions even if none of the substrate languages has them—is now confirmed from an unconnected
and wholly unexpected source.

But, neat though that is, it's just one detail in an overall plan,
the plan for building a language wherever one is needed, where
there wasn't one before. And, since all biological plans operate
across the board, wherever normal members of a species are born,

it's hardly a big surprise that a small detail like a difference in modality should be powerless to affect the outcome. For the inborn faculty of language doesn't worry about how language is expressed. Sound or sign, it's all the same to that faculty. And if a group of people had to depend on semaphore flags or Morse code to express themselves, it would still be the same. Like magma seeking a volcanic rift, the language in all of us will find some way by which it can break out into the world.

Six or seven hundred miles from Nicaragua, across the southernmost bulge of the Caribbean in northern Colombia, lies El Palenque de San Basilio.

El Palenque, as we saw in Chapter 4, symbolized the attitude of Colombians toward people of African descent. That attitude was—there's nothing black in Colombia! The Creole Palenquero was dismissed as a hodgepodge of poorly educated white folks' grammatical solecisms. The citizens of El Palenque were left in their rural isolation, without power, running water, or any of the amenities that modern societies take for granted. Although at least a quarter of the population carries African blood, although Africans have profoundly influenced Colombian music, cuisine, and many more aspects of its culture, the Colombian establishment either entirely ignored the African contribution or, if directly challenged, flat-out denied it.

In most respects since my visits in the late sixties, Colombian society had gone to hell in a handcart. The left-wing insurgencies had, if anything, grown stronger. They had been answered, not just by the government, but by right-wing paramilitary death squads. The cocaine cartels now made a third party in these internecine wars, siding sometimes with the lefties, sometime with the righties, but mostly pursuing their own lethal agenda. In the chaos that ensued, the nominal government had minimal control; judges, journalists, politicians could be assassinated in broad daylight and no one would be arrested, let alone sentenced. Abroad, "Colombia" and "cocaine" became synonymous. Flying from Caracas to San José with a two-day stopover in Cartagena, we were strip-searched by the Costa Rican customs police. They were very polite, even apologetic, about it—Ticos are nice people, even the cops—but they told us they did that to everyone who'd stopped in Colombia long enough to pick up a mule consignment.

But in one respect at least things had improved.

Colombia—at least the official government and the intelligentsia; there's still discrimination at other levels—gingered by revisionist historians, slowly changed its attitude toward Afro-Colombians and their culture. The constitution of 1991 officially recognized their rights and those of other ethnic minorities, while a subsequent law known as "70/93" created a special constituency to give blacks two seats in the National Congress, and allowed autonomous community organizations to own land collectively. In academia, Palenquero was now a respectable field of study, attracting younger scholars.

I hadn't given the language a thought for at least ten years. But I had been the first to publish a linguistic article on it, and so, out of the blue, came an invitation from the University of Cartagena to attend a conference entitled "Palenquero, Colombia, and the Afro-Caribbean: Language and History." Would I present a paper there?

I couldn't not go. I hurriedly boned up on recent Palenquero studies. Monogenesis, or a watered down version thereof, seemed to be alive and well in this little corner at least. Once more it was the Portuguese who did it. They brought the slaves from their African possessions into Colombia, and en route the slaves picked up that old Afro-Portuguese contact language (pidgin or Creole?—no one was saying) that most creolists, in the late sixties to early seventies, had accepted as the source of Creoles everywhere. At least, that was what some of my fellow conferees were saying.

I wrote a paper, nothing fancy, just basic nuts-and-bolts linguistics, to show that Palenquero could be better explained by assuming that, like other Creoles, it had sprung up right where it lived, and that what was attributed to Portuguese influence could just as plausibly be derived from Spanish. And off I flew with it. Have paper, will travel—that's what life in academe's about.

I love Cartagena. Outside the old city walls, the walls African slaves sweated blood to build and that Domingo Bioho fled from to found El Palenque four centuries ago, there's nothing you'd want to see—just the yucky, formless sprawl of almost all the cities of the Americas. But within them, on the cobbled streets among the cream, pink, and green stucco buildings, you could be back in the eighteenth century.

The conference was a surprise. Some people were actually reading their papers in Palenquero. Some of them even *were* Palenqueros. You have to realize how extraordinary this was. Things aren't quite so bad nowadays as they were at Mona in 1968, when Douglas Taylor astonished his colleagues by uttering just a few Creole sentences. But apart from the odd prodigy like Michel DeGraff, a native speaker of Haitian who now teaches at MIT, Creole conferences don't usually hear from native Creole speakers, and native Creole speakers who lack resumes like Michel's don't usually have the self-confidence to address an international cast of specialist scholars.

Well, the populist in me was delighted to find that this lot did. Indeed, there was a kind of celebratory air about the conference, a bonding between scholars and community activists as pleasant as it's rare. I met again with my old coauthor, Aquilas Escalante, attended now by a small court of admirers, basking in his unexpected eminence as the Father of Palenquero Studies after the long years of isolation and indifference. I also made the acquaintance of Matthias Perl, a German prof I'd savaged in a review, and found him so jolly and genial that I was bitterly ashamed and apologized profusely. No, he assured me, he hadn't taken offense, and to cement our relationship we went out to dinner with a mutual friend, Nicolas Del Castillo, where we all drank too much.

Taking us back to our hotel, Nicolas was expounding some abstruse point in Afro-Colombian lexicography when I suddenly realized that (a) he was driving at around five miles an hour, (b) he was driving on the wrong side of the road, and (c) a pair of headlights were rapidly approaching us.

"Nick, look out!"

". . . and in fact the same word can also be used to describe . . ."

The headlights got bigger real fast.

"NICK!"

He swung the wheel at the last second, or you wouldn't be reading this.

Naturally, the conference included a visit to El Palenque. This
time, instead of a converted truck on a dirt road, we rode in an air-
conditioned bus on a broad and recently resurfaced highway. And
the village was so totally changed I wouldn't have recognized it.
Gone were the wattle-and-daub huts, the palm-thatched roofs, the
areas of beaten mud that passed for streets and plazas, the chickens
flying in and out of everywhere. In their place were tarmac and
paved surfaces, tidy little cement-block houses with galvanized iron
roofs, neat wire fences around them to keep hogs and chickens in
place. There were street lights everywhere; power lines drooped
over the little houses and through open doorways you could see the
erratic blue flicker of television screens.

The modern world had arrived, with a vengeance.

We ate and drank and listened to speeches, then we were free
to wander around and talk to the villagers. I went into several of
the houses; as I'd guessed, the galvanized roofs kept them far hotter
than the old palm-thatch, but some folk had built palm-leaf shel-
ters out front where you could sit and drink and talk far into the
tropical night, keeping all the doors and windows open so the
house would, eventually, cool down.

Were they happy with the changes? Yes, of course, who
wouldn't be? Life was far from perfect, naturally. Crime was worse
nowadays. And somehow there wasn't the closeness, the camaraderie there'd been in the old days. It was every man for himself
now. But then they would square their shoulders and say, well, at
last they've taken notice of us. We're not marginalized, bastard
speakers of a bastard tongue, not anymore. We count for something
now.

Cartagena put a nice period to my Creole career. But one thing
continued to haunt me.

It was, of course, from the place where this book began—the

thought of what we might have accomplished on Ngemelis if the Island Experiment had been funded. Could it ever have worked? Could any language experiment involving people ever be carried out? If not, how could you ever rigorously and empirically test the proposition that language is biologically instantiated in every human brain?

For despite all I had discovered, the most crucial question remained:

- Younger children can create a full human language out of ???

What was the content of that ??? What was the absolute minimum input that children would have to have in order to acquire a full human language? How much could the human mind alone contribute to the task of creating language anew? Just some of it, or all of it?

But surely we know that zero input gives zero results.

Well, do we?

At first sight the answer's an unconditional "Yes!" We know of the so-called wolf children, children abandoned in infancy who (whether or not they were really suckled by wolves) somehow managed to survive for years before they were discovered. None of them ever subsequently acquired a full human language or anything close; most gave only inarticulate grunts. Then there was the case of Genie, the unfortunate Californian girl who was kept isolated from all human contact by her demented father—"The world will never know," he wrote in his suicide note after Genie's rescue—until she was thirteen, probably past the end of the critical period within which language must be acquired. Dozens of caregivers struggled to give her language, but all she wound up with was, in terms of its grammatical structure, exactly like a pidgin.

But with both wolf children and Genie, one essential factor in language building was absent: within the critical period, someone to talk back to you.

Whether two or more children together, without any access to language of any kind, could succeed in creating a language remains an unanswered question. To answer that question requires an experiment, and indeed such an experiment has been carried out at least four times. The goal of these experiments, admittedly, was not to discover whether children could create language. Up until at least the Renaissance, most people believed they didn't need to. They believed that children without input would still speak a language, and that the language they spoke would be the original language of humankind. But the basic experimental conditions they chose—infancy, company, isolation, zero language input—were such that, other things being equal, they might have told us whether the presence of at least one potential fellow speaker would have let language begin again from scratch.

Unfortunately, other things weren't equal.

To give them their due, at least two of the experimenters were well ahead of their time. In the ancient world, indeed until the Renaissance, the empirical method didn't exist. You discovered things not by doing experiments but by sitting and thinking. It took centuries for people to begin to wonder, "If I actually did so-and-so, what would happen?"

So it's not surprising that in detail and in execution (not to mention ethics!) these experiments leave much to be desired. Plus the reporting was execrable. Nobody who wrote about them actually witnessed them, and where there are two or more accounts they contradict one another. We can't even be certain that the experiments actually took place, but they have been reported with, in most cases, enough detail to convince one that something happened, so here they are.

Pharaoh Psamtik of Egypt (663–610 B.C.), known to Greeks as Psammetichus, isolated two newborn babies with only a shepherd to look after them, instructing him not to speak with them. After two years, Psamtik checked on them, and they said *becos*, which was Phrygian for "bread." Phrygian was therefore pronounced to be the original human language.

Frederick II of Sicily (1194–1250), a.k.a. Stupor Mundi, "Wonder of the World," was an early devotee of empirical research; one of his experiments involved killing a knight and cutting open his stomach to see how far his digestion had progressed. His language experiment, basically the same as Psamtik's, concluded prematurely when the children, who according to the chronicler "could not live without clappings of the hands, and gestures, and gladness of countenance, and blandishments," died.

James IV of Scotland (1473–1513) isolated two babies with a "dumb" (presumably deaf) woman. When they came to "lawful age," whatever that is, the two "spak goode Hebrew," if you can believe that.

The fourth version of the experiment was conducted by Akbar the Great, Emperor of India (1542–1605). Several conflicting accounts exist. The number of children may have been twenty or thirty. The nurses may have been deaf or merely instructed not to speak. The result was either "the noises of the dumb" or (in one account) some form of sign language.

Some obscure references suggest that an early-nineteenth-century French anthropologist performed a fifth experiment, but this can't be confirmed.

Would it be possible nowadays, given our immensely greater knowledge of what language is and how it works, to find a humane and ethical way to do such an experiment? Let's try.

We're somewhere in, say, South America. To a mansion on a large estate obtained for the purpose, a dozen or two orphans less than one year of age are flown in. A rich environment is provided for them, limitless quantities of toys and activities, plus all the "clappings of the hands, and gestures, and gladness of countenance, and blandishments" a child could wish for. Just no normal language. Words, but no grammar, no syntax. The caregivers use an artificial vocabulary, just as in the Island Experiment. Hidden microphones are everywhere, and any caregiver who utters a grammatical sentence will be out of there fast. We're not interested in whether children can make up their own vocabulary. We know vocabulary can't be innate because every child that learns a different language learns a different vocabulary. We want to know if, given a basic vocabulary, children can produce regularly structured sentences with-out ever having heard one. We want to find out, once and for all, whether syntax comes from experience or from the human mind.

Is there a genuine ethical objection here? What about informed consent? Well, who gives informed consent for infants in orphan-ages? They sure don't give it themselves, and there are no parents to give it for them.

What's the worst that could happen? Well, the children might grow up without ever getting a real language. But that risk could be reduced to a minimum, perhaps zero, with some simple precau-tions. We know from studies of normal acquisition the approximate ages at which different levels of structural complexity are achieved, and different kinds of complex sentence produced. Benchmarks could be set—the last date by which a normal child should have reached a given target—and if those benchmarks are not met, the plug would immediately be pulled on the experiment. (This means that whoever ran the experiment would have to be hard-nosed, deeply ethical, and self-confident enough not to regard an aborted experiment as professional suicide.)

In any case, if the hypothesis is correct and children don't re-quire structured input to acquire structured language, they'll pro-duce language just as fast as children in normal circumstances. And children aged three who've learned under normal circumstances al-ready control a wide range of syntactic structures. There'd be no point in going on after they reached that age—they'd either have created a language, or they wouldn't. So the maximum time length for the experiment would be a little over two years.

Children of three are still only in the early stages of the critical period. Immediately after the experiment ends the orphans are re-turned to their own countries. Arrangements have already been made for each to be adopted into a family with children around their own age (large financial incentives available). There they get total immersion in Spanish, Portuguese, or whatever their language would have been if they'd been left in the orphanage. Plus a small trust fund that with the magic of compound interest enables them, later in life, to buy a house, start their own business, whatever. If all we know about language learning at that age is correct, they should have native mastery of Spanish or Portuguese in a matter of weeks. And what kind of future could a South American orphan look forward to, otherwise? There are countless thousands already trying to survive on the streets (and as often as not, failing)—thousands facing abject poverty, sexual exploitation, death squads, drug abuse, degradation in every shape and form. But for some reason, the near certainty of causing harm by doing nothing is outweighed, for most people, by a remote risk of causing harm by doing something. After all, they're not our children, not even in our country, so how could we be responsible if they get raped and beaten to death on the street? And the mere uttering of the dire words "human experiment" clouds the reason with a red haze of righteous indignation.

So is this still too barbarous? Let's see if we can think of something a little less scary.

We're in a large American city, large enough to contain recent immigrants of a dozen or more nationalities. From those recent immigrants are chosen as many as possible, up to a dozen, each one speaking a language as different as possible from the others, each of whom has a child under two, but not too far under, so as to minimize the length of time the experiment takes. In each case, both parents are working; if there's a single parent, better still. Parents should have as little English as possible; none would be best, but how realistic is that nowadays?

Centrally located in the city is a day care center. The dozen children of the immigrants are the only ones there. There's a high staff-to-child ratio and a rich environment, as described in the previous experiment. The staff are sworn to speak to the children only using the prepared vocabulary and unstructured utterances, single words for preference, again on pain of instant dismissal for infractions. Surveillance cameras and concealed microphones record everything that happens.

The children are there for eight to ten hours, five days a week. At night they return to their families. The families are instructed not to use English with the children for at least a year and to try to ensure that they do not play with English-speaking kids. English is the most serious source of possible contamination. The kids use their original native language in the home, and acquire it normally, so there's no risk of language loss. They may try using that language in day care, but that won't matter so much. As we've seen, pre-Creole pidgins and even Creoles themselves in the early stages usually have a mixed vocabulary. '

In some ways this situation resembles that of a Creole more than any other experimental model. On plantations, children of that age, too young even to do simple weeding jobs, were placed in the care of one or two elderly slave women, played with one another during the day, and returned to their mothers at night. If rules from the substrate grammar do start to leak into their day care speech, at least, unlike the Creole case, we'll know what all the substrates are, and again, in contrast to many Creoles, there won't be any numerically predominant substrate to skew the balance.

So, hopefully, they will taˡˡ to one another in a language of their own invention. The danger is, since English is all around them, and since children have a keen ear for the language of the place, that they will instead begin to try out on one another whatever scraps of English they've managed to pick up. Nothing comes without a trade-off; risk of contamination is the price that has to be paid for avoiding the hazards of other methods, lack of informed consent, risk of arrested linguistic development, and the like.

You pays your money and you takes your choice, as the amusement-stall barkers used to shout in the old country. Either way, the results would tell us things about the human brain that we couldn't learn any other way.

And talking of money, how much would this cost, anyway?

Probably less than a million dollars. But in today's climate, no government organization is likely to fund it. As one scientist cynically remarked, the only way to get funded nowadays is to do the research first, prove it can be done, then ask for money so you can do it all over again.

The best chances lie in the private sector. The sum needed is chump change for all the billionaires floating around nowadays. For any who want to be remembered, it's a great deal. Under normal circumstances, who'll remember them five years after they've gone?

Who'd remember Psamtik, pharaoh or no pharaoh, if he hadn't done a language experiment? Anyone who finances one now will be remembered long after death, because we now know enough to do the thing right and because the findings, whatever they may be, will be crucial for future understanding of both language and human cognition.

I'm out of it. I'll consult, if asked, but anyone else is welcome to organize it and run it and take the credit for it. All I care about are the results. Other sciences at least have the luxury of temporary certainty. Newton's explained the universe, oops, no, Einstein's explained the universe, er, well, now there's all this dark matter and dark energy we have to account for. In linguistics we don't even get that far, we just argue back and forth. Some linguists, like Steve Pinker (whose book *The Language Instinct* is, after this one, the most fun book on language you're likely to read), have what they are pleased to call "labs," but the kinds of experiment they can do in them, even in the fancier ones where you can get pictures of the inside of your brain, yield results that are always interpretable in at least two contradictory ways. And so the arguments go on. I'd like to see a stop put to all that word wastage, at least on the issue of how much language structure the brain can create.

But even without experiments, the evidence from bastard tongues shows beyond doubt that a major part of language learning comes from the brain rather than experience. In those languages we see the unmistakable signature of a capacity all of us share, or rather have shared earlier in our lives—unless you're a really precocious reader, you've probably lost it by now. It's the capacity to acquire a full human language under almost any circumstances—even a language that could not have been learned, since it did not exist before the first generation that acquired it.

All of us have used this capacity once in our lives, when we acquired our first language. We didn't learn the language of our parents by rote, as is shown by all the "mistakes" children make—things that would not have been mistakes if what we'd been learning had been a Creole. We didn't really "learn," in the accepted sense of the word. Rather we re-created our parents' language. But in those rare cases where most of the community doesn't know that language, and there's no other established language they all do know, children will take whatever scraps of language they can find and build as efficiently with those scraps as they would with the words and structures of a long-established language like English.

What they build from those scraps won't be exactly the same everywhere. It can't be, because the scraps will be different in different places and they will incorporate into the new language whatever they can scavenge from the scraps—more in some places than in others. But the model into which those scraps are incorporated will reveal the same basic design wherever those children are and whoever they are, and similar structures will emerge, no matter what languages their parents spoke.

For Creoles are not bastard tongues after all. Quite the contrary: they are the purest expression we know of the human capacity for language. Other languages creak and groan under the burden of time. Like ships on a long voyage, they are encrusted with the barnacles of freaky constructions, illogical exceptions, obsolete usages. Their convoluted recesses facilitate lying and deceit. But Creoles spring pure and clear from the very fountain of language, and their emergence, through all the horrors of slavery, represents a triumph of all that's strongest and most enduring in the human spirit.

GLOSSARY

anterior: a tense used to express actions that occurred prior to whatever is being currently discussed (i.e., "past before past").

anterior marker: a particle indicating that the following verb expresses anterior tense.

ASP: abbreviation for "aspect marker."

aspect marker: a particle preceding a verb that shows whether the action described by the verb was completed or not (e.g., "has tried" versus "was trying"), is currently in progress, or is habitual (e.g., "is trying" versus "tries").

bakra: in the Caribbean, any person of Caucasian origin (see **haole**).

bioprogram: see **language bioprogram**.

calque: a literal translation of an expression from one language into another.

case marker: a particle or affix indicating whether the adjacent noun is nominative, accusative, genitive, and so on.

CM: abbreviation for "case marker."

code-switching: varying one's language when speaking to different types of person, in different social situations, on different topics, and so on.

cognate: a word with roughly the same sound and meaning as a word in a different (and presumably related) language.

consonant cluster: a group of two or more consonants at the beginning or end of a syllable.

continuum: a range of closely related dialects, usually of an English-related Creole, stretching from one unintelligible to uninitiated English speakers to one almost indistinguishable from standard English (as in "post-Creole continuum").

copula: a linking verb, most commonly the verb "to be."

Creole: a full language that emerges when children acquire a pidgin as their native language.

creolization: any process through which a Creole is formed.

decreolization: the process through which a Creole, when spoken alongside its superstrate, loses typically Creole features and replaces them with superstrate features.

diffusion: any means by which a language gets from one place to another.

diffusionism: the belief that Creoles were created in places other than where they are now spoken and subsequently spread there; **-ist:** one who holds this belief.

epenthetic vowel: a vowel inserted between adjacent consonants or at the end of words ending with a consonant in order to preserve consonant-vowel syllable structure.

generative grammar: the systematic theory of syntax originally developed by Noam Chomsky and taken by him through several mutations; **generativist:** one who believes in generative grammar.

haole: in Hawaii, any person of Caucasian origins (see *bakra*).

implicational scaling: a method for sorting data that displays in logical order the various varieties of a language.

irrealis: a modality that expresses actions that have not taken place (covers the same ground as "future" + "conditional" in traditional grammars).

irrealis marker: a particle indicating that the following verb expresses irrealis modality.

LAD: abbreviation for "language acquisition device."

language acquisition device: a mental organ hypothesized by Chomsky without which children would be unable to learn a language.

language bioprogram: the biological program for language that underlies the similarities between various Creoles and the human language faculty generally.

lexifier: a language that supplies words for a Creole language.

locative: anything indicative of where something happens.

macaronic: involving a mixture of words from several languages.

main lexifier: see **superstrate.**

marker: a particle or affix that expresses a semantic (e.g., tense) or a grammatical (e.g., case) relationship.

maroon: a member of a community of escaped slaves, or the descendants of these (from Spanish *cimarrón*, "wild").

MOD: abbreviation for "modality marker."

modality: the reality level of a state, event, or action—whether it is actual or hypothetical, located in the future, and so on.

monogenesis: a theory that claims all or most Creoles are descended from a single original contact language (most commonly, an Afro-Portuguese language spoken in West Africa in the 1500s).

noncount noun: a noun (sometimes referred to as a "mass" noun) representing something that cannot normally be counted (e.g., bread, sand).

nonpunctual: an aspect that covers habitual, repeated, or prolonged actions (what traditional grammars refer to as "habitual," "progressive," or "continuous").

patois: a rude name for Creole languages.

pidgin: a much reduced form of language used when people speaking two or more mutually incomprehensible languages have to communicate with one another.

pidginization: any process through which a pidgin is formed.

PL: abbreviation for "plural marker."

polygenesis: the belief that most Creoles originated separately in the communities where they are now spoken.

punctual: an aspect form indicating an action that happens on a single occasion and is neither prolonged nor habitual.

relexification: a process by which a language substitutes words from another language for its own words.

serial verb construction: a sentence containing two or more verbs with the same subject throughout but no conjunction, uttered with no pause under a single intonation contour.

SOV language: a language where the predominant word order is subject-object-verb (e.g., Japanese, German).

substrate: a language or languages spoken by the ancestors of Creole speakers and supposedly influencing the Creole.

substratism: the belief that substrate languages constitute the most important factor in the creation of Creoles; **-ist:** one who holds this belief.

superstrate: the language of the dominant group in a Creole society.

superstratism: the belief that the superstrate language constitutes the most important factor in the creation of Creoles; **-ist:** one who holds this belief.

SVC: see **serial verb construction.**

SVO language: a language where the predominant word order is subject-verb-object (e.g., English, French).

tense marker: a unit (in Creole languages, almost always a full word) that indicates the (relative) time at which an action or event occurred.

TMA system: a subsystem consisting of those particles that express tense, modality, and aspect, in Creoles always preceding the verb, in that order.

TNS: abbreviation for "tense marker."

VSO language: a language where the predominant word order is verb-subject-object (e.g., Hawaiian, Tagalog).

zero form: a word or affix that is not actually uttered but "understood," so that you know what is being referred to (e.g., the plural marker of "sheep," or the subject of "see" in "I was expecting to see you").

SUGGESTED READING

Pidgins and Creoles: An Introduction, by Jacques Arends, Pieter Muysken, and Norval Smith. Amsterdam and Philadelphia: John Benjamins, 1995.

> Introductions to Creole languages are an unimpressive lot, but this is probably the least misleading, and covers quite a number of topics other introductions skimp, as well as giving useful thumbnail sketches of some of the most important languages.

Early Suriname Creole Texts, by Jacques Arends and Matthias Perl. Frankfurt and Madrid: Vervuert, 1995.

> Not easy to get hold of, but if you can, it offers what's even harder to get hold of anywhere else—actual texts in Sranan and Saramaccan from the eighteenth century. A must-read for serious Creole buffs.

Dynamics of a Creole Continuum, by Derek Bickerton. Cambridge University Press, 1975.
Dimensions of a Creole Continuum, by John Rickford. Palo Alto, California: Stanford University Press, 1987.

> Between them, these books say pretty much all there is to say about Guyanese Creole. They sometimes complement each other and sometimes contradict each other, but Rickford is a reliable observer and a native speaker too.

Isle de France Creole, by Philip Baker and Chris Corne. Ann Arbor, Michigan: Karoma Press, 1982.

> The first and in some respects the most thorough attempt to reconstruct the early development of a Creole, it opened people's eyes to what you could do with historical sources. (You can skip the nitpicky bits aimed at Robert Chaudenson.)

SUGGESTED READING

Roots of Language, by Derek Bickerton. Ann Arbor, Michigan: Karoma Press, 1981.

The book that set the bioprogram ball rolling. Less lively than the present volume, but not your stuffy academic tome, either. The final chapter, on evolution, should be read cum grano salis.

Language Creation and Language Change, edited by Michel DeGraff. Cambridge, Massachusetts: MIT Press, 1999.

If you want an overview of all the ideas on Creoles afloat around the millennium, this is your book. Has the added advantage that it puts Creoles squarely within the framework of modern general linguistics, historical linguistics, and language acquisition theory. Contains a fairly full treatment of Nicaraguan sign language, among much else.

Pidginization and Creolization of Languages, edited by Dell Hymes. Cambridge University Press, 1971.

The proceedings of the 1968 Mona conference. Shows what the field looked like when I entered it. It ought by rights to be out of date but (except for the strong version of monogenesis) most of the ideas in it are still around. Noteworthy for one or two historic papers, e.g., David DeCamp on the Jamaican continuum.

Issues in the Study of Pidgin and Creole Languages, by Claire Lefebvre. Amsterdam and Philadelphia: John Benjamins, 2004.

I'm not exactly recommending this book, but if you want to see what a really hard-nosed version of substratism looks like (Haitian Creole is just relexified Fongbe), this is it. I mean, you gotta be fair to the competition.

The Ecology of Language Evolution, by Salikoko Mufwene. Paperback edition. Cambridge University Press, 2006.

Same caveat as with the previous volume. Think of them as two opposed bookends—this one is a hard-nosed version of the superstratist case (Haitian Creole is just a kind of French). Ignore the title—the book has nothing to do with evolution, or ecology of any kind you may be familiar with.

Maroon Societies: Rebel Slave Communities in the Americas, edited by Richard Price. Third edition. Baltimore: Johns Hopkins University Press, 1996.

The classic account of maroons, including all those mentioned in this book—Palmares, El Palenque de San Basilio, the Saramaccan, and many more.

Language and Dialect in Hawaii, by John Reinecke. Reprint edition. Honolulu: University of Hawaii Press, 1969.

A reprint of Reinecke's pioneering 1930s study. Not always accurate (he grossly underrates the role of Hawaiian in interethnic contacts) but contains lots of useful statistical information about immigrants to Hawaii. Helps to complement Takaki's book *Pau Hana* (see below).

Stedman's Surinam: Life in an Eighteenth-Century Slave Society, by John Stedman. Abbreviated edition, edited and with notes by Richard and Sally Price. Baltimore: Johns Hopkins University Press, 1992.

Perhaps the most vivid firsthand description ever of what it was like to live in a Creole plantation community (as a white person, of course) in slavery days. Not much about the languages, but if you want to understand the circumstances under which they arose, this book is essential reading.

Pau Hana: Plantation Life and Labor in Hawaii, 1835–1920, by Ronald Takaki. Honolulu: University of Hawaii Press, 1983.

Unquestionably the best and most complete history of Hawaiian sugar plantations. Again, not much on language, but very good on the matrix in which Hawaiian Creole was formed, and full of details you won't find in any of the guidebooks to Hawaii.

ACKNOWLEDGMENTS

In writing about one's own life, even if only one aspect of it is covered, it would be an impossible task to thank all those who have contributed in one way or another. First and foremost, of course, is the person to whom this book is dedicated, without whom it could hardly have been written, since without her I would probably not have survived long enough to write it. I must confess I grudge every minute it took me away from her, but writers gotta write, and it's the one addiction that brings in money instead of wasting it.

Over the years, the University of Hawaii has played tolerant and understanding host to my erratic activities, largely thanks to the late and much-lamented Don Topping, former head of the Social Sciences Research Institute, and to Byron Bender, for many years chair of the Linguistics Department, peacemaker par excellence. I've also, as you've learned here, benefited enormously from shorter stays at the University of Amsterdam (courtesy of Pieter Muysken) and the University of Provence (thanks to Robert Chaudenson). The National Science Foundation (apart from the Island Experiment) has consistently supported my research, and I am deeply indebted to Paul Chapin, who oversaw that organization's linguistics grants during the period in question.

Probably the most indispensable contribution to my work came from the kindness of ordinary working people in Guyana, Hawaii, Mauritius, the Seychelles, and elsewhere. They uncomplainingly endured what I'm sure seemed to them bizarre lines of questioning, and freely gave of their time and, on a number of occasions, their hospitality, even though the motives of this inquisitive stranger may sometimes have baffled or even upset them. (I'll never forget Kathy Kesolei's indignant "You think you can get to the bottom of a culture in *three days?!*")

Thanks too must go to my students, especially Frank Byrne, Thom Huebner, Sabine Iatridou, Bill Peet, Sarah Roberts, and Bill Wilson. Students are more fun when you're learning stuff from them than when they're learning stuff from you, I've found, and each of these has made some substantive contribution to my knowledge, hence to the research that you read about in the preceding pages.

Colleagues without number have helped shape my thinking, dispelled my ignorance, disabused me of mistaken notions, and in general, through personal contact or their writings or both, lit up my way in ways that they themselves may not always have been aware of. Among them I must particularly note those—Beryl Bailey, Chris Corne, David DeCamp, John Reinecke, and Douglas Taylor—who, alas, will now never be able to read what I wrote about them. To those who are still with us—Dany Adone, Mervyn Alleyne, Charles-James Bailey, Philip Baker, Peter Bakker, George Cave, Penda Choppy, Danielle d'Offay-de Saint-Jorre, Glenn Gilbert, Tom Givon, Ian Hancock, George Huttar, Sylvia Kouwenberg, Bill Labov, Juergen Meisel, John Rickford, Ian Robertson, Gillian Sankoff, Armin Schwegler, Norval Smith, Joyce Trotman, Margot van den Berg, and Tonjes Veenstra—my sincerest thanks.

Without my superlative and ever-resourceful agent, Natasha Kern, this book might have remained one of those projects that flit around the rear of one's head, or founder after a couple of half-written chapters. She has nurtured it all the way from conception to maturity (incidentally making total sense of what had always been a mystery to me, the publishing trade) and finally found it a happy home with my editor, Joe Wisnovsky, a source of constant encouragement, whose laid-back style has proven the perfect complement to my shoot-first-ask-questions-afterward approach. If imperfections remain, as in this imperfect world they inescapably must, don't blame any of these good folk—it's my fault and mine alone.

INDEX

171, 181, 188, 198, 201, 206, 233;
children and, 110–11, 140–43, 190,
201
Language Instinct, The (Pinker), 246
Latin, 57, 84
Latin America, 49, 84, 231
Leeds, 6, 19
Lefebvre, Claire, 190
LePage, Bob, 30, 94
leprosy, 211
Lesser Antillean, 27
leveling, 112–13
linguistics, 5, 6–9, 13, 22, 43–44, 111,
191; "street," 46–47
Linguistic Society of America, 13, 137
literacy, 210, 227
loan words, 54
locative, 83, 84
London, 67, 68
Louisiana, 153
LSN (Lenguaje de Señas Nicaragüense),
233–34
Lynch, John, 126–27

macaronic, 176–77, 217, 228; pidgin,
217–18
Machado, Antonio, 177
Madeira islands, 79
Mahe, 198, 199
Malaysia, 55
Marianas, 228
Markey, Tom, 137–38, 140, 143–44,
145, 151
maroons, 51, 108, 139, 155, 166, 177;
colony, 51; Saramaccan, 177–78
Marshall Islands, 116–17, 121, 228
Matjau, 177
Matuari, 166
Mauritius, 141, 151–52, 182, 190–95,
199; Creole, 190, 193–95, 199–201;
serial verb construction in, 190, 193,
199–201; slavery, 200–201

Medellín, 59–60
media, 132, 214
memory, 6, 43
Middle English, 147
migrations, 85
Mill on the Floss, The (Eliot), 4
Milosevic, Slobodan, 21
MIT, 185, 238
mixed-language marriages, 69, 101
modality, 41, 42, 43
modality marker (MOD), 41
Molokai, 211
Mona conference (1968), 25–27, 33, 40,
48, 49–50, 238
monogenesis, 14, 27, 47, 68, 161, 237
monolingualism, 123, 163
Moon-Gazer, 31
Morisyen, 200, 205, 206
Mormons, 145
Morse code, 236
motherese, 102
Murray, Bill, 9–10, 15, 69–70, 73
Muysken, Pieter, 185
My Father's House (Matthew Carr), 15

Napoleonic Wars, 194
NASA, 128
National Science Foundation, 89, 116,
126–29, 131–34, 213
Native American languages, 133, 176
Nauru, 228
nautical jargon, 86–88
Netherlands, 184–88, 201
Netherlands Antilles, 56, 57
New Guinea, 116, 124, 125, 172, 200,
228, 235
New Hebrides, 124
Newsweek, 144
Newton, Isaac, 43–44, 246
New York City, 45, 59, 128–29, 131–32,
134–35, 174
New York Review of Books, The, 144

Printed in the USA
CPSIA information can be obtained
at www.ICGtesting.com
LVHW091139150724
785511LV00005B/423

9 780809 028160